P9-ECW-128

Maybe You Know My Kid

A Parents' Guide to Identifying, Understanding and Helping Your Child with Attention-deficit/Hyperactivity Disorder

by Mary Fowler

A BIRCH LANE PRESS BOOK
Published by Carol Publishing Group

Copyright © 1993, 1990 by Mary Cahill Fowler
All rights reserved. No part of this book may be reproduced in any form, except by a
newspaper or magazine reviewer who wishes to quote brief passages in connection with a
review.

A Birch Lane Press Book
Published by Carol Publishing Group
Birch Lane Press is a registered trademark of Carol Communications, Inc.
Editorial Offices: 600 Madison Avenue, New York, N.Y. 10022
Sales and Distribution Offices: 120 Enterprise Avenue, Secaucus, N.J. 07094
In Canada: Canadian Manda Group, P.O. Box 920, Station U, Toronto, Ontario M8Z 5P9
Queries regarding rights and permissions should be addressed to Carol Publishing Group,
600 Madison Avenue, New York, N.Y. 10022

Carol Publishing Group books are available at special discounts for bulk purchases for sales
promotion, fund raising, or educational purposes. Special editions can be created to
specifications. For details, contact: Special Sales Department, Carol Publishing Group, 120
Enterprise Avenue, Secaucus, N.J. 07094

Manufactured in the United States of America
10   9   8   7   6   5   4   3   2   1

Library of Congress Cataloging-in-Publication Data

Fowler, Mary Cahill.
      Maybe you know my kid : a parents' guide to identifying,
understanding, and helping your child with attention-deficit/
hyperactivity disorder / by Mary Fowler.
         p.   cm.
      "A Birch Lane Press book."
      Previously published: 1990.
      Includes index.
      ISBN 1-55972-209-6 (pbk.)
      1. Attention-deficit hyperactivity disorder. I. Title
RJ506.H9F68
618.92'8589—dc20   93-35870
                                                          CIP

For my sons,
David and Jonathan—the spirit behind the words—
and my mother

Contents

Acknowledgments

I am especially grateful to the researchers and practitioners who graciously contributed their time and knowledge to me. Their devotion and work in Attention-deficit/Hyperactivity Disorder (AD/HD) has made significant differences in the lives of those challenged by this disorder:

Russell Barkley, Ph.D., director of psychology and professor of psychiatry and neurology at the University of Massachusetts Medical Center, where he established the Center for Attention-deficit/Hyperactivity Disorder. Dr. Barkley is the author of numerous books and articles, including the gold-standard text for practitioners. A clinical practitioner, scientist, and educator, Dr. Barkley is internationally recognized for his work in the field.

C. Keith Conners, Ph.D., professor of medical psychology in the Department of Psychiatry at Duke University Medical Center, where he is director of the AD/HD Clinic and co-director of the Research Training Program. Dr. Conners has written numerous books, articles, and the Conners' Rating Scales. His work has received international acclaim.

Sam Goldstein, Ph.D., is a psychologist in private practice specializing in child development, school psychology, and neuropsychology. He has written numerous books and created an award-winning video.

Melvin Levine, M.D., professor of pediatrics and director of the Clinical Center for the Study of Development and Learning at the University of North Carolina, Chapel Hill. Dr. Levine has published extensively.

Bennett Shaywitz, M.D., professor of pediatrics and neurology at Yale University Medical School and director of a federally funded center to study learning and attention.

Sally Shaywitz, M.D., associate professor of pediatrics at Yale University Medical School.

Paul Wender, M.D., professor of psychiatry and director of pediatric research at the University of Utah Medical School. Dr. Wender, author of numerous books and articles, pioneered much of the work in both child and adult AD/HD.

I also wish to thank the following experts who contributed to this second edition:

Edward Hallowell, M.D., faculty member at Harvard Medical School, a child and adult psychiatrist in private practice who specializes in AD/HD and has published a book on adults.

Kevin Murphy, Ph.D., chief of the Adult Clinic on AD/HD at the University of Massachusetts Medical School.

Charles Popper, M.D., faculty member at Harvard Medical School and editor of the *Journal of Child and Adolescent Psychopharmacology*.

Ron Reeve, Ph.D., a psychologist and associate professor of education at the University of Virginia, where he coordinates the School Psychology Program.

David Shaffer, M.D., Irving Philips Professor of Child Psychiatry at Columbia University/NYSPI.

Alan Zametkin, M.D., senior staff psychiatrist of the Clinical Brain Imaging Section, National Institute of Mental Health.

Sydney Zentall, Ph.D., professor of special education and psychological sciences, Purdue University, and immediate past-president of the Division for Research at the Council for Exceptional Children.

My appreciation to Gabor Barabas, M.D., Jean Bramble, R.N., Kathy Collins, M.S.W., Randy Mendelson, Ph.D., William McMahon, M.D., Richard Reuter, M.D., and Judy Welch, Ph.D., for their contributions to the first edition.

Special thanks to my close personal friend Sandra Thomas, immediate past-president of CH.A.D.D., for her incredible support and encouragement; to Fran Rice, director of Advocacy Associates of Northern New England, who taught me about the laws governing the education of children with disabilities, and to Richard Zakreski, Ph.D., for his contributions to the text, review of my work, and support of our family.

To Margaret Bambury, Sylvia Boyd, Anne Gridley, and Pat

Rosiak, thanks again for your continued friendship and moral support through yet another part of my writing journey.

And to the mothers, fathers, children, and siblings who took me into their confidence, I am forever indebted. Your stories are an important part of this book and I thank you for your trust and honesty. Finally, love to my children for your patience and love.

Preface to the Second Edition

Five years have passed since I undertook to write the first edition of *Maybe You Know My Kid*. Much has changed in my life since I sat down, an idealistic mother, anxious to tell a story that might help families and children come to grips with Attention Deficit Disorder (ADD). Then I had no idea of how much my interest in the subject would lead to my personal growth and development. Within a month of finishing the manuscript, I found myself part of a national advocacy effort to improve the lives of children with ADD, particularly their lives in America's public schools.

I had the privilege of volunteering my time to Children with Attention-deficit Hyperactivity Disorders (CH.A.D.D.), the national support organization for children and adults with ADD. On behalf of CH.A.D.D., as a board member serving in the capacity of vice president of federal affairs, I along with then-president Sandra Thomas and co-founder Harvey Parker had the opportunity to go to our nation's capital and speak in support of our children with ADD and their parents.

That Washington effort truly broadened and enriched my life. Seldom does growth happen, however, without some type of humbling experience. For me, humility came when I realized that there I was in Washington, banging my chest, expressing my outrage at the fact that too many people in America's public schools did not take ADD seriously, when I too had a lot to learn.

I went to Washington full of empathy and compassion for the children and parents I represented. But I also went with little understanding or appreciation of disabilities. In fact, if the law we were attempting to change did not use the word "disability," I probably would never have come to conceive of ADD in this light. I would have stayed comfortably naive, paying lip service to the idea that ADD has no cure, yet inwardly stoking the illusion that if "we" just hit on the right combination of whatever, "we" could change the children and make ADD go away.

Like the mythical character Sisyphus destined for eternity to struggle with pushing a boulder to the top of a mountain only to have it roll downhill each time, the futility of my thinking and blatant ignorance about the nature of disabilities, particularly the disability named ADD, became readily apparent. As with many people, for me the term "environmental barrier" evoked the image of a wheelchair at the beginning of a staircase. I saw environmental access as a wheelchair ramp. By spending time with people who had physical disabilities, I came to understand that environmental barriers are not simply physical structures. Often the greatest barrier to overcome is attitude. With the passage of the Americans with Disabilities Act, we have come a long way in changing our attitudes to fully include people with disabilities as part of the montage that comprises mainstream America.

Yet I fear as a society we have a long way to go when applying these egalitarian principles to changing our perceptions and attitudes and what we do to assist people with hidden disabilities. Too often, they are blamed for their difficulties, their disabilities either discounted or minimized. Take ADD for example. I recently read a newsletter in which ADD was referred to as a "lifestyle." Until I read that line, I thought I had heard it all. We parents of children with ADD have been accused of labeling our perfectly normal kids because we are pushy parents hell-bent on having our children be overachievers. I have also heard ADD referred to as the yuppie disorder of the nineties. Translated, that means, like having a BMW in the garage, no home is complete without a child with a disability named ADD. How absurd! And how devaluing to the children and families who struggle every day with this disability.

Our society does not tend to think about people with hidden disabilities, such as cognitive processing deficits, dyslexia, and ADD as being at the mercy of environmental barriers, which often arise as expectations. Seldom do we even know to question what such barriers might be.

Today, I am haunted by the voice of a man who spoke out at a conference I attended on rehabilitation. The subject under discussion was advancement in technology. This man who walked into the room on both feet, who had no apparent disability, raised his hand and asked the discussion panel what technology had been created to provide him access. He told about his cognitive processing disorder, about how he could not enjoy a movie because the words and pictures got too muddled in his head.

This fellow did not look disabled, nor did he sound disabled. Yet he spoke of the many jobs he had gained and lost because his cognitive processing deficit interfered with his performance and the ability to meet expectations. He asked about his chances for a future when he had no present. He told the audience that he doubted he could attend the conference next year since he had no money, no job, and was living in his car. I guess we could say this man has a "lifestyle" too.

This man's "lifestyle" forced me to think about ADD in a much different fashion. Too often, even when we acknowledge that ADD is a disability requiring special intervention, we focus our efforts on how to change the children to meet the demands and expectations of the environment. Shouldn't we be creating and/or adapting environments to provide access to children with ADD?

Acceptance of ADD as a disability with the potential to cause significant difficulties for its sufferers certainly changes our attitude and belief system. But that is not enough. ADD has been called an "environmentally dependent" disability. As such, different environments present unique barriers. Typical environmental barriers for children with ADD arise in settings where the child is expected to pay attention for prolonged periods of time, to think before acting, to inhibit bodily movement, and to "get with the program." None of these environmental expectations are unreasonable. Unless, of course, the child's neurobiology interferes with the ability to meet such environmental expectations on a consistent basis. Under those circumstances, if we do not adapt the environment to meet the child's unique needs, then we are in essence asking the child with ADD to fend for himself or herself. We might just as well ask the child in a wheelchair to climb a staircase.

During these past five years, I have also come to know that I am not the mother of an ADD child. I am the mother of a child who has dark hair, blue eyes, a quick wit, a marvelous charm, an engaging smile, a silver tongue, and an ability to see things as they are, and who happens also to struggle with a disability named ADD. I invite you to know this too. We do not have disabled children. We have children with disabilities.

Yet I also caution you to be wary of descriptions that refer to our children's ADD as a "difference" rather than a "disability." People may have different lifestyles and learning styles. But ADD is not a "style." It is a disability. With use of these euphemisms, I worry that we may lose sight of this fact.

Frankly, for too long, children with ADD have been called merely "behavioral problems," and viewed as the masters of their own deeds. Needed educational services have often eluded them. Consequently, our children with ADD frequently stepped into America's schools and fell through the cracks. Rather than being viewed as children with special needs, instead these children with ADD received blame and punishment for the difficulties stemming from their disability.

That is why we parents felt the need to go to Washington and fight to have ADD recognized as a disability which afforded these children their rights to eligibility for special education and freedom from discrimination. We believed then, as I do now, in the integrity of the laws governing the education of children with disabilities. These laws, passed by Congress in the 1970s, are the educational bill of rights for children with disabilities. Though these laws are well-written and inspired, unfortunately their intent sometimes gets muddled in practice.

Consider the current trend of using the term "at risk" to identify children with learning and behavioral disabilities. At risk for what? I wonder in labeling children "at risk" if we might not be setting up a prophecy of failure and an attitude of "less than." Where cracks now exist, let's not create craters.

For children with hidden disabilities such as ADD, quite possibly the diagnostic label is the only cue we have to remind us that they have special needs, that they are in trouble and not the cause of trouble, and that we, their parents and educators, must make the environment accessible to them.

Perhaps the most debilitating effect of this disability is the loss of self-esteem, the breaking of spirit. For the children with ADD left undiagnosed and untreated, feelings of inadequacy color their worlds. Our role as caregivers is to enable the children to see that they are "can-do" kids, able children.

This second edition has been revised and updated to reflect the latest scientific advances in knowledge and understanding of this disorder. The most current information regarding educational problems and promising practices along with the responsibilities of schools to address the educational needs of students with ADD has been included to assist parents and educators in reaching and teaching these children. The chapter on adolescents and adults discusses the manifestations of the disorder during these life phases and provides detailed information regarding appropriate diagnostic procedures and recommended interventions for this burgeoning field of service delivery.

May you find the help you need to face the challenges presented by ADD.

October 1993

Maybe You Know
My Kid

CHAPTER ONE

An Overview of Attention-deficit/ Hyperactivity Disorder

Maybe you know my kid. He's the one who acts before he thinks. It's usually upon some rash impulse that scares the living daylights out of me, like seeing how fast he can ride a big wheel down a long, steep, curvy hill. He's the one who says the first thing that comes to his mind. It's usually with a loud voice in a quiet crowd, and it makes me wish I could evaporate into thin air.

And he cannot remember a simple request. So I long for a trained parrot that can tell him ten times in five minutes 365 days a year to go upstairs, brush your teeth, get dressed, and make your bed. He's the kid who scrapes his knee and screams so loud and long that I worry the neighbors think I am beating him. Then, when I'm about to call the doctor, he eyes a monarch butterfly and chases it through the trees until it disappears, just like his hysterics of seconds before. He's the kid in school with ants in his pants who could do the work if he really tried. Or so we have been told over and over.

Maybe you know my kid really well. Maybe he reminds you of your own or someone else's. But maybe you didn't know that children like this are not really pain-in-the-neck kids with lousy mothers. They are the children with Attention Deficit Disorder, commonly called ADD. This syndrome, characterized by inattentive, impulsive, and/or hyperactive behavior, affects an estimated 3 to 5 percent of the child population. Many adults also suffer from it.

ADD is not a new phenomenon. Physicians first noticed a very similar pattern of behavior in the late nineteenth century. Their patients, who suffered from either brain injury or illnesses affecting the central nervous system, appeared overactive, impulsive, and distractible. Eventually similar patterns of behavior became noticed in children without any brain injury. Over the years, numerous investigators delved into the reasons behind the cause of such behavior in children who otherwise appeared perfectly normal.

As a result of these investigations, the name of this symptom complex changed numerous times to reflect advances in the scientific community's understanding of the disorder. During the 1960s, the syndrome became known as Minimal Brain Dysfunction or MBD. Around 1970, excessive motor activity was the most visible symptom, so the children formerly said to have MBD came to be called hyperactive or hyperkinetic. Since the hyperactivity slowed considerably around the time of puberty, many practitioners believed the child's problems ended then.

By 1980, inattention appeared as the primary problem of most children. But not all children who exhibited attention difficulties behaved in a hyperactive, "always on the go" fashion. So researchers divided the disorder into three subgroups: ADD with Hyperactivity (ADD-H), ADD without Hyperactivity (ADDnoH), and ADD-RT (residual type), meaning symptoms carried into adolescence and adulthood. People frequently described the ADDnoH children as the "spacey" or "absent-minded professor" types. Often their inability to focus and sustain attention did not seem problematic until school demands for attention and concentration. The notion that one need not be hyperactive and that symptoms could exist beyond puberty proved a breakthrough in the understanding and treatment of this disorder.

In 1988, the name changed again to reflect the consensus among researchers that inattention, impulsivity, and hyperactivity were all central characteristics of the disorder. Thus, the disorder came to be called Attention Deficit Hyperactivity Disorder (ADHD) and a single list of 14 criteria containing features of inattention, impulsivity, and hyperactivity were used to make the diagnosis. A separate category called Undifferentiated Attention Deficit Disorder was created to diagnose individuals who had attention difficulties but little problem with hyperactivity and impulsivity.

I find it helpful to think about the name changes like a kaleidoscope. As scientists advance their knowledge and understanding about the disorder, they refine the name and the diagnostic criteria just as you or I turn the kaleidoscope to sharpen the image. Certainly, as explained by noted ADD researcher Keith Conners, the disorder has not changed. The children studied forty years ago had the same symptoms as children studied today. Only today, much more is known about ADD.

ADD is not a disease, but rather a medical syndrome. As with all medical syndromes, the diagnostician must decide if a given constellation of symptoms characteristic of a specific disorder is present in an individual before making a diagnosis. To complicate matters, an individual with a medical syndrome does not necessarily exhibit all the characteristics associated with that syndrome. Thus, determining if an individual has ADD is not a cut-and-dried matter.

ADD happens to be a very complex syndrome. No single profile can be used accurately to describe all children or adults who have the disorder. Now the prevailing view among researchers points to three subtypes of ADD. This view will be reflected in the fourth edition of the *Diagnostic and Statistical Manual of the American Psychiatric Association* (DSM IV), due for publication by 1994. The DSM is used by medical and mental health professionals to identify child, adolescent and adult psychiatric, learning, and emotional disorders.

In this fourth edition, the name Attention Deficit Hyperactivity Disorder remains unchanged from the previous 1988 edition. There is, however, a slight variation in the way the name appears in print. Unlike the 1988 version, the 1994 version is written Attention-deficit/Hyperactivity Disorder. The slash within the label is there to indicate that a person could have primary symptoms of Attention-deficit or Hyperactivity Disorder or a combination of both.

Following are the DSM IV Draft Criteria as of March 1, 1993:*

ATTENTION-DEFICIT/HYPERACTIVITY DISORDER

A. Either (1) or (2):
  (1) Inattention: At least six of the following symptoms of inattention have persisted for at least six months to a degree that is maladaptive and inconsistent with developmental levels:
      (a) often fails to give close attention to details or makes careless mistakes in schoolwork, work, or other activities

*Reprinted with permission from the DSM-IV Draft Criteria (3-1-93). Copyright © 1993 American Psychiatric Association.

     (b) often has difficulty sustaining attention in tasks or play activities

     (c) often does not seem to listen to what is being said to him or her

     (d) often does not follow through on instructions and fails to finish schoolwork, chores, or duties in the workplace (not due to oppositional behavior or failure to understand instructions)

     (e) often has difficulties organizing tasks and activities

     (f) often avoids or strongly dislikes tasks (such as schoolwork or homework) that require sustained mental effort

     (g) often loses things necessary for tasks or activities (e.g., school assignments, pencils, books, tools, toys)

     (h) is often easily distracted by extraneous stimuli

     (i) often forgetful in daily activities

  (2) Hyperactivity-Impulsivity: At least four of the following symptoms of hyperactivity-impulsivity have persisted for at least six months to a degree that is maladaptive and inconsistent with developmental level:

     Hyperactivity

     (a) often fidgets with hands or feet or squirms in seat

     (b) leaves seat in classroom or in other situations in which remaining seated is expected

     (c) often runs about or climbs excessively in situations where it is inappropriate (in adolescents or adults, may be limited to subjective feelings of restlessness)

     (d) often has difficulty playing or engaging in leisure activities quietly

     Impulsivity

     (e) often blurts out answers to questions before the questions have been completed

     (f) often has difficulty waiting in lines or awaiting turn in games or group situations

B. Onset no later than seven years of age

C. Symptoms must be present in two or more situations

D. The disturbance causes clinically significant distress or impairment in social, academic, or occupational functioning.

E. Does not occur exclusively during the course of a Pervasive Developmental Disorder, Schizophrenia, or other Psychotic Disorder, and is not better accounted for by Mood Disorder, Anxiety Disorder, Dissociative Disorder, or a Personality Disorder.

Code based on type:

314.00 Attention-deficit/Hyperactivity Disorder, Predominantly Inattentive Type: if criterion A (1) is met but not criterion A (2) for past six months

314.01 Attention-deficit/Hyperactivity Disorder, Predominantly Hyperactive-Impulsive Type: if criterion A (2) is met but not criterion A (1) for the past six months

314.01 Attention-deficit/Hyperactivity Disorder, Combined Type: if both criteria A (1) and A (2) are met for the past six months

Coding note: for individuals (especially adolescents and adults) who currently have symptoms that no longer meet full criteria, "in partial remission" should be specified.

314.9 Attention-deficit/Hyperactivity Disorder Not Otherwise Specified: This category is for disorders with prominent symptoms of attention-deficit or hyperactivity-impulsivity that do not meet criteria for Attention-deficit/Hyperactivity Disorder.

Even though the name remains relatively the same, DSM IV has changed from its predecessor, DSM IIIR, in three significant aspects. First is the addition of subtypes. Some children and adults are primarily seen as having difficulty with attention. Others will show a hyperactive, impulsive pattern of behavior with some attentional difficulty. The third subtype, the combined type, has considerable difficulty with attention, impulsivity, and hyperactivity.

The second change, which closely relates to the first, is the move to three distinct symptom groups: inattention, hyperactivity, and impulsivity. Previously, under DSM IIIR, to be diagnosed, a person had to have any eight of fourteen possible symptoms contained in a single list of items. Now individuals must meet the specified amount of symptoms under each category.

The third major change has to do with adult diagnosis. As explained by Dr. David Shaffer, chairman of the DSM IV Work Group for Child and Adolescent Disorders, there was concern that the previous criteria with emphasis on childhood behaviors of play and school were not appropriate for adults, so the criteria were rewritten to reference work and recreation, making them less age-specific than they had been. Adults can either meet the full criteria or be diagnosed as "in partial remission" when they have symptoms but no longer meet the full criteria.

Dr. Shaffer also commented that the subtypes seem to predict functional impairment and that the predominantly inattentive subgroup appears to be the least impaired. "They are also the group that have the largest proportion of girls," he added. As might be expected, the combined subtype (i.e., inattention hyperactivity, and impulsivity) likely has the greatest degree of impairment, including a higher incidence of social rejection.

As previously stated, ADD is a complex disorder with potentially serious effects. I strongly advise readers not to diagnose their children, spouses, or selves unless trained to do so. Diagnosis is a complicated process. For a thorough discussion of diagnostic procedures, please see Chapter 5.

Though I, along with many others, have gotten quite comfortable referring to this disorder as ADD, I will refer to the disorder by the AD/HD label throughout the rest of this book. When reading about my child, please understand that he would be considered Attention-deficit/Hyperactivity Disorder, Combined Type. Your family member may have one of the other subtypes.

No one knows for certain what actually causes AD/HD. We do know that it does not come from diet, allergy, or bad parents. Strong scientific evidence suggests that the disorder is genetically transmitted in many cases. That does not mean, however, that AD/HD can be linked directly, for example, from a father to a son, or a mother to a daughter. According to Dr. Paul Wender, "On occasion, it skips generations, and it blurs so that if you look at siblings in a family, they come in all shapes and colors.

"One sibling may have AD/HD and be poorly coordinated. Another might have AD/HD, good coordination, and possibly some other disorder." Of course, some siblings will not have AD/HD.

Scientific evidence also strongly suggests that AD/HD is neurologically based. The director of pediatric neurology at Yale University Medical School, Dr. Bennett Shaywitz, says most children are believed to have AD/HD because of "inherited disturbances in certain chemicals in the brain's neurotransmitter systems." Neurotransmitters are chemicals which regulate brain cell function. Thus, these chemicals help the brain regulate behavior. Still, the exact cause of AD/HD remains unknown, though recent research advances offer promise. Results of a 1990 landmark study by Alan Zametkin, M.D., and his colleagues at the National Institute of Mental Health showed that the rate at which the brain uses glucose, its primary energy source, is lower in subjects with AD/HD than in subjects without AD/HD.

What causes AD/HD, or even what name it has, does not change what is known about this condition. Though once considered predominantly a childhood disorder, we now know that AD/HD continues to cause problems into adulthood in approximately two-thirds of the cases. Children with AD/HD come in all shapes and sizes. Some have very severe cases and have all of the symptoms. Many areas of their lives are affected. Others have symptoms so minor that the condition almost goes unnoticed. Some have associated disorders as well.

Most clinicians and researchers agree that certain symptoms constitute the disorder. However, an individual need not have all the primary symptoms to have the disorder, a point clarified in DSM IV by the addition of subtypes.

We know that at different ages, different features of the disorder prove more problematic. For example, impulsive behavior is a danger for a toddler, but attention is not a skill required or expected at this stage of development. The symptoms can create problems in all areas of a person's environment or in just one area. For instance, the child with AD/HD who has moderate attention difficulties may have trouble in school but not at home, where there are fewer tasks that require concentration. Further, the adolescent with AD/HD may have done reasonably well in school and at home during earlier years, with problems not becoming evident until increased demands for self-responsibility occurred.

We know that in half the cases, children evidence signs of the disorder prior to age four. But we also know that these signs often go unrecognized until the child goes to school. Boys are more commonly diagnosed, but we now know girls also have the condition. Researchers have only recently begun to study AD/HD as it affects girls. Leading expert Dr. Russell Barkley notes that the disorder is prevalent in boys by a 3:1 ratio, and that boys tend to be more aggressive. Given the absence of aggression, little difference in the manifestations of AD/HD is noted between males and females.

These children come from all socioeconomic, racial, and cultural backgrounds. But underachievement appears as a unifying theme.

Outcome studies paint a picture of serious academic failure. These children's underachievement is not a function of their capability. Children with AD/HD span the range of below average, normal, above average, and superior intelligence.

Despite all that is known about AD/HD, many children go undiagnosed. Instead, they are misunderstood. Some are even blamed for behaviors which are the very features of this disorder. Children with AD/HD act in a way that comes naturally to them. Thus, they are at the mercy of their disorder and its symptoms. They are the children *in trouble, not the cause of trouble.* Parents may suspect that all is not as it should be. But without knowledge and understanding of AD/HD they are puzzled and worried by what they see.

As the fellow parent of a ''difficult'' child, you probably know that I hurt too, and have felt alone and scared, frustrated and angry, helpless and hopeless. Maybe you also suffered from the looks you were flashed by people who did not know your kid couldn't help it. Maybe you did not know this either. Maybe you cried and hollered when you sent your child to school hopeful that he would succeed and he returned home angry. Maybe you were scared when you realized the system understood him less than you. And maybe you saw what little self-esteem your child had go down the tubes.

Presently, there is no cure for AD/HD. But our children and families do not have to be stressed to a breaking point. Some of the qualities that comprise AD/HD can be assets for the child and adult who learn how to channel them. A positive outcome is best accomplished through diagnosis and proper management of the symptoms of this disorder.

The recommended approach is multidimensional. It begins with education of the parent, child, and child's teachers about AD/HD; parent training in behavior-management techniques; an appropriate educational program for the child designed to address the AD/HD-related difficulties; and medication when indicated. Family and/or individual psychotherapy to address self-esteem and peer-relationship problems is also suggested at times.

I am one of the lucky mothers. I now understand why my son behaves the way he does. I know what to expect from him and how to manage his AD/HD. I know when and where to go for help. I know now that the disturbing behaviors which appeared at various stages of his development were not of his own doing or my fault. I also know now that above all else, my child needs to feel competent. If you are the parent of a child with AD/HD, I want you to know this too.

This book is intended to serve as your guide. The following chapters present a picture of what Attention-deficit/Hyperactivity Disorder is and what to do about it. The chapters are organized in a developmental fashion. Each one describes the patterns and characteristics of AD/HD at a particular stage of the child's development and, where possible, outlines the recommended treatment for the disorder.

Chapters are divided into two sections. At the beginning of the first section, signs and symptoms of the disorder are discussed and illustrated using anecdotes from my family's personal experience. The second section presents the manifestations of the disorder predominant in the particular developmental stage. Since there are various types of AD/HD, and thus every child with AD/HD does not manifest the exact same signs and symptoms, the second section of each chapter discusses the experiences of other mothers, fathers, siblings, and children affected by AD/HD. In order to observe the child's right to privacy, these others have been given pseudonyms.

That this disorder presents differently from child to child is a point to be emphasized. As you read, try to identify with the patterns of the disorder and how they may pertain to your situation. Try not to compare your situation to these others, for as we know, many factors contribute to each child's development whether or not he or she has a disorder. No two children are the same.

Section two also provides a clinical point of view based on interviews I had with practitioners nationally and internationally recognized for their work with this disorder. For the sake of readability, their credentials are described in the Acknowledgments rather than throughout the text. These sections also contain information from professionals in private practice. The effects AD/HD has on those who interact with the child is discussed throughout. Each chapter ends with a summary highlighting main points.

I offer this book with the hope that it will broaden the general knowledge of Attention-deficit/Hyperactivity Disorder. Its information is well documented and its treatment recommendations proven. You may recognize your child or someone else's within these pages. If so, you are on the road to getting help. But again I caution against self-diagnosis and self-treatment. Just as you would seek the expertise of an eye doctor for a problem with your vision, find a practitioner who is reputed to be knowledgeable about Attention-deficit/Hyperactivity Disorder.

Facts About AD/HD

- Estimated to affect 3-5 percent of childhood population in varying degrees of severity
- More prevalent in males, but also occurs in females
- Affects individuals of all socioeconomic, racial, and ethnic backgrounds and intelligence levels
- Often continues through adolescence and adulthood
- Is neurobiologically based
- Characterized by symptoms of inattention and/or impulsivity and hyperactivity
- Is comprised of three subtypes:
  - inattentive type
  - hyperactive-impulsive type
  - combined type (inattentive and hyperactive-impulsive)
- Diagnosed through criteria set forth by the American Psychiatric Association Diagnostic and Statistical Manual
- Symptoms must be maladaptive, developmentally inappropriate, and present in two or more situations
- Self-diagnosis and self-treatment are not advised
- Often results in underachievement in school and career
- Usually causes very low self-esteem
- Managed through multiple treatment approaches including:
  - Parent education and training in behavior-management techniques
  - Appropriate educational program
  - Medication, when indicated
  - Possible individual or family psychotherapy

CHAPTER TWO

The Infant

I have always believed that when it came to the birth process, mother and child worked together. But David, my firstborn, is and always has been his own person. His birth came on his terms in the form of a swift hard kick that ruptured the amniotic sac and left me in a puddle of water alone and wondering at 1:00 A.M. if this was the long-awaited moment. The doctor's examination just hours before revealed that I was nowhere ready for birth. Yet at 2:00 A.M., without having so much as one single contraction, I was admitted to labor and delivery. My egg had decided to hatch.

Nineteen hours later, my son was born on his due date, September 25, 1979, the United Nations Year of the Child—a good omen for a superstitious mother like his. David was 7 pounds 7 ounces, 19½ inches, and beautiful. Except for the fetal monitor tangled in his long, black hair, his voyage into the world of newborn didn't leave a mark on his body. His face was perfectly rounded, and though slightly blue at birth, his color improved within minutes.

As I lay on the delivery table watching the nurses wrap him in the garments of the outer world, I was struck with a sense of astonishment. Here was this little tiny body, having just emerged into our world after what had turned out to be a very long day, alert, moving his limbs, full of life, while I, his mother, could barely move a muscle. I've always tried to make sense of what seems contradictory and so I rationalized that this was as it should be. After all, I had done the work.

Six hours later, when the nurses brought the babies to the room for feeding, I had my first taste of motherhood. No more dress rehearsal. Though physically I felt like a dishrag, my sense of excitement became so great that it didn't take more than a second before I was fully awake and holding my baby, who was sound asleep. He

11

looked and smelled as all babies do, so innocent and pure, though to me he was not like any other baby. I felt such a sense of pride and joy and bewilderment that within so short a period of time I could go from taking care of my own needs to suddenly having the responsibility of someone else's. For a brief second, I allowed that I felt unsure about the kind of job I would do. Then I quickly dismissed this thought and went back to feeling elated.

From the very beginning David seemed to have a profound effect on everyone. Visitors to the hospital would go to the nursery first and then report to me. "Oh Mary," my sister said, "he's a beautiful baby and what an active soul!"

My sister-in-law exclaimed, "He's really strong. The little guy bucked himself to the top of the bassinet. He lifted his head and looked straight at me! I can't believe how he looks all over the place. The other babies just seem to sleep."

Well, being a proud mother, what could I think? That he performed feats of strength could only mean that he was naturally a super athlete. Being highly stimulated by his environment must mean that he was exceptionally bright. Both his father and I felt this child was a gift we would have to manage very carefully.

So with this attitude, it is not surprising that I grew furious at the events of his second day on Planet Earth. At 4:00 P.M., the nursery staff buzzed my room to inform me that David had raised such a ruckus, the staff could not comfort him after two hours of trying. "So, Mrs. Fowler, would you please come get your baby?" What was wrong with those baby nurses that it took them two hours to realize that this newborn needed his mother?

I brought David to my room, gave him my undivided attention, fed him, and changed him, and off to sleep he went. Simple. Until day three. Then I had trouble quieting my child. He screamed so uncontrollably I thought certainly something must be terribly wrong. Rocking made him squirm so hard, I feared dropping him. I put him in the bassinet and held a water bottle to his lips. Gradually he went to sleep. I couldn't understand why my roommate could hold her baby all day long and I would have to put mine down after ten minutes. A seemingly logical answer came to mind. Her baby was a girl and girls cuddle; mine was a boy and boys do not.

By the end of day three, I realized I was off to a bad start with parenting. I became very high-strung. To make matters worse, some minor complications restricted my activity, and David developed jaundice, which is quite common in newborns, but nonetheless upsetting. Then he added a new twist to his repertoire. Choking! Every time I tried to feed him, be it breast or bottle, he gagged. Even my roommate, the picture of serenity, suggested I call the nurse.

Congestion. That was all. "Nothing for you to worry about," said the nurse as she stuck a long rubber tube down his throat and sucked through the other end. After removing the worst of the mucus, she gave me the baby and for the first time in two and a half days he slept once again peacefully in my arms. Congestion. No wonder this little fellow had been so disagreeable. I became calm.

That was a big mistake! The pressure I felt in the hospital could not compare to the stress in store when I had the full responsibility for the baby at home. His dad expected I knew what I was doing. I expected he knew what he was doing. God only knows what the infant expected. Whatever he figured on, I did not meet his needs. The baby cried every twenty minutes from eight at night to six in the morning. His high-pitched voice pierced my ears and ran through my body, jangling every nerve ending. No sooner would I fall asleep than "screech" and up I would get. First I tried to feed, then change, then rock, then let him cry himself to sleep. After three weeks I was beating my pillows, screaming into them, feeling furious that I had ever conceived this kid, ashamed that I could feel this way about my son.

I tried to tell his dad that I felt strung out. He acted as though David's behavior was normal, that all babies keep their mothers awake round the clock. Since he had a son by a previous marriage, I figured he knew what he was talking about. Yet I desperately wanted reassurance that I was not just one of those women reputed to be "not cut out for motherhood," so I turned to friends and family for guidance and backing.

Some, like my one sister-in-law, were sympathetic and assured me that eventually baby David would establish a routine. My mother seemed very empathetic, but above all she was a mother and thus needed to share the wisdom of the ages, which is, "That's what babies are like." Since she had five, she could recall numerous incidents to verify her point. And she happily reminded me that at least my husband helped with the baby when he wasn't away on his weekly business trips.

That certainly was true during the daylight hours. But David Sr.

and I agreed he needed sleep to be alert for his very demanding job. So during the night, our son fell entirely into my care. After all, I could grab a nap with the baby during the day. That is, if the baby napped, which he did not. Deep inside I felt abandoned.

Fortunately, we lived near many relatives who pitched in. My first good night's sleep came when my sister-in-law Terry spent the night to care for the baby, as I was ill and David Sr. was away on an overnight business trip. The next morning I felt reborn and for-ever grateful for that night. Terry was exhausted but seemed to have developed a new respect for me. This was no easy kid.

Yet I could not help feeling that somehow David was special, different from other children. He just seemed so alert, so active, so advanced. When I reported that he rolled over at two weeks another sister-in-law, the mother of three, told me in no uncertain terms, "It's not possible, Mary. Babies can't do that." When I insisted that I put him face down and found him face up, she quoted from Dr. Spock and allowed this was no doubt a freak inci-dent that would not happen again. I began to question myself. I knew I saw what I saw, but it was not clear how David had per-formed this feat. I surmised that through crying and screaming, David rolled over by accident.

I called the pediatrician, not so much to say that he had rolled over, but to ask if maybe the baby had colic and could that explain why he screamed so much. He said it was possible but improbable since he would scream round the clock if he were colicky. He then suggested that maybe David was one of those hungry babies "who need solid food in addition to breast milk." At four weeks he had solids. And he loved them. Though I had made the commitment to breast-feeding, I did not in the least mind the compromise. At this point I would have killed for a good night's sleep.

The solid food seemed to do the trick, and once again I thought we were bound for smooth sailing. David only woke periodically, and though he still did not sleep much during the day, I at least had more energy to deal with the constant attention he demanded. Though he had a wealth of toys, little seemed to keep him interested very long. He hated the playpen and the crib. By two months, he perched himself on his hands and knees and rolled across the floor from one place to another. Our son's every move thrilled us. Friends and relatives marveled at his stamina and persistence. My sister Margaret affectionately nicknamed him "wiggle worm."

It has always been my nature to make light of situations when I am scared. So at two and a half months when David came down with bronchitis and was placed on a bronchodilator medicine, I assured myself that this was perfectly normal. But a few hours later David had a reaction to the medicine. He behaved like Superboy until he lost all control. His body flailed so wildly about that I could not restrain him. The pediatrician told me to keep him safe and ride it out. A few hours later he crashed into a sound sleep. I spent the night on the floor next to his crib, terrified. From then on it didn't take much for me to call the doctor, who within the first ten months of David's life saw him twenty-six times. Some of those visits were for normal checkups. Most were for upper-respiratory and ear infections.

Did he ever have ear infections! But he never simply cried or screamed in pain. Instead he would "dolphinize," a term I coined to describe his high-pitched wail. This sound reached such a high pitch that friends who telephoned would hang up because it drove them crazy. David's dolphinizing was like a rising barometer. As the shrill increased, he became more difficult to manage. When I tried to hold and quiet him, the sound would grow louder. Distracting him worked only momentarily. After hours of hearing him cry, my ears would start to hurt. The more I tried to soothe my son the more disturbed he became and the more frustrated I felt until eventually I was totally distraught, screaming at him to shut up. When I reached the point where I wanted to jump out a window, I knew to call the pediatrician.

"Why don't you bring him in, Mrs. Fowler," he would say. Then, after he examined him, "Mrs. Fowler, his ears are infected. Look at this." I peered in the scope and saw a blister the size of a pea. No wonder the poor child screamed. "What are we going to do with this kid, Mrs. Fowler?"

I simply did not know what I was going to do with this boy. Only a few things seemed to work. Humor became a coping tool I used. For the first six months of David's life, I would joke with the pediatrician and ask if he knew where to find a band of roving gypsies who might want to add a beautiful blue-eyed boy to their troop. Once I suggested that I didn't really need a pediatrician, that perhaps an exorcist could drive out the evil demons who deemed that he behave horrendously instead of crying like normal babies when he was ill. Though the doctor understood my attitude and laughed along with me, others found me disrespectful. I could not imagine why. After all, not much in our house smacked of calico and apple pie.

By the time David turned six months, our house became a crazy place. I remember one night when a business associate of my husband's stopped by unexpectedly. We still functioned under the misconception that infants do not really interfere with a routine, and so we invited this traveling salesman for some good company and a home-cooked meal. The child seemed to have radar. Though he was usually dead to the world from 6:00 to 10:00 P.M., on this particular night he awoke at eight, dolphinizing. Realizing that I would be preoccupied, Dad offered to barbecue the chicken.

Hank, our guest, watched in amazement as little David crawled up my leg, down my arm, over my head, across the back of the chair, and up his leg. Though a bit astonished at the energy level of this little baby, Hank found a ready explanation, "He's just like his dad, isn't he!" We all laughed, though it was not a belly laugh. It was more like the laugh you make when you are not sure what behavior is appropriate.

The chicken came in from the grill black. No one had to worry about the risk of infection from this bird. We sat down to dinner with little screaming David lying on his stomach across my knees, my elbow pinning him while I tried to sway him into sleep. I decided not to mention the spider dangling from a long strand directly over Hank's rice. Fortunately, the insect retreated from the grating sound made by our guest's knife as he sawed through his chicken. Our companion thanked us profusely for a very nice evening but declined in no uncertain terms our invitation to stay the night. Hank was the first in a long line of guests who didn't overstay their welcome.

Gradually, my husband and I became separated from our friends with grown kids and our friends with no kids who preferred the more civilized pleasures. Our home was quite simply chaotic and not at all soothing to the nerves. Only on rare occasions did we function as a team. Since my husband traveled on business trips at least three full days each week, I saw his evenings at home as an opportunity to break away from what was fast becoming a prison. When I returned to find the baby had given his dad a hard time, instead of offering sympathy, I seized the opportunity to complain.

David Sr. would acknowledge that managing the baby could be

difficult, but certainly no reason for me to lose my temper. That statement sent me into orbit, which only proved his point. I knew I had to do something to get myself on an even keel.

I soon developed a group of friends, all of whom were young mothers, figuring that maybe if I had a social life during the daytime I would feel more satisfied and might even speak in sentences again. Most afternoons, we would gather at my house since David was the only baby who would not nap if the daily routine changed in any way. Unlike my friends and relatives with grown children, who thought I was ridiculous to remove all perishables from harm's way, the other mothers liked the security my home offered. It was not just childproof. It was a veritable fortress.

But even these seasoned mothers found David's antics to be phenomenal for a six-month-old. When they observed me change him, one asked if I had developed a unique technique for diapering boys, who are prone to hose down whatever leans over them. As you know, most babies are placed on their backs and the old diaper is removed. But David had to be placed on his stomach while my elbow pinned his chest to the table. Otherwise, I was apt to catch him in midair as more than once he catapulted off the table. Had it not been for the modern-science wonder of stickum diaper tabs I would have been unable to change him. While the other women thought my solution to be clever, some relatives thought maybe I bent over backward for this kid. "You should make him stay still," I heard them say more than once. It seemed to me they thought I took some perverse pleasure in complicating matters, that I liked the sensationalism and encouraged David's behavior.

After spending a lot of hours together with me, the gals began to tell me how exhausted they became just watching me keep up with my daredevil who knew no fear. At seven months, he stood and climbed, and soon the floor no longer sufficed as his playpen. He found the view from on top of the tables and the backs of chairs to be far more inviting. The stairs gave him absolute delight. When we gathered at the kitchen table, he discovered he could join the party if he climbed up the rungs of the ladder-back chairs.

This stunt proved relatively harmless until the time I didn't know where he had gone. Seeing my baby sprawled on the floor with a chair on top of him while he screamed at the top of his lungs scared me to death. I thought for sure he had been crushed. The more I tried to comfort him, the louder he hollered. I lost patience and finally out of sheer frustration plopped him in the playpen, where he soon found a suitable distraction and stopped crying. My friends stood by with looks of horror on their faces. I felt like a total failure, believing that a mother's gentle touch was the best curative. With David, my touch only made him scream louder.

On days such as these, when Dad came home from a hard day's work or a week on the road, I would recite a litany of antics David had pulled off during his absence. Proud Papa loved having a rough-and-tumble boy and never thought his behavior to be abnormal. Instead, he thought my response to our son was overstated. He said I lacked patience. That attitude stung! My emotions became totally confused. I realized I had trouble coping with my son. Still I loved him. I simply did not know what I was supposed to do to please him.

With David the rewards were few. As long as I watched from afar or provided a myriad of stimuli to keep him constantly occupied, peace reigned. But the minute I tried to have a peaceful moment with my baby, there was no rest. I eventually learned that holding David meant bouncing him on my knee or throwing him in the air. Though he still breast-fed, he never concentrated on suckling. His eyes flitted all over the room while his hands tangled my hair or tore at the hoop in my ear. With the least little distraction he interrupted his feeding entirely. I couldn't understand why this baby was unreachable. Again I concluded that boys will be boys and mine seemed so alert he must be destined for great things.

After eight months, a pattern began to emerge in David's behavior. While he was always very active and inquisitive, sometimes his behavior crossed the line from being overly stimulated to frenetic. When this happened, I recalled the kitten we had named O.B. O'Brien. One day, when O.B. was barely ten weeks old, we left him outside while we went off to shop. Upon our return we found O.B. wildly racing in circles around the yard. At first my husband and I laughed, but as O.B. persisted, we somehow saw that he was in a pathetic way. I picked him up and discovered his eyes were swollen shut and his fur was coated with a mass of bee stingers. It seemed that poor O.B. got tangled up with a hive and had been driven crazy. Though he eventually calmed down, O.B. remained somewhat neurotic after that.

Whenever David reached that frenetic state where nothing I could do would calm him, I began to feel that maybe I too behaved like O.B. O'Brien and would do something rash if I had to spend one more second with this baby. This reaction supported my suspicion that I lacked the nurturing abilities which make for a good mother. Though I loved my child, I felt ashamed that I could not cope with this little boy who was my own flesh and blood.

I covered these painful feelings with a veneer of bravado and entered what I call the black-humor stage of motherhood. Some people thought it funny that I nicknamed the baby Rasputin. Others found me irreverent. Naturally I spent most of my time with the gang that liked to laugh, which included my sister-in-law and her fifteen-month-old. Every day we met at the beach. This was no simple feat. First, we had to carry the boys across the hot sand and find some unsuspecting stranger or friend to watch them for a few minutes while we ran back to the car to get the diaper bag, the toy bag, the wooden corral, which easily weighed ten pounds, the blanket, the towels, the umbrella, and the cooler. Then we set up all this paraphernalia for a relaxing day of sun and surf.

My nephew Johnny, an industrious toddler, entertained himself for hours. When he fussed, he was generally hungry or ready to nap under the shade of the umbrella. Not David! He hated that corral and alternated between throwing the toys outside, "dolphinizing," and taking the toys from Johnny. I jumped up and down like a yo-yo, and after an hour had about all I could take. Yet getting there always turned out to be such a major production, I could not bear to leave early. Rasputin was simply going to do things my way.

David proved so disruptive, he became the center of attention by default. The gals who sat with us would remark about his escapades and his activity, but always they ended by saying, "He's such a good-looking boy!" "Look at those blue eyes," or "He's really beautiful."

My reply was, "He needs to be." Some were nice enough to tell me to ignore him and enjoy myself. People not sitting with us just glared at me with that look, "Why doesn't she do something about that kid!" If only they knew.

After two weeks of his pick-me-up/put-me-down routine, David realized he could wedge his big toe into the parts of the corral that formed a "V" shape and pull himself up. I dubbed him Spiderman and watched with the others in awe as he climbed to the top and then out. "There goes the neighborhood," was my comment. There went any chance of sitting peacefully.

David quickly discovered the ocean. Since he hated the feel of the sand on his knees, he improvised by walking on hands and feet, and like a little crab headed straight for the sea. I expected that the pounding surf and cold water smacking him in the face would dissuade him, but this lemming kept to his march. So I learned to tie a long rope around his middle.

At ten and a half months he walked. It didn't take long for me to realize that once again we would do things his way.

That August David had yet another ear infection. The ear specialist told me that a very minor surgical procedure called a myringotomy was indicated. Panic set in. Though I knew older children who had had this procedure, this was my child the surgeon would operate on, my little fellow he would put under anesthesia. When I told his dad the news, he reacted with as much panic as I.

Unlike me, however, on the day of the operation David's father appeared totally composed. He even calmed me when the nurse told me hospital policy did not allow parents to accompany their child to surgery. The nurse suggested we put his favorite stuffed animal in the bed with him. But my baby had no favorite toy, no special animal he would fall to sleep with night after night, no blanket he would cuddle for comfort. Dad handed the nurse his pacifier. I felt so helpless when on the way to the operating room young David saw me sitting in the hall, and jumping to his feet, he almost fell off the gurney. "Boy, he's an active fellow. I've never had one do this before," the nurse commented. His fragile and frightened look tore me apart. This was the first time I realized just how much my son and I depended on each other. While he slept off the sedation, I held him close. I felt like a mother who knew how to care for her baby.

Once again I saw David as being special. Since his first birthday fast approached, I no longer expected him to be a cuddly teddy bear. Junior Frolic, a nickname given by his dad, seemed more than appropriate. Weaning him from the breast was not traumatic. I knew it was time, and besides, I was pregnant again and ready to part with his infancy stage. The day before his twelve-month checkup, David ran full speed through the hall, stopping abruptly when he crashed into the bathtub. He now sported his first shiner. He too became ready to enter the world of the toddler.

I am given to sentimentalism and thought I would mark my

son's first birthday and each subsequent birthday by writing him a letter. In that letter I intended to write about all the milestones he had achieved during the year. I began, "Dear Junior Frolic, your dad gave you this name because you were so active, so full of life." But as I went on I found it increasingly difficult to report just what exactly had occurred during the year. Much that I had to say was uncomplimentary. Much that I had to say seemed unmotherly. And so we gave him the usual toys: a little big wheel, a set of building blocks, and puzzles.

David was not the only family member to receive puzzles that first year. Both his dad and I were frequently confused by his behavior. On the surface, most of the things he did seemed ordinary. At times all babies fuss and cry, refuse certain foods, have difficulty establishing routines. But these behaviors are not ordinary when they are consistently exhibited to the extreme. Though David could be charming, engaging, and interesting, "difficult" is a more accurate overall description of him then.

At this stage there was no way for anyone to now that David had Attention-deficit/Hyperactivity Disorder. AD/HD is a hidden disability. Its presence or absence must be determined through careful analysis of behavioral patterns over time. Furthermore, difficult, demanding behavior in infancy is not even considered a marker for the disorder. Most children with AD/HD were not difficult infants. Thus, obtaining this diagnosis often proves to be a matter of trial and error.

Five years ago, though some children were diagnosed as toddlers, the average age at which a child was determined to have AD/HD was around eight years, or during third grade. At this age, the greater environmental demands for self-control and attention marked these children as unable to meet age-appropriate expectations. By age eight, the developmental gaps widened to the extent that the child's age-inappropriate behavior could no longer be excused as a simple problem of immaturity. Thanks to greater public awareness of this hidden disability, more children are being identified and diagnosed at earlier ages.

Unlike the core symptoms of impulsivity and inattention, the symptom of excessive motor activity is visible early in life. As a symptom, however, hyperactivity alone cannot be diagnostic of AD/HD. First of all, hyperactivity is only one of the possible core symptoms that can comprise the disorder. Second, a child can have all the other symptoms of the disorder and still have a normal activity level, that is, not be hyperactive at all. Some children with AD/HD are even underactive and may appear lazy or lethargic. As explained by Dr. Paul Wender, "Hyperactivity is a red flag. It is analogous to a fever or temperature in medicine. A fever tells you somebody is ill, but it does not indicate which illness the patient has."

Certainly David was more active than the typical baby. When I described his behavior to the pediatrician, though he acted sympathetic, I got the distinct impression he thought I was the nervous and overreactive type. I accepted that kind of response back then. I do not today. Then, having only limited information, I guessed that I was a big part of the problem.

So did most of the fifteen mothers I spoke with who had children eventually diagnosed with AD/HD. Most of these mothers typically described their babies as colicky, given to frequent and persistent crying, not easily soothed. Some of these babies, but not all, had a high energy level as well. Many of these infants were poor sleepers and fussy eaters. At the very least, you would think that difficult, demanding, overactive infants could be earmarked as children who will eventually be diagnosed with AD/HD. Yet research indicates that these traits in infants do not predict the disorder. Such traits, however, do identify the infants as "at risk."

Dr. Richard Reuter, a neurodevelopmental pediatrician and director of the Child Evaluation Unit at Monmouth Medical Center in New Jersey, believes some infants are difficult because they have a hard time regulating their state of being. They are the babies who, for instance, cannot calm themselves after a frenzied crying. Rather than respond to parental attempts to settle them, Dr. Reuter notes, these infants tend to continue crying until they wear themselves completely down.

Throughout the course of a day, infants pass through many different states of being. As described by Dr. Reuter, they may go from quiet and alert to quiet and sleepy, or from awake and irritable to full crying. The ideal state for a baby is quiet and alert because that is the time the baby is able to respond to and learn from stimuli in the environment. Dr. Reuter thinks at-risk babies, babies with AD/HD for example, have a hard time getting to the quiet-and-alert state. Once there, they often are not able to maintain that condition. Thus, these infants are deprived of the good interactions with the environment which are a natural by-product of being in the quiet-and-alert state.

Like myself, the mothers of the difficult infants I interviewed thought they were bad mothers, some because they could not seem to please the baby no matter what they tried, others because they found it difficult to cope with the constant effort the baby required. We assumed we must be doing something wrong. Most of us felt ashamed of and responsible for the negative responses provoked by the baby's difficult and demanding behavior. We assumed "good mothers" would never respond to an innocent little baby with anger and frustration. Though we may have suspected that the baby could not be held accountable for his or her behavior, we felt uncertain about our role in causing the baby's distress.

Lynn White felt particularly guilty. The pregnancy which produced her daughter Susie was unplanned. The only way she could explain such an active and aggressive little nine-month-old girl was to surmise that her baby daughter acted out because she somehow sensed her mother's reluctance to have another child. As it happened, Susie had to be sent in mid-year from second grade back to first before her symptoms were identified as AD/HD. Yet Lynn White characterized Susie's overall behavior as problematic dating back to the first months of her life.

In addition to the guilt many mothers place upon themselves, Dr. Reuter has noted that quite often others reinforce the mothers' guilt feelings. The classic example is the irritable breast-fed baby. Dr. Reuter says mothers of such babies often get advice from the baby's grandparents, aunts, or uncles that she is not feeding the baby enough, or the baby needs food, or her milk is no good. As a result, many of these mothers switch from nursing to bottle-feeding, or if bottle-feeding may switch from one formula to another in an attempt to satisfy the baby. Dr. Reuter explained that the baby, of course, cannot be satisfied because the problem is not a food problem, but rather a problem regulating state of being.

Besides feeling guilty, Dr. Reuter has observed, parents of difficult and demanding infants often feel cheated. Their expectations of what the interaction should be with their babies and what actually occurs are quite different. They tend to feel angry, frustrated, and embarrassed. Dr. Reuter notes relatives and other people are often too quick to make derogatory remarks to the parents of difficult, demanding babies, such as, "You are spoiling the child" or

"You don't punish the child enough and that's why he acts that way." Such comments fuel the parents' negative feelings. These negative feelings that parents, and more commonly mothers, have about themselves and toward the child feed on each other. Unfortunately, sometimes these feelings cross the realm of rationality. Children with AD/HD are at risk for physical and emotional abuse.

Dr. Reuter believes parents of difficult, demanding infants need some anticipatory guidance to recognize that these sorts of angry feelings are natural when a baby cries a lot and nothing they do soothes the baby. They also need support. He advises parents to acknowledge such feelings when they occur and to deal with them, for example, by calling somebody and talking about what they are experiencing. This step generally diffuses the frustration so parents can handle the situation better.

For coping with difficult and demanding infants, Dr. Reuter emphasizes the importance of parents recognizing that the problems are not the result of something they are or are not doing. He advises parents to expect babies who do not regulate their state of being easily to have trouble with transitions and changes in routine. In addition to everyday transitions, Dr. Reuter says parents also need to recognize that "virtually anything that comes along, such as illnesses or routine immunizations, will challenge this type of baby more than others." In preparing parents for what to expect from different situations and at various times, physicians help them avert even more difficulties. Forewarned is forearmed.

Once parents understand the whys and wherefores of their baby's behavior, Dr. Reuter says they can then work on various techniques that might help the baby. These include smoothing transitions and establishing steady routines. Dr. Reuter advises parents of difficult infants to establish routines by doing the same things at the same time, in a set manner each day, and to be consistent about these routines, because these infants need that kind of order.

Parents also need to avoid overstimulating the difficult baby. Along this line, Dr. Reuter explained that these babies will often become overly excited by a simple, routine play activity. Parents will continue play interactions when the baby has gone beyond the point of being responsive to such activities. Thus, parents need to learn to recognize the cues given by the baby. For instance, sometimes these babies will cry irritably or avert their gaze and withdraw from the situation to avoid the excess stimulation. If the stimulus is physical, the baby may arch or pull away. When the parents interact with the baby, Dr. Reuter advises they do so when the baby is quiet and alert. But as he pointed out, difficult babies may only be quiet and alert for a few minutes out of each hour. Trying to push the baby beyond his or her internal limit will only result in further aggravating the situation.

Besides not overstimulating the baby, there are techniques parents can try to soothe the agitated baby. Their usefulness, Dr. Reuter says, depends on the individual baby. Some babies respond to swaddling. Others respond to the stimulation that comes from being walked or rocked. And still other babies will only fall asleep easily when they are riding in the car. Like myself, there were nights when Claudie Kreiger resorted to drives in the car to settle her baby. I guess this technique is somewhat common since Dr. Reuter told me that today there is a device you can attach to the crib that provides the sensation of a car traveling at 55 mph.

Parents of difficult infants also need to take care of themselves. Dr. Reuter advises they get some type of a respite. He suggests that if one parent does most of the caretaking, then the other parent should assume a greater share. In cases where both parents are stressed, hopefully they can leave the baby with a relative or a friend for short periods of time while they get a break away from home.

Not all difficult infants will continue to have problems as they grow older. However, parents of hard-to-manage infants still need support during these months whether the baby's difficulties are self-limiting or not. Anyone who experiences parenting difficulty, regardless of the cause, should take the initiative and ask a health care professional for help. But I offer a word of caution. Not every doctor can give what is needed. As many of us know quite well, some doctors dismiss parental concerns too readily. Dr. Reuter says that very difficult behavior is not a normal phenomenon of infancy and that such responses do little to help the parents who really need guidance and instruction. Support will come from a doctor who, as Dr. Reuter outlined, treats your concerns seriously, offers information about why a baby might behave in a certain way, and who has specific recommendations to help ease the distress.

Dr. Reuter explains that many pediatricians tend to dismiss these types of concerns, particularly when they are raised during routine visits. He advises parents who have difficult, demanding infants to set aside a special appointment to speak with their pediatrician specifically about their concerns. Once a parent makes a special effort, if the doctor is unresponsive, Dr. Reuter suggests the parents look for someone or some place that deals with infants who have special problems.

A good starting point to find support for the difficult infant is the local hospital. If that hospital does not have a child evaluation unit or any specific programs to deal with infants who have difficulties, it might have a referral system where it can provide names of physicians in the area who deal with this kind of situation. If the local hospital cannot be of help, Dr. Reuter recommends parents contact either the county or state chapter of the American Academy of Pediatrics for the necessary information to obtain these types of services.

Everyone needs to realize that "bad parents" and even "good parents" do not cause Attention-deficit/Hyperactivity Disorder. Dr. Paul Wender says the studies he conducted on adopted children "show fairly convincingly that there is a genetic transmission." Dr. Wender reports that current research is focused on finding the chromosomes which carry the disorder, and perhaps within the next ten to twenty years, investigators will be able to identify the specific gene or genes involved with AD/HD.

The child's environment does not cause the disorder either. However, the child with AD/HD does not exist in a vacuum and we cannot overlook the interplay between this child and environmental conditions. Research indicates that the child's environment often exacerbates his or her AD/HD symptomatology. For instance, practically every mother I interviewed said her child with AD/HD did well in school under the guidance of a sympathetic and understanding teacher. Conversely, with a stern and rigid teacher, the same child did not fare as well.

Conditions at home also affect the child with AD/HD. Dr. Wender explained that parents do not cause AD/HD, but they may aggravate the child's symptoms. "Kids with AD/HD need a parent who is consistent, sympathetic, even-tempered and unflappable," Dr. Wender said. Instead, he noted that the parents of a child with AD/HD often have any number of problems themselves such as depression or even AD/HD. When present, these parental problems often restrict the parent's ability to cope in a calm, consistent manner. I do not suffer from depression or AD/HD, yet certainly my emotional reactions to my son's behavior helped make his problems worse. I intend no blame. Rather, I think every family member suffers and that to aid in recovery, we need to place our responses to the child's behavior in context, particularly when we are operating without a diagnosis and knowledge of the disorder.

AD/HD is not user-friendly. As Dr. Wender explained, the child, because he has AD/HD, may be overreactive to ordinary or more than ordinary family troubles. Just as the child overreacts to ordinary family troubles, the family's troubles become intensified by this child's behavior, which dominates all daily interactions. The stresses created by the disorder leave little time or energy to deal with ordinary problems and pressures, let alone complications such as marital discord. Usually, every individual's needs go unfulfilled. Families gradually become enmeshed in a dysfunctional pattern which begins so subtly that family members grow accustomed to negotiating in a disordered environment. The abnormal takes on the guise of normal. A vicious cycle is created because the child with AD/HD feeds on family troubles and family troubles feed on the child's behavior.

We cannot blame the child for his disorder. Nor can we blame the parents for the difficulty they have coping with the situational demands. Until researchers solve the genetic puzzle, we need to know how to cope with the effects of this disorder. One such way is to maintain a sense of humor. And so I offer you Dr. Paul Wender's aside about the lesson he has learned from genetic studies to date.

Said Dr. Wender in jest, "You should breed with exquisite care, then marry whomever you choose." Since this notion is probably too revolutionary for most people, early diagnosis and treatment might be a suitable alternative. The sooner the child is diagnosed and the family is in treatment, the better the opportunity for families to break that vicious cycle and be restored to normalcy.

Summary

- Average age of diagnosis between six and eight years
- AD/HD is not predicted by "difficult" infant behavior
- Difficult infant behavior identifies at-risk infants
- At-risk infant behavior:

- — evidenced by problems regulating state, e.g., going from quiet to alert, wake to sleep
- — interferes with positive interactions
- — does not meet parental expectations of infancy
- — can result in physical/emotional abuse
- Parents of difficult infants, particularly mothers:
  - — often blame themselves and think they are bad parents
  - — often feel guilty, ashamed, embarrassed, angry, frustrated, resentful
  - — develop a negative self-concept frequently reinforced by relatives and friends
- Parental support for coping includes:
  - — talking with others about difficulties
  - — professional guidance to recognize and anticipate potential problem areas, e.g., transitions, overstimulation
  - — tips for avoiding and managing problems
  - — respite time and shared parental duties
  - Finding professional help
    - — make a special appointment with physician to discuss concerns
    - — avoid physicians who discount or minimize difficulties
    - — utilize child evaluation unit at local hospitals for referrals or help
- Changing perceptions
  - — disorder is not the result of parenting
  - — environmental factors can exacerbate difficulties
  - — affects all family members

CHAPTER THREE

The Toddler Years:
Ages 1–3

Around the time David's life passed the six-month mark, I developed the rather elaborate theory that his embryonic body placed restraints on his attempts to explore, which stifled his curiosity, and that was why he became frustrated so easily. So I welcomed the toddler stage of development with the foolish belief that David would be more content once he came into his own realm. "Toddlers are supposed to be active," I told myself. "They are supposed to get into things. Toddlers are supposed to be somewhat independent, not like a baby monkey on its mother's back."

But I did not know what the toddler with AD/HD could be like. Within a few short months, I found the monkey on my back was now loose in the house. I no longer had full control of him. David had mobility. He had strength. He had the ability to run circles around me, which he did. Being four months pregnant did not make coping with this one-year-old boy any easier. To keep a semblance of order in our house, I realized David, unlike other toddlers I knew, needed undivided attention unless he was asleep.

And to think, once his dad and I foolishly pretended not to notice the great deal of time and energy required by this one small child. I gave up trying to restrict his activity level. Instead I became a mother–vacuum cleaner who followed him around, swept up after him, and swallowed all traces of disorder. Friends who marveled at this display of spit and polish asked in awe, "How do you keep the house so neat with a one-year-old around?" Little did they know it turned into a full-time job.

When David woke from his nap, he not only threw the toys from his crib, he also tossed out the sheet and blankets. And when he wasn't in the process of rearranging the house, David became engaged in inventing new uses for household objects. By thirteen months of age, he knew the stairs were for climbing, but found they could be turned into a slide. A banister became a jungle gym to be scaled from outside the staircase. It was not unusual to find him dangling in midair.

No matter what the activity, David gave it new meaning and purpose. Pots and pans turned into flying disks. Windows made wind chimes. (When you bang on them with a truck they make a shrill, melodic sound.) The drapes became rope swings, electric cords lassos. The dog he chased. David refused to acknowledge the word "No." Unless, of course, it spilled from his lips.

When I called friends and relatives to say, "You won't believe what he did today!" they laughed and said, "He's a piece of work." No one branded him as exceptionally wild. Not even as they watched him progress to the point where he always walked one step ahead of me. Based on their responses, I assumed I over-reacted to his behavior until my mother asked, "How are you ever going to manage little David and a new baby?" I knew I could barely manage my first child, and I had absolutely no answer for my mother's question. Since I was a few months pregnant, within a short time I indeed would be faced with finding a solution.

Meanwhile, David's energy level physically drained me. Yet I knew I could keep him from harm for at least another year before he developed better judgment skills. But his contrary response to my efforts to please him left me disheartened. We never got into sync and I never knew what to expect.

On Halloween, I thought for certain he would be thrilled to give out candy to the neighborhood ghosts and goblins. But when a seven-year-old witch appeared on our porch, David screamed bloody murder until I closed the door. I figured this sinister crea-ture had proved a little too chilling for his bones. But even with the princesses and fairy godmothers he threw a fit. When nothing I did calmed him, I surrendered the notion that mother's instinct was a guide I could rely on through his darkest nights.

By the time David's dad came home, my nerves were shot. "You should have stopped answering the door," he said. To my way of thinking this answer was no solution but rather a stopgap measure. Years later, when once again a witch swept our home into an uproar, I remembered we lived under a very strange spell.

Perhaps then if we knew our son's extreme reactions to be symptomatic of an underlying problem, his dad and I might have had a chance to address the difficulties more effectively. But we did not. Instead, we took each symptom as an isolated behavior and tried to rationalize it as best we could. When illness could not be considered a factor, we blamed ourselves or each other.

Over the course of my second pregnancy, our preoccupation with David's finicky eating patterns grew in direct proportion to my girth. When I told David Sr. I felt frustrated because our son would eat nothing except cereal and milk, he responded as though I said David would only breathe on alternate Tuesdays. "He needs green vegetables. He's probably sick all the time because of what he doesn't eat. Maybe if you had better eating habits . . ." Bang!

I knew my eating habits did not cause David to be such a fussy eater. I even knew my cooking could not be considered at fault. Maybe, I thought, the problem existed because it was I who fed him. But that possibility did not make me feel good. So I decided I simply did not know what kids like to eat. My friends with small children told me what they prepared. But when I placed these tidbits in front of David, in one fell swoop he brushed them to the floor, which made Pogo the dog/vulture very happy.

Shortly before the birth of our second baby, David Sr. moved his office into our house, which gave Dad more time to spend with our son and gave me some respite. There were times, though, I felt inadequate and jealous, especially when I watched them play together. While my instincts about how to nurture this child seemed lousy, Dad's roughhousing pleased young David. While I complained about how frustrating he could be, Dad found him to be "a real kick!" But where we had hoped for a boy our first time around and had one, this time I hoped for a nice, quiet, cuddly little girl.

It was so hard for me to see that I meant anything at all to my son. Whenever I tried to share my affection, David ran in the opposite direction. At times, I felt guilty for believing this little guy set the tone of our relationship. At times, I just felt very sad.

In order for a pleasant interaction to occur, we needed a calm place and a routine activity. Every morning I made sure we sat side by side on the floor of his room and did puzzles together before nap time. At age one and a half, this child could piece together puzzles geared for a five-year-old with very little help. Nurturing David came in quiet moments such as these.

The rest of the day, however, was spent in an effort to keep David out of trouble. This task proved much harder with each month that passed. Whenever I talked on the phone or visited with a friend, David waged an all-out assault on the house. Seasoned mothers told me "Don't worry. David's just one of those kids who is into everything. You'd rather have him inquisitive instead of dull." True. But what concerned me was David's seeming lack of fear.

After his new brother, Jonathan, was born that May, David lost all caution. His stunts became dangerous. I lived in constant fear that one day David would move just a little too fast, do something just a little too impulsive, and not be able to stop the course of action. I worried that one day I might bring my son home in a box.

My fears about David's ability to harm himself were not unfounded. One July morning while I changed the new baby, twenty-two-month-old David quietly left the room. Seconds later, I found him standing on a second-story window sill. Both his hands pushed the thin screen, which was fastened to its frame by only a hook and eye. Until I could find a way to distract him, I froze in the doorway, afraid that my sudden movement might propel David into a forward thrust and free-fall to the pavement below.

That day I decided to buy iron bars for the windows but soon learned even bars were not childproof. The pediatrician emphatically suggested I do whatever it took to keep David safe. "Even if that means you have to tie a rope around his waist and fasten its other end to your wrist."

I already learned to put a harness on him when we walked. David had no respect for traffic. He would run across the street without pausing a second. No matter how many times I tried to teach him to stop, to look, that the street was a dangerous place, he just never listened. But tying us together with a rope? This lifeline was an umbilical cord the likes of which I never expected. I worried he might inadvertently strangle himself. So I followed my mother's advice and watched him like a hawk instead.

Such hypervigilance came with a price. Any semblance of a warm, nurturing relationship severed. Now I was tense, irritable around my older child. My mother asked, "Why are you so uptight? Is anything wrong?"

"No, Mom. I'm just tired," I rationalized.

Her inquisition was relentless. "Are you sure? Are you and big David having trouble? Is it the new baby?" I did not want to admit how petrified David's impulsive actions made me. However, I could definitely state that Jonathan in no way contributed to my anxiety.

Unlike his older brother, Jonathan was a peaceful baby, easy to manage, a happy soul. As he progressed through the early years, he took his time and studied a move before he made it. He left his environment intact. He loved to be held. Around him, I felt like a good mother. I could not understand how two boys born of the same parents could be so entirely different. Only years later did I learn that Jonathan had not inherited the AD/HD disorder as his brother had, and therein lay the difference between my two sons. Where Jonathan proved the essence of joy, David remained an enigma until his dad and I learned the nature of our older son's problem.

Meanwhile, the stress created by a child who constantly seemed to be testing his limits and ours took its toll. Now my husband and I argued, blamed, and pointed the finger at who did what to cause David to do whatever. Even when we agreed David behaved in thus and such a way, we argued about the reasons why.

My husband's explanations vacillated between "There's something wrong with him" and "We must be doing something wrong." Afraid the something wrong might be me, I immediately assumed a defensive stance and dismissed these comments by saying, "Quit making such a big deal out of everything. That's just how kids are."

But I didn't know too many kids as testy as David. My mother said, "He doesn't respect you. He's allowed to get away with too much."

"He really loves to bust your chops," my sister observed.

Since the babysitter, Mrs. Hutchinson, never found him to be a bother, I thought the observations of my mother and sister were correct. My sister-in-law, the mother of five, suggested I "make him sit in a chair when he's naughty. That's what I do with my kids." So I tried. The only way to get David to stay seated would be to sit on top of him.

Days with David became more and more like a game of Russian roulette. I could not predict either what he would do or how he would react, nor could he predict how I would respond to his behavior. He flung himself into the "terrible twos" with a vengeance. He met with constant disapproval and increasing anger from

me. "Don't do this. Don't do that. I said stop that. That's bad."
Instead of soothing lullabies, he heard this daily barrage of commands. He followed very few orders.

Jonathan, on the other hand, received only positive and loving
attention. As David became more his own person, his behavior
became increasingly sullen and aggressive. Everyone, including
me, thought he had an extreme case of sibling rivalry. In actuality,
David did suffer serious blows to his self-image. Now I realize he
had to watch someone else get the nurturing he could not take for
himself.

Maybe that's why David stopped calling me Mommy. Who
knows? When I first heard him address me as Mary, I thought my
two-year-old was just going through the stage when some toddlers
hear their parents refer to each other on a first-name basis and do
the same. Relatives found this behavior cute and to some degree
we all encouraged him. I figured in a short time he would again
call me Mom. That did not happen for a year and a half.

During this time, our family dynamics mimicked a three-ring cir-
cus. David misbehaved. I reacted generally by yelling, since reasoning never worked. Of course, yelling did not help either. Dad
criticized my reaction. Then we argued. When David created
another naughty diversion, we repeated the entire scene until his
father and I, the adults, eventually withdrew in angry silence.
Unknowingly, I gravitated to Jonathan and my husband to young
David. Neither of us could see that our reactive interactions only
served to drive a wedge into our family.

Nonetheless, we all felt the tension. I complained about it frequently. One afternoon at a coffee klatch, my friend Pat suggested
I call the "Totline," a phone service mothers called for answers
from a psychologist to questions regarding their child's behavior.
In the child development books I read, David appeared only
vaguely in evidence on the pages. Thus, when I turned to them for
information, I found instead of answers, more questions. This service, I hoped would provide me with a plausible explanation.

When I mustered the courage and called the Totline, my throat
tightened as soon as I spoke. In a strange way, I felt as though I
had betrayed young David. A sense of relief followed after the
psychologist assured me most of David's behaviors were normal
for his age. "You just have to be consistent with your responses,"
she advised. When I asked her how to handle his refusal to eat

nutritious foods, she suggested I "make a game with the food. You know. Show him how broccoli is like a little green tree." Well, I only knew about airplanes. I couldn't wait for that evening to serve broccoli. But David did not like little green trees either.

I should have predicted such a simplistic solution would not fool David. All along, people told us how bright they found this child. Some even said, "He's too bright for his own good." I wondered if he was too bright to follow the norms.

After all, this child demonstrated he could understand and conceptualize complex events. When David was eighteen months old, his dad and I watched the televised landing of the first orbiting space shuttle. Young David, who sat at my feet seemingly preoccupied with a flashlight, apparently tuned in more than we realized. After the *Columbia* rolled to a stop, he turned to us and said, "I wish I could go up there someday." Neither one of us could believe what we heard.

Mysteries began to make sense to me. I reasoned David was hard to handle because his intellectual abilities far exceeded his physiological development. We only had to wait for his mind and body to get into sync. Then, I figured, he would surely behave appropriately. Meanwhile it seemed sensible to nurture David by responding to his intellect. But in doing so, I perceived David to be older than his years. Once again, in an attempt to explain the nature of this child, I took a wrong turn. I expected David to be smart enough to have greater self-control.

He was not. There were so many days I wished he, like the *Columbia,* could go up there too. Frequently I told him in various tones of voice, "David, you are driving me nuts." I made similar comments to friends and relatives as well. It did not occur to me to question how such feedback affected this two-and-a-half-year-old boy.

But I did realize David's attention-demanding behavior was not the only aspect of life "driving me nuts." During this period, major life stresses bore down on our family. First we had to adapt to a new baby. Then my husband's father died suddenly. My father became terminally ill. When David Sr. came home from the office and announced he had been transferred to another city hours away, I exploded.

Patience has never been my strong suit, but now I had even less. When I brought both boys to the pediatrician for checkups, he asked, "How's it going, Mrs. Fowler?" We had a long history of kibitzing about the trials and tribulations of being David's mother. Generally, the doctor joked with me and shook his fist while he smiled and said, "He needs a good punch in the nose."

This particular winter's day, I was in an ill humor. Instead of making light of David's antics, I held back tears and angrily told the doctor in no uncertain terms, "This kid is driving me nuts. There has to be something wrong with him." The pediatrician quickly retorted, "Maybe there's something wrong with the mother."

That remark did everyone a great disservice because I thought to myself, "Maybe he's right." After all, I took my children to him because I respected his medical judgment. I thought David's lack of control probably was my fault. This thought prevented me from seeing any clinical reason for David's difficult nature.

And this thought also made me really angry, but instead of reacting to the doctor's remark, I took my anger out on David. I decided to declare war on his behavior. Whatever it took, this kid was going to slow down, be careful, and do whatever he was asked, or else. Fortunately, before I chained him to a radiator, the business of moving distracted me. For the time being, David had a reprieve from the iron fist of Mom, the disciplinarian.

Clearly, David did not behave like a typical toddler. But I did not know that. Nor did most parents of children with AD/HD. Granted, many of our kids stood out in a crowd. Still we assumed they were just going through a stage. Perhaps this idea was not too farfetched. After all, there had to be a reason this time in a child's life is called the "terrible twos." Most of us shared the point of view of Brian Doyle, a father who said to me, "I thought he would grow out of it."

The "it" to which Brian referred is the classic out-of-control behavior exhibited by many children with AD/HD. These kids do not grow out of "it" at an early age. If anything, the symptoms of AD/HD intensify as demands from the environment for quiet, in-control, attentive behavior increase.

Dr. C. Keith Conners believes the pattern of AD/HD can be recognized as early as one or two years of age provided you can identify the clues. But at this age, most parents and even many practitioners do not spot the behavior so characteristic of AD/HD.

Dr. Conners describes children with this condition as restless, impulsive, incapable of sticking to a task, and constantly on the go. Traditionally, the likelihood of early diagnosis remains minimal, even for children who are moderately hyperactive and thereby call attention to themselves.

According to Dr. Russell Barkley, mothers often fail to recognize the behavior of the young child with AD/HD as problematic and out of ordinary bounds for a number of reasons. First, new mothers or mothers of only children often lack experience with youngsters and do not know how to identify abnormal behavior. Second, some children with AD/HD have mild problems and consequently do not evidence much difficulty in the years before elementary school because they mainly play. As these children grow older, Dr. Barkley notes, more work is demanded by parents who assign chores and teachers who assign schoolwork. This work taxes children with AD/HD and their difficulties become noticeable. Third, some of these children are exceptionally bright and do not have to study or pay attention until they are in the higher grades, so they compensate for their AD/HD deficits in the early school years through their brilliance.

Beyond this basic inattentive, impulsive, restless framework of behavior, what parents generally see in toddlers with AD/HD are variations of the theme. Most toddlers with AD/HD have unstable moods. They explode in emotional outbursts over a seemingly minute problem or for no apparent reason at all. They are persistent and not readily soothed. They frustrate easily and exhibit very little self-control. They also may be highly curious, which might explain why so many toddlers with AD/HD get lost in shopping malls or why family treasures often are found lying in bits and pieces around their feet. Disturbances in the parent-child attachment are frequently noted. In fact, Dr. Barkley's research shows a higher incidence of negative mother/child interactions prior to identification and management than afterward.

These early signs and symptoms are usually misunderstood. By the time some children with AD/HD reach the preschool age, they are tarred with much rejection and their world has become a very damning place.

The toddler with AD/HD often appears to behave in a willful and deliberately noncompliant way. Child psychologist Sam Goldstein reports that parents usually attribute the child's behavior to a conscious choice on his or her part. In actuality, the child has little control.

To further complicate matters, on some occasions the child with AD/HD does behave appropriately. Such inconsistency confuses those who do not know that the child has AD/HD, or even those who may know. The inconsistent behavior also perpetuates the myth that these children have control when they want. Truth is, these are not the children who *can't* or *won't*. They can and do. It's just that can and do come harder for them, particularly without extra help. The attitude that the child *could* behave if he or she chose to places guilt and blame on the child.

Children who wreak havoc upon themselves and their families do not need rejection. They need the attention of a professional who can determine whether or not there is an underlying problem creating distress. For the child with AD/HD, early diagnosis in and of itself becomes prophylactic.

There are a couple of guidelines parents can follow when troubled by their toddler's behavior. If you suspect a problem exists, regardless of the child's age, acknowledge it and seek a solution. Do not let friends or relatives talk you into believing you have conjured up this notion. That happened to Claudia Kreiger and her husband, both trained child development professionals. They were told, "You're just two professional people looking for something. Leave him alone and he'll be fine." Fortunately, they only waited until their son Jay turned two to learn he had a communication handicap and AD/HD.

For those of us lay people who are unknowledgeable about either childhood behavioral problems or the social service system, finding the appropriate support services takes on the magnitude of a quest. The major questions most of us must answer are: (1) Does my child really have a problem? (2) What is my child's problem? (3) What type of help do I need? (4) Where do I find that help? (5) How do I know I've found the right help? and (6) How will I afford the help? Since AD/HD is both a physical and a mental health problem, there are a number of roads to travel in search of answers.

Once you suspect your child has a problem, even if you are uncertain that your assessment is correct, try to identify the problem. You will probably begin with your child's doctor, and may want to follow the suggestion made in the previous chapter, that is, make a special appointment to discuss the problem. Ask the doctor whether the child's behavior is indicative of any specific childhood problem. Do not ask if the behavior is normal. If the child's behavior was normal, it would not bother you to the point that you sought help. Once you inquire, if you are told, "It is too early to tell," "I don't know," or "Your expectations are too high," travel along and seek the advice of another professional who is well versed in childhood behavioral problems. In this regard, I am reminded of the sage advice given by one of the fathers I interviewed. "Listen to the mother," Ben Green said. "She is with the child every day and sees the problems." The message to mothers is TRUST YOUR INSTINCTS.

The exact nature or cause of the child's problem and the help the child will need are closely related. Often the person who determines the nature of the child's problem also manages the treatment of the problem. Parents must find a competent clinician with expertise in their child's particular problem, which in this case is AD/HD. Like myself, many parents when first presented with a need for professional services do not have the vaguest idea of where to begin to find these services.

According to Kathy Collins, a social worker who is the director of Consultation and Education for CPC Mental Health Services in New Jersey, parents should not blame themselves if they get confused and frustrated as they try to find their way through the complicated maze of health care services. When a parent is concerned about a child's behavior, Ms. Collins suggests a mental health center as a good place to begin the answer-seeking journey. Though the size and services offered may vary, she says most communities have mental health centers, and most of these centers are equipped to diagnose learning and behavioral problems. People can locate mental health centers through listings in the phone book or through referrals by their child's doctor. In addition to community agencies, many universities also have mental health clinics that will assess behavioral and learning problems.

Another alternative Kathy Collins suggests as a first place parents might call is the local hospital, particularly if the hospital is large and/or a teaching facility. Such hospitals often have child evaluation services equipped to diagnose and make recommendations for a wide range of childhood disorders.

Parents who suspect their infant or toddler has special needs, for

instance AD/HD, can also look to their local school districts for information about where to go for help. Thanks to a law passed by Congress in 1975 and its subsequent amendments, early intervention
services now exist for infants and toddlers with special needs (ages
birth up to three), and special education services for preschoolers and
school children with disabilities (ages three to twenty-one). This law,
which was originally named the EHA, is now called IDEA — the
Individuals with Disabilities Education Act.

Assessment is one service mandated by this law. An infant or
toddler with AD/HD might be found eligible to receive services
because of cognitive problems such as inattention or disorganization, or psycho-social problems such as difficulty following rules
or planning and completing tasks. To learn more about these laws
and programs, obtain a free copy of "A Parent's Guide to Access-
ing Programs for Infants, Toddlers, and Preschoolers with Disabilities," published by NICHCY — the National Information Center
for Children and Youth with Disabilities. (Please see NICHCY listing in Appendix A.)

Head Start programs also offer an avenue for assessment and
intervention services for four- or five-year-old children with AD/
HD found eligible for enrollment in them. The 1993 federal Head
Start regulations consider AD/HD to be a chronic or acute health
impairment entitling the child to special education services when
the child's inattention, hyperactivity, and impulsivity is developmentally inappropriate, chronic, and displayed in multiple settings,
and when it severely affects performance in normal developmental
tasks, for example, planning and completing activities or following
simple directions.

Just as there is a wide array of agencies available to help parents
of children with special needs such as AD/HD, professionals who
diagnose and treat AD/HD come from many different specialities.
These professionals include clinical psychologists, pediatric neurologists, pediatricians, child psychiatrists, and clinical social workers.
Exactly which of these to use depends on the individual's training,
expertise, and area of interest.

Most pediatricians are trained in childhood behavioral problems
and often prove to be the first doctor parents contact. Many pediatricians, however, have very demanding practices. Beyond medication, they often do not have the time to coordinate and manage the
other areas of treatment which AD/HD requires. Parents must

determine if their child's pediatrician has the time or inclination to devote to the child's treatment.

Pediatricians often refer AD/HD cases to pediatric neurologists or child psychiatrists, both of whom are physicians who can treat the AD/HD disorder medically. Neurologists tend to be more involved with the organic basis of the disorder, while child psychiatrists deal with the emotional aspects of the disorder. Child psychiatrists, unlike pediatric neurologists, are also trained to do clinical work with the children and their families. Similarly, child psychologists are trained to treat the disorder clinically. However, they use nonmedical interventions, often in conjunction with medication prescribed by a physician. Unlike the other specialities, child psychologists have the advantage of being trained to administer psychological tests.

Any of the aforementioned practitioners may choose to specialize in the treatment of neurodevelopmental problems. To do so, they must seek additional training. Social workers are also competent professionals. However, they do not have specialities and often do not receive formal training in the treatment of neurodevelopmental problems. Parents are wise to inquire about training and experience when choosing any practitioner.

Referrals for a therapist who may be well suited for your needs can come from a variety of sources. Some of these sources will have formal referral procedures. Others may do a word-of-mouth type of recommendation. According to Kathy Collins, every state and most counties have mental health associations and these agencies generally have a referral system of mental health professionals including information about their specialities. In addition, the same sources you would go to for information and assessment, i.e., community mental health centers, university mental health clinics, hospital child study evaluation units, school-based assessment teams, and family physicians, can also prove beneficial for therapist referrals.

Support organizations such as CH.A.D.D. (Children and Adults with Attention Deficit Disorders) also are a source of invaluable up-to-date information. CH.A.D.D. National promotes public awareness and advocates on behalf of people with AD/HD. It also offers newsletters featuring articles from nationally recognized authorities, and an annual conference. CH.A.D.D. has over four hundred local chapters throughout the United States. (Please see listing in Appendix A.) If you are looking for a therapist highly trained in the treatment of AD/HD, many of the local ADD parent support groups offer referrals. Dr. Paul Wender applauded the service provided by these organizations and said, "Support groups do what medical societies are unwilling to do. They will tell you that Dr. Jones is available and Dr. Smith is not, that Dr. Jones listens to you carefully and Dr. Smith does not."

I think parents need to be wary of practitioners who only address a child's behavior in theoretical terms. Deep-seated psychological problems do not cause AD/HD. Even if they did, the symptoms require treatment. We parents need practical advice. Whatever practitioner you use, be sure you receive good, solid information based on his or her training and common sense. TRUST YOUR INSTINCTS.

When you seek the services of a therapist, Ms. Collins suggests you follow these guidelines. First, when you call to make an appointment explain your problem and determine if this practitioner can help. Second, when you go to your first appointment, do not commit yourself to being the therapist's client. Ms. Collins explains that the first appointment is part of an assessment process and should be a mutual interview. Both parties, the therapist and the parent, must decide if the therapist can help. Then the parents need to decide if they want to work with this particular person. Third, if you know, for instance, that your child has AD/HD, be sure to determine the amount of training the therapist has with the disorder. If you do not know what your child's problem is, Ms. Collins advises parents to describe the child's behavior along with steps the parents have already taken, and ask for a diagnosis and assessment based on those facts.

As everyone knows, health care can often be somewhat expensive. Ms. Collins says every community mental health center receives state monies and most of them also receive local and federal funds to provide affordable services for everyone. Each agency has some type of mechanism to provide these low-cost services. Some offer discounts; others have sliding-scale fees. Most agencies take medical insurance. Many private practitioners will also take insurance payments. Some private therapists will even discount their services or treat a small percentage of patients without financial resources for no charge. In addition, university mental health clinics and hospitals might also offer low-cost services. Ms. Collins advises that people with need inquire about the mechanisms in place at the various agencies to provide low-cost services and not to be embarrassed or think they are asking for something unusual.

Along the line of health care and insurance benefits, you should be advised that many companies severely limit the amount of coverage they will allow for mental health problems. I personally believe such shortsightedness is a step back into the Dark Ages. Much documentation exists to demonstrate that untreated mental health problems lead to physical ailments, reduced productivity, and other difficulties that are more costly to society over the long haul. AD/HD is a combination physical and mental health problem. I think our children with AD/HD, and adults as well, should have the same rights to treatment and affordable services as others with chronic disorders. In this current climate of health care reform, you may want to contact your legislators and stress the importance of legislative action requiring affordable and accessible health care and insurance coverage for all people with disabilities, including those with AD/HD.

In addition to diagnostic services, most parents of children with AD/HD need some form of training to effectively manage children with these difficulties. One way to acquire such training is through parent training groups, which are generally facilitated by mental health professionals. Private practitioners who specialize in AD/HD sometimes offer group training. Most will also conduct private training.

Other avenues of parent training exist as well. Two mothers I spoke with, Colleen Patterson and Donna Rothman, turned to Parents Anonymous when they experienced behavioral difficulties with their children with AD/HD. This nationwide organization is set up primarily for parents who are in danger of abusing their children, and some Parents Anonymous groups offer parent training. Parent training courses might also be offered through child guidance clinics, mental health centers, local child protection services, municipalities, community colleges, and adult schools of education.

Dr. Richard Zakreski is a clinical psychologist in private practice who works primarily with children, adolescents, and families and has a special interest in AD/HD and learning disabilities. I spoke with Dr. Zakreski about the general principles parents need to follow when rearing a child with AD/HD. The following information is in essence an overview of behavior management principles for these children. Literally hundreds of books exist on this subject alone. The information below is meant to be informative. In no way should it replace a clinical approach to parent training. It can be used, however, as a guide to determine if your family is getting the type of help needed to effectively manage the behavioral difficulties that frequently accompany AD/HD.

Dr. Zakreski explains that all children, including those with AD/HD, need their parents to provide a structure to guide their behavior. This structure must provide rules and limits and parameters so that the child has a clear picture to follow in order to determine what behavior is or is not appropriate and acceptable in given situations.

Children without AD/HD are quick to regulate their behavior to follow the rules inherent in the structure. For instance, they will know to stop talking when seatwork begins. Children with AD/HD, on the other hand, often have difficulty recognizing rules that are not explicitly stated. They tend to misbehave and frequently break rules because of their impulsive, uninhibited, and disorganized nature. Yet children with AD/HD behave better when they have a clear picture to guide their behavior. Thus, they need to be guided by a structure that is consistent and predictable. In other words, the structure must be so clear that the child fully understands what behavior is expected and the consequences for meeting or not meeting those expectations.

These children also need a considerable amount of feedback about the behavioral choices they make, and they are to be held accountable for those choices. When managed accordingly, children with AD/HD have an improved ability to regulate their own behavior to external limits. This type of management approach is not really aimed at controlling children. Rather, the point is to provide these children with a clear picture of rules followed by consistent consequences so that they develop routine responses to everyday situations and thereby develop self-control. To get there, though, at first parents (and teachers) might have to be very much involved.

Parents need to understand that children do not follow rules simply because the rules exist. A verbal understanding of a rule does not mean the child will automatically internalize the rule so that it guides his or her behavior flexibly and adaptively in different situations on different days. For instance, ask a child with AD/HD what the rule is about running inside the house after he or she has done so and broken an object. In all likelihood, the child knows the rule about running indoors. Yet just talking about the rule rarely makes the child embrace it, particularly when the child is younger or a child with AD/HD. Rules work because they are applied consistently and enforced over time in ways that are meaningful to the child. If running inside the house is frequently ignored, then the child will not always follow the rule. From the child's perspective, the no-running rule sometimes but not always creates confusion about what the parents actually expect and may even teach the child that running inside is okay provided that nothing gets broken.

Even though AD/HD is an involuntary, nondeliberate condition, when creating a system to effectively manage the behavior of the child with AD/HD, therapists use the premise that the child is making choices about that behavior. How a parent responds after the child has made a behavioral decision is what makes the structure work. Thus, behavior management systems are a critical part of the structure. These are designed to influence the child's choices by how parents (or teachers) respond to them.

Influencing behavioral choices is basically a four-step process:

1. Tell the child what behavior is expected in a given situation.

For example, at dinnertime, you might tell the child you expect him to eat all the food on his plate within twenty minutes.

2. Tell the child the consequences for doing or not doing what is expected.

In the dinner example, the child is given dessert after eating the meal in the specified amount of time; otherwise there will be no dessert and no food for the rest of the night.

3. Give the child an opportunity to make a behavioral decision.

The child in our dinner example has the choice to eat or not eat all the food in the specified amount of time.

4. Hold the child accountable for his or her choice by applying a consequence for the behavior.

If the child decided to eat dinner and did so in the specified time, dessert is given along with praise.

As simple as these steps and the example appear, we parents can often get into a lot of difficulty using this four-step process in real-life situations. We need to anticipate where problem areas could arise. For instance, if we expect the child to eat all his dinner in twenty minutes, we must also decide if that means the child begins eating as soon as dinner is served and does not leave the table during the meal. Does eating all the dinner mean all, or is the child allowed to skip the lima beans, which you know the child will never eat no matter what you offer in return? Does nothing to eat for the rest of the evening mean nothing to eat, or does it mean if the child keeps whining about how hungry he is and maintains that he would eat if only you would cook the meals he likes, you give in and give him a bowl of cereal instead of the snack he might usually have?

To influence behavioral choices, parents sometimes have to be very firm and rigid. Otherwise, the child gets trained to look for loopholes. In so doing, the child actually learns to manage parental behavior more effectively than the parents manage the child's behavior.

The use of consequences to shape the behavior of the child with AD/HD by influencing his or her choices is extremely important. By definition, the word "consequence" means "that which follows." Usually people think of consequences as being negative. In actuality, consequences can be either positive or negative. When kids do something well, a positive consequence delivered by a significant other, e.g., parent or teacher, helps them to recognize that they made a good decision. Praise and recognition increase the likelihood that the good decision means a good consequence will follow. Conversely, when the child misbehaves, he or she suffers a negative consequence. Then the child understands that a poor decision led to an unpleasant consequence.

Positive consequences come in many forms: an oral acknowledgment, such as "good going"; a kiss on the cheek; material rewards, such as food or toys; or the receipt of certain privileges, such as television time. Always give oral praise along with any other positive consequence.

Negative consequences similarly range from disapproval or an oral reprimand, such as "I do not like it when you . . . ," to a withdrawal of privileges and punishment where indicated. Although a parent may be quite frustrated or angry about the child's misbehavior, it is important that punishment be communicated to the child in a matter-of-fact, emotionally controlled manner. However, parents of children with AD/HD need to realize, as Dr. Conners said, "They are human beings under extraordinary stress." Thus, if mistakes are made when delivering punishment, rather than wallow in guilt, parents need to try better next time. The best advice I've ever heard is, "ACT, DON'T REACT." Sometimes, to avoid reacting, you may have to leave the room or count to ten. If so, when you are calmed, take action and give the child a negative consequence for inappropriate behavior.

One action proven effective for use with all children is time-out. Time-out means that the child is sent to a predetermined location and literally timed out of rewarding activities. For example, if the child smacks a sibling, time-out becomes a reasonable consequence for that behavioral decision, because the child has violated the social contract of shared living within the household, i.e., no hitting. In time-out, the child no longer has the privilege of choosing location or activity, or how he or she will spend his or her time.

The actual location of the time-out spot is chosen by the parent. Once sent to time-out, in general, the child is expected to stay there for five quiet minutes, with emphasis on quiet. For younger children, two minutes is a more appropriate time. Similarly, fifteen minutes may be more suitable for a twelve-year-old. After time-out, the child should be rewarded with an approving statement for a positive change in his or her behavior.

Consequences can also be either logical or natural. Whenever possible, consequences should be logically or naturally related to the original behavioral decision made by the child. Logical and natural consequences can be either positive or negative. A natural consequence means the behavior and the consequence are naturally related. For example, the child who does not eat dinner will be hungry and not satisfied. The baseball glove left in the rain and not put away will be ruined. Logical consequences have a logical connection between the behavior and the consequence and are imposed by people. For example, if you do not put your toys away, you will not be allowed to play with them for X amount of time. If you stretch out your bedtime, you will have to go to bed earlier. If you come home late, you will have an earlier curfew or be grounded.

To create a clear and predictable structure in order to effectively influence behavior, we might need to use a systematic approach to behavior management. Specially designed behavioral programs for home or school use provide that structure. Such programs become more effective when both parents work together. To date, behavior charts have proven the most widely used and effective approach to systematically managing behavior. The benefit of charts is that they tell the child what behavior is expected and provide daily feedback in a consistent fashion. The charts help to shape the child's behavior, and, even more important, the child develops an inner sense of self-control. We want the child to view his behavior as a series of choices he makes and to feel that he is responsible for those choices. Because good choices are paid with positive outcomes, the child learns to make appropriate decisions.

Behavior management systems should be instituted when children are young and kept in use into the teenage years with modifications made in the program to suit age and need. These programs prove harder to implement with the teenager who has AD/HD, especially if the teen with AD/HD has not previously been exposed to behavior charts. He or she will predictably balk. Nonetheless, the program should be instituted despite any resistance.

Dr. Russell Barkley feels that behavior charts are "nothing glitzy—just good hard work at learning to manage a disabled individual." The hard work stems from the fact that the charts require daily implementation on a long-term basis, parental organization, and regimentation. After a while, as parent Hope Clark explained, "I just want to take things as they come and live like a normal family, so I stop using the chart. Of course, Tommy's behavior deteriorates within a few short days."

Many varieties of behavior charts exist, as do many books which explain the use of behavior management techniques. Various examples of charts are included in Appendix C. Behavior charts, however, need to be tailored to each individual child's needs. Certain guidelines have to be followed. Charts can be a "do-it-yourself" project, but behavior management is a sophisticated skill, especially when used with children who have special needs. To get started, professional guidance is generally advisable. (For further discussion, please see Chapter 6.)

Dr. Zakreski suggests the following as guidelines for the use of behavior management charts:

1. Select behaviors to manage.

The parents with input from the child need to select the behaviors to be managed on the chart. The child also needs to understand exactly what is expected from him or her in terms of these behaviors.

2. Choose a limited number of behaviors to work on at any given time.

With young children, only a few behaviors should be selected at any given time since they do not have the developmental capacity to work on more. With older children, it is generally advisable to start with just a couple of behaviors and then add additional behaviors as the child meets with success. However, no more than five behaviors should be charted at any one time so as not to overwhelm the child (or parent). As the child meets with success in shaping the behavior, then additional behaviors can be added one at a time.

3. Chart the behavior you want the child to use.

Behavior management is designed to encourage the use of appropriate behavior. In charting, you want to be sure the child is working to meet behavioral expectations. Thus, behaviors are phrased to tell the child what you expect, rather than what you don't expect. For example, suppose you don't want the child to hit other family members. Instead of writing "no hitting" on the chart, you would write something along the lines of "treats other family members, including pets, in a polite, courteous way."

4. Chart only routinely occurring behaviors.

The behaviors selected for the chart should occur every day. Examples of such behaviors include going to bed on time, doing homework, and getting ready for school on time. In using everyday behaviors, the child is afforded the maximum opportunity to develop control over them. Once you and your child have developed some expertise with this type of system, you can depart from using daily-occurring behaviors and use behaviors which occur less frequently or more irregularly. Whether or not you use a chart for these irregular behaviors, they should still be responded to with natural and logical consequences.

5. Build consequences into the chart.

Once you establish the behaviors, you have to give the child the choice to behave appropriately. Then you must pay attention to the child's behavioral decisions throughout the day and give the appropriate feedback. When the child makes good behavioral choices, he or she should be rewarded with approval messages and some form of tangible marker such as tokens, stickers, or points.

6. Determine daily performance.

The points, stickers, or tokens earned are tallied at the end of each day. In doing so, the child is held accountable for the overall daily performance. Tallying the score at the end of the day is preferable because then the child is held accountable for patterns of behavior rather than specific acts. If the child has little or no markers, then he or she did not comply or meet minimal expectations for behavior.

7. Give consequences for daily results.

The parents use the child's total daily score to determine the positive or negative consequences earned for his or her behavior over the course of the day. The positive and negative consequences will come in the form of the granting or withdrawal of certain privileges agreed upon when the chart is first designed. Such privileges could include going to bed a half-hour later, having time to play Nintendo or watch television, having a friend over, or going out for pizza or ice cream. When the system is used in conjunction with natural and logical consequences throughout the course of the day, the behavior is dually consequated.

As you can readily see, such behavioral management systems are, indeed, good hard work. Dr. Zakreski cautions parents to be consistent and stick to the program once they decide to use it. In so doing, they give the child the impression that the behavior is important and that they mean what they say. Dr. Zakreski points out that when you make a rule and then fail to enforce it, the child does not respect you and gets the message that he or she can turn your "no" into a "yes." For instance, if you withhold food as a consequence after the child makes the behavioral decision not to eat and then whines and cries and wears you down, and two hours later you back down and give him or her food, the child's gotten control and you have increased the likelihood that he or she will challenge you in the future. Firmness and consistency are the operative words in behavior management.

The point of behavior management is for parents to get better at making the child's behavior his or her own problem than the child is at making his behavior the parent's problem. Even if you are tired or involved in other things, when the child makes a poor behavioral decision, you have to enforce the consequence. If behavior management does not work, then the parents have been unsuccessful at making the child responsible for his or her behavior by experiencing the consequences for it.

Another common pitfall of behavior management is complacency. Dr. Zakreski knows many parents who develop a good program, implement it, and produce positive changes. Then they get really happy and are lulled into a sense that the child is doing great now, so they stop the program. Within a short period of time, the child's good behavior slides and the family is back to square one.

"In order to control their behavior successfully, children with AD/HD do not need different parenting. But they do need extra parenting," Dr. Zakreski said. Thus, the skills used with children with AD/HD are the same skills used with all children. However, for kids with AD/HD, these skills must be used in a more articulate, more consistent, more deliberate way because children with AD/HD need that extra management and organization and feedback from parents.

Summary

Manifestations During Toddler Years
- Symptoms intensify as environmental expectations increase
- Generally, toddlers exhibit an impulsive, restless, always-on-the-go behavior pattern
- Other behavioral difficulties include:
  — unstable mood
  — problems with sleeping or eating
  — extreme curiosity
  — intense responses to stimuli
- Disturbances in parent-child attachment often occur
- Children are viewed as choosing to be noncompliant

Guidelines for Finding Help

- Discuss difficulties with physician
- Identify assessment and treatment resources at community mental health centers, hospital child evaluation clinics, local school districts, private practitioners
- Use a practitioner knowledgeable about AD/HD: clinical psychologists, pediatric neurologists, pediatricians, child psychiatrists, and clinical social workers trained in diagnosis and treatment
- Referral sources include AD/HD parent support organizations, community or university mental health centers, school-based assessment teams, family physicians
- Interview practitioners

— determine amount of AD/HD training and number of cases

Help for Parents

- Training in behavior management techniques to:
  - set rules
  - give commands clearly
  - limit amount of demands made
  - institute consequences
  - follow through on consequences
  - consequences must be consistent
  - consequences can be positive or negative, logical or natural
- Act, don't react to inappropriate behavior
- Use time-out
- Use behavior charts
  - to help structure the environment
  - to develop the child's sense of self-control
  - with consistency

CHAPTER FOUR

The Preschool Years:
Ages 3–5

Once I grew accustomed to the reality of our impending move, I told myself this geographic change would be a new beginning. Without the lure of friends and relatives to escape from home activities, I planned to devote my full attention toward shaping David into a quiet, ordered little boy.

But David now approached the time when a child's horizons expand to the world beyond, the preschool era of children aged three to five years. Neighborhood children and nursery school beckoned. Soon I would have even less control of him. No longer would we conduct most of our business in the privacy of our own home. Like most parents, I hoped my son would shed the difficult skin he wore and ease into the world beyond his front door.

My husband and I left the children with their aunt the day we physically moved into our new home. When they arrived the following day, their rooms were ready. Childproof locks secured all cabinets; curtains laced some of the windows. However, before I unpacked his toys, David took ill. As always, I attributed this fever to an ear infection, but the new pediatrician said, "A virus, probably brought on by the stress of the move."

His diagnosis surprised me. Though I knew David overreacted to silly little changes, I expected him to handle the relocation with ease. After all, unlike myself and Jonathan, David, as with his dad, seemed to thrive on adventure. A few days later, he perked up when we attended a welcome coffee given for me by a neighbor.

Stacy Birdwell invited all the neighborhood ladies to meet me. One of them also brought along her three-year-old son so David would have a playmate. Over the din of our voices we all heard the noise from the other room where David was trying to convince Ryan to "relinquish" a toy. The little fellow stood his ground until my son's persistence forced him to retreat into the folds of his mother's skirt. When our hostess attempted to appease David with another toy, he threw it to the floor. Totally mortified, I slunk further down into my chair.

This image was not the one I wished to portray in our new neighborhood. I wanted our family to be like the one in the sitcom "Leave It To Beaver" where everyone interacted in a polite, courteous fashion, where parents asserted their control and the children aimed to please them, where all problems subsided quietly and calmly behind closed doors, always within a half hour. But from that fateful spring morning, Ryan's mom always made an excuse whenever I suggested we get the boys together.

David Sr. attributed our son's aggressive behavior at the coffee to frustration. "David probably felt ignored," he said. Over time, however, I noticed he even played roughly with our dog Pogo despite the fact he had grown old enough to know better. David never behaved nastily. He just ran at that dog with so much exuberance, the poor beast turned her tail and ran in the other direction whenever she saw him. Our neighbor commented many times about our pet's good nature.

These days, so much of David's behavior proved inappropriate and could not be ignored. Every activity became an ordeal, even simple walks through the neighborhood. Logic would dictate after a few bad experiences, a sensible person would know when to quit and make changes. And I did really cut back the number of outings. I stopped taking David to shopping malls and grocery stores, but I hungered for adult company and so persevered with our daily afternoon jaunts through the streets where we lived. People always stopped me to admire the kids. After a while, I met some of them on a regular basis.

If we happened to speak for more than a few minutes, David, ever in search of action, impatiently tried to pull me away. Failing this first attempt, he then rode his Big Wheel full throttle and, on his more impish days, headed it directly toward my legs. If this action did not achieve the desired effect, he played bumper cars with Jonathan's stroller. Jonathan accepted these jolts with good nature.

But most everyone else remarked about David's demands for my attention. His actions embarassed me, and I grew increasingly resentful that he interrupted my conversations. I assigned motives to his actions which reinforced my incorrect perception that David deliberately chose to create trouble. Before long, I found myself in the habit of making sarcastic comments about him. When someone stopped to say, "He's so adorable," I invited them to stick around. Those who stayed usually saw my point.

Through no conscious effort on my part, such comments reduced the shock value of David's actions and placed them in the Peck's Bad Boy category. They prepared people to expect the worst. If the worst did not happen, all the better. My remarks also shielded me from my feelings of incompetence and allowed the observer to know though I acknowledged David's "bad" behavior, it nonetheless remained out of my control.

While my negative comments minimized the effects of David's behaviors on others, they went far to keep the wedge between us. Today, I'm certain such feedback tore at my son's self-worth. Instead of his best fan, I appeared his worst critic. I felt ashamed of my reactions to this child. Our mother-child bond had stretched to its limit. I now depended more and more on my positive interactions with Jonathan to feel like a good mother. David, to the contrary, became increasingly resentful of his younger brother. Our family had all the trappings of a miserable mess.

When the time for nursery school arrived, David Sr. and I, despite our ambivalent feelings, decided to enroll David. He thought David too young. I worried the teachers might not understand such a loud and unruly child. But I also had concerns about his social development. With the one neighborhood child out of the picture, Jonathan remained his only playmate. David bossed his younger brother so much Jon and I both needed a few hours' peace.

The school's director listened to my concerns about David's readiness for nursery school. She told me not to worry, "Most children need to adjust." The curriculum centered around play and social interaction. Since David never balked about going, after a time I figured nursery school agreed with him.

One winter day, his teacher, Mrs. Able, stopped my car to hand me an owl he crafted from kidney beans. "David worked so hard on this owl, Mrs. Fowler. I just wanted you to know what an effort he made," she said. Well, I beamed with pride. His mosaic depicted a flawless owl. How sweet of her, I thought, to commend David's obvious talent in person.

When the first parent-teacher conference arrived a month later, I could not wait to hear more about my son's ability. After I sat down and Mrs. Able said, "Oh, David's coming along nicely," I scratched my head. That comment did not sound at all like the glowing report I expected to hear.

"Hasn't he been doing well?" I asked.

She hesitated and then told me the kidney-bean owl represented one of the rare days when David stayed on task. She felt pleased for him and figured if she made a big fuss over his accomplishment he might repeat it again. But most days, David became frustrated about his work and lost his temper quite demonstratively.

"He's not a problem," she assured me. "I just say 'David, attitude, attitude, attitude!' and he catches himself."

What a great response, I thought, but when voiced by my lips, Mrs. Able's words brought an even angrier attitude.

Though these days David's attitude also presented an annoyance on the home front, other improvements in his behavior compensated for the nuisance. No longer did I worry about his physical well-being. David, now three years old, seemed less fragile, his actions less rash. Sure he ran across the field during a high school football game while a play was in progress, but he saw his dad on the other side and the shortest distance between two points is a straight line. And he did stop cold in his tracks when the referee blew the whistle to prematurely stop the play.

He now called me Mom again. True, I had to force the word from his lips, but he gave me this courtesy. He even showed signs of affection. When I landed in the hospital with a mysterious illness, I came home to find a teddy bear David had propped on my pillow. I praised him and bragged to everyone about this loving gesture he made. For years after, though I still did not get bedtime kisses, every night I received a stuffed animal which my son selected with the greatest care.

I'm not certain why David's behavior improved. Perhaps the change could be attributed to the fact that he had grown older. Or maybe since I had a respite while he went to nursery school, I felt less tense and did not overreact to everything he did. Who knows? But I thought David even handled the jealous feelings toward his brother in a better fashion. One day as I prepared to leave for an overnight trip, David said, "Jonathan goes too."

Shocked at this gesture of goodwill, I skeptically asked, "You want me to take Jonathan?"

"Yes," he replied, "take Jonathan to Granny's and leave him there." Now that young David verbalized his feelings, I figured with speech for a tool, he no longer needed to act on every whim. And so I anticipated an improvement in life around our house, at least where David was concerned.

Even though young David's behavior seemed less problematic, tensions within our marriage flared. Most of our problems did not arise as a result of trying to manage our son. We each brought problems to the marriage in the first place. If anything, David's difficulties enabled us to avoid facing the harsh realities. My husband and I found ourselves entangled in a negative interactional mess wherein he blamed me, and I, of course, blamed him, for the unhappiness. Before we could address the issues, life handed us a few major stresses within a period of two months. Our marital situation deteriorated from bad to worse.

David Sr. made a career move, and a year to the day, we once again relocated. Since this change brought us back home, we didn't anticipate that this move would be stressful. We had not learned that new jobs and even brand-new houses upset the status quo. This time I flew into orbit because of the additional stress resulting from the death of my father the day after we moved.

No one during this journey had been stamped "handle with care." Only our belongings arrived intact. But these things broke soon after being unpacked. First, a family-room lamp smashed when three-and-a-half-year-old David clipped it with his feet while somersaulting off the couch. A teacup met its destruction next, though not by accident: when David Sr. made a critical remark, I hurled the cup at the kitchen wall. For months, until I wallpapered the room, tea stains bore witness to my loss of self-control.

Young David's reactions, however, proved impossible to cover up. He unleashed his temper with a fury that rocked the nursery school walls. In one morning, he hit a child, pushed another off the slide, and threw sand at yet a third. The teacher, totally exasperated, sat him in the corner for over an hour and even after I arrived, she refused to allow him to leave that spot until she vented her frustration on me.

He looked so frightened. I could not believe David behaved in such an aggressive manner without provocation. Since this teacher clearly played favorites and my little boy did not make her list, I rationalized that she might be partially to blame for his behavior by doing nothing to ease his transition to this new school. I bit my tongue so as not to scream at her, "Why don't you give him a break? Can't you see how this move affected him?"

When I recounted this incident to David Sr. he agreed with my assessment of the nursery school teacher's role. But, as always, he carried his comments a step further and insisted this new teacher did not recognize David's need of special attention. By now, I suspected young David might have some underlying problem that made his life intense. But honestly accepting the possibility that my son could have a hurt which I could not fix threatened me, and so I tried to ignore my suspicions, to bury my fears. I had no conception of what more I could do for my boy.

A few weeks after the school episode, David's outbursts at home intensified with such magnitude, his rages scared me. I confiscated the croquet set along with all sticks and blunt objects. When David got mad, he let them fly at whatever or whoever happened in his path. Punishment had little, if any, effect. His temper could not be controlled.

With the tea from my rampage still a blot on the kitchen wall, I felt responsible as though somehow he patterned his actions after what others now referred to as "my high-strung behavior." His father continually said to me, "You're the one having the problem." There seemed no other explanation but the obvious, his mother. My self-esteem hit an all-time low. I slipped into a depression.

Life in our home became enshrouded in unpleasantry. Young David blamed everybody and everything for his behavior. When he ran in the house and crashed into a table, he smashed that "bad table" to bits. When I said, "David, you did the running," he got angrier. If he fell off his bike, instead of crying like other children, David repeatedly threw it to the ground or into the garage door. Even when playing nicely, David managed to break all his toys. His room always looked as if a tornado had just passed through. None of the neighborhood children invited him to play except one very mild-mannered young boy. Often Jonathan received the full thrust of his brother's fury. But unless he had been physically hurt,

Jon just sort of took David's actions in stride, and I felt somewhat gratified that at least my younger son was mellow.

David's dad coped with the turmoil by denying its existence and burying himself in work. I buried my head under the covers minutes after the boys went to bed. During the daylight hours, I felt tired all the time. A friend suggested I get out more with the boys and take them to the beach. Well, I thought, that couldn't hurt. But after a week my stomach went into severe spasms.

David refused to obey the club rules. Such audacity always resulted in a reprimand from the owner, who then flashed me a dirty look. Time and again I redirected young David's attention, but he did not learn to stop even when I forcefully removed him from off-limits places. He pushed and pulled until he became free and immediately returned to the scene of the crime. Eventually he wore me down and I either gave in to his whims or left the beach in a huff. The other mothers gave us a very wide berth.

That summer ended when Jonathan landed in the hospital from the effects of a mysterious virus. The week before, my mother had commented about how awful and pale he looked, but Jonathan never fussed, so I assumed his health was fine. Years later, our child psychologist explained this incident to be a prime illustration of his favorite cliché, "The squeaky wheel gets the oil." David became the center of all that happened in our house by demanding so much of our time and energy, everyone else's needs went unattended.

Relatives warned both David Sr. and me that our younger son did not receive enough attention. Still, everyone laughed when I referred to our boys as Charley McCarthy the dummy and his ventriloquist Edgar Bergen. David consistently interrupted his younger brother to finish Jon's every sentence. Though I agreed with my family that David clearly usurped center stage, I quickly dismissed their comments. "But the attention Jonathan gets is always positive," I explained. "David gets nothing but negative press," his father concurred. I could not understand why these people did not see how little we, as parents, had left to give.

Anyone who walked through our door could not avoid the tension. My husband and I reacted through shouting matches or angry silences. By fall, the hostility proved impossible to submerge. We individually sought private therapy which eventually led to marriage counseling.

The therapist needed time to sort out the mess of our marriage. Yet he almost immediately realized that our son's behavior, though not the cause of our problems, acted as a catalyst wherein our negative patterns surfaced. However, why all our family outings ended in disaster and why chaos constantly surrounded us remained a mystery.

After the events of David's fourth birthday party, neither his dad nor I could continue to make excuses for our son's outrageous behavior. That day after all the little guests arrived, David flipped into a frenzy. His mood grew so dark he zapped all the joy from the event. The birthday party ultimately degenerated into an ugly scene when at the petting zoo David smacked a horse in the mouth, an action which totally stunned his dad and me.

All along we figured our son's aggressive behavior to be a reaction to some provocation. Clearly, he hit the horse for no apparent reason, and though initially we felt like strangling him, after the shock subsided, we realized David had no control. Where I once viewed him as the master of his deeds, now I saw he needed help. Though his dad still didn't believe our son could have a problem, we set out to find the source of what troubled him.

That journey turned into a pathetic comedy of errors. We spent eighteen months going from one professional to another before we obtained an accurate diagnosis. Our search began at the pediatrician's office. In my initial conversation I told the doctor everything about David's behavior which puzzled me. After recounting the horse-hitting incident, I chronicled his behavior from infancy to date. I ended this diatribe with an observation. "Doctor, he will not allow his dad and me to have a conversation at the dinner table. His behavior is not normal, is it?"

The doctor replied, "No, Mrs. Fowler, the behaviors you describe are not normal."

The pediatrician sent us to an allergist who saw David in November of 1983. The allergist observed David to be hyperactive. He told me no one really understood the cause of hyperactivity. Since David reacted positively to house dust, he received shots every week.

The allergist also placed David, a finicky eater to begin with, on an elimination diet to see if foods exacerbated his problems. We then used the Feingold diet, which promised to alleviate hyperactivity by restricting certain foods such as additives, preservatives, salicylates, and sugar. The promises of the Feingold diet proved worthless. I figured I must be doing something wrong. Though none had tried this diet personally, every mother I knew said she heard this diet worked miracles with other mothers' kids. A year later we learned diet and allergy do not cause AD/HD and no miracles cure it.

Next we landed in a child psychiatrist's office in January. After taking a family history and observing David interact with us, the child psychiatrist said, "David is hyperactive." He then told us our son would outgrow his hyperactivity around puberty and we could use medication if we needed to "slow him down" until then.

The real issue of treatment, he believed, centered around David's angry and ill-mannered behavior. When I asked why our son acted so horrendously, the child psychiatrist said, "Because he has an extreme case of sibling rivalry. You introduced another sibling at the crucial individuation/separation stage of development." At ninety dollars an hour in 1984, I figured he knew his material.

This doctor ended the session with the suggestion that I read about separation/individuation. He gave me Margaret Mahler's book *The Psychological Birth of the Human Infant,* a clinical text offering an in-depth discussion of this critical stage and other stages as well. He then made a recommendation which validated my gnawing suspicion that I was a horrible mother. The psychiatrist told David Sr. to give our son at least two hours a day of individual attention so young David could work through this stage again. When we pointed out that Dad traveled every week, the doctor said, "Hire a neighborhood teenage boy as a substitute father." Though our marriage wavered on shaky ground, neither of us believed David Sr. could be that easily replaced. In May, we ceased using this doctor's counsel when he recommended we gag David to stop him from releasing his ear-piercing shrieks when riding in the car. Nothing improved in our house under his care.

With the school year drawing to a close, my husband and I faced the decision of whether or not to enroll our soon-to-be-five-year-old son in kindergarten. Having no confidence left in our parenting abilities, we attended a seminar on "Kindergarten Readiness" for direction. As usual, the norms did not fit David. The speaker, a licensed and certified school psychologist, suggested he evaluate David privately.

That evaluation lasted an hour and a half. Though David could sustain performance a full year ahead of his age, the psychologist recommended we not place him in kindergarten. In his three-page report to us, the psychologist wrote, "David is very active and has a poor attention span. He is easily distracted and will not stay with tasks for very long. He is a very intense young child and given to open displays of anger and yelling. David does not like new or different situations and cannot re-adapt even after some exposure to them." He had described a child who displayed all the behaviors that are the very hallmarks of Attention-deficit/Hyperactivity Disorder.

Instead of telling us the source of David's problems or referring us to a clinician who specialized in the disorder, his report contained these recommendations. "I would prefer David to be in a very structured and controlled setting at home. If things are always organized and predicted, and quiet and arranged so as not to stimulate David, he can calm down readily and have some control. His activity is not beyond him."

How ridiculous! David's activity proved beyond him, beyond me, beyond the entire family. For some reason a knowledge and understanding of Attention-deficit/Hyperactivity Disorder proved beyond this child development specialist, just as it had eluded the other professionals from whom we sought counsel and guidance.

The signs and symptoms of AD/HD become highly visible at the preschool stage. Except in the very mild cases, children with AD/HD between the ages of three and five generally experience problems in at least one major setting: at home, in school, with peers. Children like David, with moderate to severe degrees of the disorder, exhibit difficulties in all three areas.

Typical reports from nursery school teachers indicate the child's inability to follow directions and stay on task. Children with AD/HD tend to be away from their desks more than do their classmates. Frequently teachers will describe the child as "immature."

Children with AD/HD evidence nursery school problems in different degrees of severity. While only one teacher made only one serious complaint about David, Jan Lawes received such unfavorable reports about her son Doug's behavior, she became a mother volunteer, her rationale being, "I thought if I did everything they could possibly want, they would tolerate my kid a little better." Unlike Doug Lawes, Steven White was not at all disruptive in preschool. Steven does not have the hyperactive or impulsive symptoms of the disorder. Still his mother, Lynn, heard frequent complaints from Steven's preschool teacher because he daydreamed so much and seldom paid attention. One day, in response to the teacher's comments, Lynn said, "Well, you know some kids march to the beat of a different drummer." The teacher insensitively replied, "And some have no drummer at all."

Between the ages of three and five, difficulties with social interactions arise as a dominant problem for many children with AD/HD. Many behave in a verbally and/or physically aggressive fashion with their peers. Though boys with AD/HD tend to be more aggressive than girls, they do not corner the market on aggressive peer interactions. According to her mother, five-year-old Maggie Anderson did not fit the "sugar and spice, everything nice" mold characteristic of young ladies. When Maggie went to a friend's house, if something did not go her way, she literally knocked her female playmate to the floor. After each incident, Maggie's mother apologized and explained that her daughter had a problem with self-control which she and Maggie's dad were trying to correct. Nonetheless, Maggie would still be banished from the other child's home for a period of months.

The overall social behavior of most children with AD/HD is aptly described as immature and insensitive. Dr. Russell Barkley explains, "Children with AD/HD lack self-awareness. They are mentally and developmentally immature and so they behave like younger children. Younger children do not pay much attention to how their behavior affects other people or themselves."

In addition to classifying them as immature, Dr. C. Keith Conners describes children with AD/HD as "socially insensitive." For example, Dr. Conners notes the frequency with which children with AD/HD will blurt out very embarrassing comments in company. Such gaffes are made, he explained, because children with AD/HD are insensitive to the demands of the situation and to how their interactions might affect others.

Children with AD/HD tend to apply rules in a hard-and-fast way rather than as guides to actions. Since they tend to be insensitive to internal states in themselves, they often prove insensitive to how others may be feeling. These children tend to misread the feedback they receive from others about their social behavior. Says Dr. Conners, "Often these kids are amazed they have had an effect on somebody."

If you consider the child with AD/HD's immature and insensitive nature and factor in the impulsivity that accompanies this disorder, you can easily see why social problems become a constant thorn in his or her side. These children generally react before they make an appropriate assessment of a situation to determine what behavior is appropriate. They also tend to be disorganized and so behave in a chaotic manner. Dr. Conners explains that the prerequisites for good socialization are being able to wait your turn, to share with others, and to follow the rules of the game. Since children with AD/HD often cannot delay impulses, impulsivity prevents them from learning these basic rules of fairness. Dr. Conners also cites two other factors which contribute to social problems for children with AD/HD. Because of their hyperactivity, these children are usually not in one place long enough to play a game or to learn the rules. Children with AD/HD frequently have associated visual-motor problems, which makes playing sports somewhat harder too.

According to Dr. Conners, "Children with AD/HD are different from the antisocial kid who wants to hurt other children. Children with AD/HD just cannot control themselves." The inability to restrain behavior and respond appropriately to the demands of a social situation often cause children with AD/HD to experience negative consequences in every arena of social interaction, be that the playground, the neighborhood, the school bus, or the classroom. These children are rejected by playmates, isolated from groups. They receive many unkind comments and are usually the last kids picked for teams if they are picked at all. Most parents know too well the sad fact that their sons and daughters often find themselves excluded from birthday parties. Dr. Conners makes the point that children with AD/HD *want* to be liked and *want* to be involved, but their AD/HD characteristics often prevent them from keeping the friendships they start.

To encourage prosocial behavior, children with AD/HD often require intervention to remediate their social skill deficits. One form of intervention is parental manipulation of the child's social interactions in the home environment. Dr. Richard Zakreski, a clinical psychologist in private practice, believes parents need to become highly involved to help their child with AD/HD build social relationships. He suggests parents create a type of therapy group at home in which they facilitate their child's social development by structuring the child's social time and by providing feedback about the child's peer interactions, so that the child with AD/HD comes to understand and appreciate appropriate social behavior.

Dr. Zakreski reminds parents that building relationships takes time and effort. Therefore, parents need to be persistent and involved. Bear in mind, most children with AD/HD can make friends, but they have difficulty keeping friends. The younger the child with AD/HD is when the parent helps him or her to build social bridges, the better the chance for success. To this extent, Dr. Zakreski described the following approach as a possible way for a parent to help and encourage the child with AD/HD to develop social relationships.

The parent must first target a child to be a playmate for the child with AD/HD. The hope is this target child will be someone who will want to continue a friendship with the child with AD/HD in the future. Preferably the parent will take advantage of any natural alliances and make the target child someone with whom the child with AD/HD has already experienced some positive connection. For instance, if the child with AD/HD came home from school one day and said, "Johnny was nice to me," Johnny would become a good candidate to be the target child. Once a playmate is targeted, the parents then must make the effort to get the child with AD/HD and the target child together at their home. To do so, the parent may have to extend the invitation. Dr. Zakreski advises the parents against leaving the invitation up to the child with AD/HD because he may never get around to it or be reluctant to make it for fear of rejection.

When beginning this social bridge-building process, the goal is to have positive interactions between the two children. Consequently, the third step in the process is for the parents to structure the interaction by limiting the amount of time the children spend together and by selecting an activity that lends itself to parental involvement and supervision. For instance, the parent might arrange for the children to bake cookies, watch a video, or go bowling. Activities such as these allow the parent to control the interactions, to intercede if problems arise, and to give the children feedback about their prosocial behavior.

This bridge-building process is repeated as often as needed to encourage a friendship and a routine type of interaction between

the child with AD/HD and the target child. As these children gradually begin to interact positively and successfully with one another,
the parent can then extend the amount of time the children spend
together and withdraw some of the parental supervision. Once the
child with AD/HD has established a friendship with this target
child, the parent should then repeat the process with a second
child. Dr. Zakreski advises parents to keep the interactions to a
one-on-one situation to avoid the possibility of the odd-man-out
type of interaction. Parents will want to withdraw their involvement to the degree that the child with AD/HD demonstrates the
ability to take responsibility for his or her own activities. Parental
involvement or lack of it is dictated by the social skills of the child
with AD/HD and not the child's chronological age.

In order to develop prosocial behavior, some children with AD/
HD may need professional intervention. Social skills training is one
available therapy for the child with AD/HD. However, AD/HD
expert Dr. Russell Barkley categorizes this treatment as promising
but still experimental. In the clinic where Dr. Barkley practices,
children must be nine years old to engage in this therapy because
he has found that "below this age they do not seem to benefit
much from that kind of instruction." He believes part of the reason
why this therapy does not work for younger children has to do
with the fact that the child is pulled out of his or her natural environment and taught the social skills and then is expected to gener-
alize those skills to nontreatment settings.

Dr. Barkley tries to circumvent this problem by training the
child's parents and teachers to incorporate social skills training as
part of what they do. He cited anger control as one social skill that
lends itself well to parent- and teacher-initiated training. Dr.
Barkley utilizes this method in the following way.

First, the child is taught in a small-group setting how to stop and
think before reacting to frustration, such as being told he or she
cannot do something. Then the parent is instructed to spend some
time each day with the child to review a potentially frustrating situation. For example, the parent may refer to a situation during the
previous twenty-four hours where the child was observed getting
angry. The parent then talks about what else the child could have
done and role-plays the situation again. As the parent walks
through the situation, the child is reminded to do other behaviors
that are incompatible with getting angry. The parent might suggest

the child think about things that do not get him or her angry, count to ten, tighten his or her lips, or keep his or her mouth closed. After the exercise, the parent rewards the child with tokens which can then be exchanged for special privileges or prizes. Dr. Barkley says, "It has been shown these children can pick up very quickly on controlling their anger, but these skills require rehearsal and practice."

Socialization groups prove to be another popular forum in which to teach children with AD/HD social skills. Betty Garver sent her son Joel to such a group because he was poorly coordinated and could not compete with the other boys. As a result, he tried to "one up" them or to boss them around, which only antagonized the other children. He did not know how to fit into a group. His mother said, "Recess for Joel was torture, like bamboo shoots under the fingernails."

Clinical psychologist Randy Mendelson, who practices in New Jersey, has been facilitating socialization groups for a number of years. He finds most children need this group therapy for at least six months to a year. According to Dr. Mendelson, a good socialization group should have four necessary ingredients: fun, structure, learning, and reinforcement. In his groups, which run for intervals of ten-week sessions, the children select the fun activity they want to use as a socialization exercise. These activities range from outside play such as tag to inside games such as "Uno." The children also make the rules to guide the activities. Just as in home behavior management charts, the rules are phrased in positive ways, e.g., "waits for turn" instead of "does not cut in front of others."

After the activity, the children sit in a circle and provide feedback to one another. The feedback is the learning part of the session. During this time, each group member hears what rules he or she has or has not followed and what type of playmate he or she has been. The reinforcement part of the process has two components. First, if a child gives honest feedback to a group member, he or she is reinforced. Second, the child receiving the feedback is rewarded (e.g., with pretzels) when it is positive. In this way, both participation and prosocial behavior are encouraged.

During the preschool years, in the absence of an effective behavior management program such as the one described in the previous chapter, most children with AD/HD continue to be hard to manage. Psychologist C. Keith Conners notes that particularly during these preschool years, since the bulk of the child care falls primarily on the mother, fathers often do not see the child as the master of his or her behavior. Many fathers tend to think the child's behavior problems are the mother's fault through being either too strict or too lenient. Ben Green, a father I spoke with, said he initially thought his wife somehow proved their son's negative behavior because his son behaved fairly well for him.

In his book *Attention Deficit Hyperactivity Disorder: A Handbook for Diagnosis and Treatment,* Dr. Barkley notes that in general these children are less oppositional with their fathers, possibly for the following reasons. Since Mom usually spends more time with the child, she is more likely to be making a greater amount of demands than the father. Consequently, moms have more opportunity to be in conflictual situations. Also, moms are also more likely to use reasoning and affection to encourage compliance with requests. Dads, on the other hand, use less reasoning and more punishment. Though Laurie Maxwell's husband did not find fault with her parenting style, friends often asked, "Why don't you spank him more?" She did not spank him more because physical punishment does not make children with AD/HD behave better.

Their behavioral difficulties usually stem from the uninhibited/hyperactive pattern of behavior so characteristic of the disorder. Because they tend to be "managed by the moment," as Dr. Barkley puts it, children with AD/HD usually do not learn from experience. Discipline techniques, such as a reprimand, which work for most children prove ineffective for these children.

"Children with AD/HD do not respond to the softer management techniques and subtle social consequences," Dr. Barkley observes. Thus, most parents of children with AD/HD need to be trained as described previously in how to set rules, how to institute consequences, how to give commands clearly, how to follow through with appropriate consequences, and how to limit the amount of demands they make upon the child.

Before many of us learn appropriate ways to manage the hard-to-handle child, Dr. Barkley notes, we parents of children with AD/HD frequently make these common mistakes. We tend to administer consequences in an extremely inconsistent way, he finds. The child on one day may have the roof fall on his or her head for a mildly inappropriate behavior. The next day when he or she repeats the behavior, the parent may make little note of it or perhaps even find it mildly amusing. Also seen in our families is noncontingent punishment by parents where the consequences are not contingent upon something the child does. The child with AD/HD becomes the family scapegoat and everyone's bad mood falls onto the child's shoulders.

In the talk/reason approach, parents try to ease the child into compliance by offering hundreds of reasons why a request was made. I have learned that reasoning only invites more opportunity for conflict, and as most parents eventually discover, children with AD/HD make great lawyers. As Dr. Barkley explained, "For children with AD/HD, reason carries no weight whatsoever."

Nor does excessive repetition of commands, another nontechnique to which most parents fall prey. Though parents usually repeat themselves to get the child to pay attention and do what is asked, excessive repetition may actually train the child not to pay attention. Think about how you respond to a back-seat-driver type of person who is always "in your face." Chances are likely that the minute you hear that voice, you tune out. These children are apt to do likewise.

These common mistakes are typically embodied in a pattern of interaction between the parent (usually the mother) and the child with AD/HD called the Coercive Interaction Pattern. This pattern may also occur between teachers and students. According to Dr. Barkley, when this pattern becomes the established manner in which the parent and child interact over parental demands made upon the child, the likelihood that the child will engage in future oppositional and hostile behavior increases significantly.

As explained by Dr. Barkley, the pattern unfolds as follows. The parent places a demand on the child which the child views as work and does not enjoy doing. At this point, the child either complies or does not comply with the demand. In families where this pattern occurs frequently, Dr. Barkley notes that reward or appreciation is seldom given when the child does comply. When the child does not comply, in most instances the parent will repeat the command numerous times. This repetition postpones any consequence the child receives for his disobedience. By talking and repeating, the parent becomes less effective because the child sees that Mom or Dad's word is not backed up. By the time the child receives punishment, the child has been allowed to continue to do things his or her way. Thus, the misbehavior is actually reinforced because the child wins at doing what he or she chooses and at waiting out the parent.

Usually, after about fifteen or twenty minutes when the child does not comply, the parent makes threats. As the child ignores the threats, the parent becomes frustrated and then begins to make threats the child knows either will not be kept or will be modified in some fashion. For example, the parent might say, "You'll never see your bike again" or "I'm going to throw that Nintendo set in the trash." With each threat, both parties become more negative and frustrated and reach a point where they are both out of control. At this point, in 70 percent of the cases, Dr. Barkley says, the parent acquiesces, which means the demand is not met in the way the parent initially specified. Either the parent actually steps in and does whatever is asked of the child or the demand is simply not met at all. About 30 percent of the time the child is punished, but the punishment occurs too late in the transaction to be of value.

Another form of acquiescence, which does not happen very often, is the situation where the parent actually rewards the child for not complying. Dr. Barkley says when the parent acquiesces in this manner, the likelihood the child will engage in future oppositional behavior increases by 400 percent. This type of situation is seen frequently in instances where the child throws a loud and obnoxious temper tantrum. The parent not only stops making the demand, but may hold the child or stroke the child's hair in a calming effort.

Increases in oppositional behavior can also result from disagreements which are known to frequently arise between spouses over the best way to manage the child. The seriousness of such disagreements caught my attention recently when a tearful mom told me about the horrendous difficulties which befell her teenage son, including a brush with the law. Since the child's earliest years, this mom, who did all the disciplining, fell into a bad-cop role because her husband constantly dismissed the child's inappropriate behavior as "no big deal." The dad's pattern was to sympathize with his son, which in turn made him the good cop. This father has continued to feel sorry for his son, who has managed to get away with some pretty serious stuff, like skipping school, without negative consequences. Thus, the mother's attempts to hold the child accountable for his behavior have become virtually useless and, sadly, almost laughable to her son.

Of course, the roles played by Mom and Dad could just as easily be reversed. Nonetheless, this scenario underscores the importance of parents working as a team. While in the toddler years perhaps parents are disagreeing over seemingly minute punishments such as withholding dessert for not eating dinner, the stakes become considerably higher when the older child is taught to play one parent against the other, as the example shows.

To defeat coercive interactions, Dr. Barkley suggests that parents make the following changes: First, he advises parents to limit the amount and type of demands they make upon the child with AD/HD. Before making one, the parents should also determine if the child is capable of meeting the demand. Once they do make a demand, parents must follow through on it and administer immediate consequences. Second, Dr. Barkley instructs the parents in how to provide substantially more rewards, such as those suggested in the previous chapter, when the child does comply with a request. Dr. Barkley views the fact that many parents of children with AD/HD do not respond to appropriate behavior as perhaps the biggest mistake they make in managing their children. Basic behavior management teaches parents to *"catch the child being good."* The best way to *decrease* good behavior is to ignore it. The best way to *increase* good behavior is to acknowledge and reward it.

Too often during the preschool period, the rewards prove few and far between for the child with AD/HD. Between the ages of three and five, some of these preschoolers display temper tantrums, outbursts of rage, and aggressive and destructive tendencies, often in public places. When asked to be accountable for their behavior, children with AD/HD commonly place the blame on someone or something other than themselves.

No one knows for certain what causes these aggressive and acting-out type of behaviors. They could be a part of the disorder itself, or a result of the manner in which the child and his environment interact, or both. I suspect the child with AD/HD is like a tumbleweed rolling over the desert where each movement gathers a little more dust and dirt. Though David as an infant evidenced a moody and irritable disposition, certainly my reactions to his AD/HD behaviors served to make his symptoms and our overall situation worse. The ultimate irony of this disorder is the child with the worst symptoms needs the greatest support, but receives instead the lion's share of negative feedback.

Though the primary pain of AD/HD falls mainly on the child's shoulders, all family members experience the disorder's negative effects. Parents frequently fall into the guilt-and-blame trap. Mothers especially become convinced they are bad parents and suffer from low self-esteem. We feel depressed, ashamed, resentful, and embarrassed because of our apparent failure as parents to raise a well-mannered and obedient child.

Dr. Conners has observed that mothers of children with AD/HD will invariably cry if he says something to this effect: "I'm surprised you're still hanging in there. You must feel awful about yourself for some of the responses this child has elicited from you. But I really admire you. You must really care about your child to do as well as you have done." He commented that these mothers feel a tremendous sense of guilt because they think they have let the child down. Dr. Conners believes parents of children with AD/HD need to understand that "the disorder creates a great deal of stress and that they are only human."

According to Jean Bramble, an AD/HD caseworker at Primary Children's Medical Center in Salt Lake City, adoptive parents of children with AD/HD, like biological parents, also feel guilty. She has observed, however, that in some cases, adoptive parents feel an additional layer of guilt as well. This other guilt comes not only from feelings of inadequacy because of their inability to manage their adopted child, but arises out of their belief that perhaps they were never meant to have children. She said, "Indeed that is not the case. These parents are loving and readily seek help for their adoptive children."

In addition to feelings of guilt and blame, marital discord often arises as a by-product of this disorder. That is not to suggest that the child causes the marital problems. As this country's staggering divorce rate reveals, many marriages are flawed and for many reasons. In the case of AD/HD, the marital discord arises because, as Dr. Conners notes, "Marriages are held together by the peace and quiet of ordinary times. Those times are missing in most of these families." Particularly prior to diagnosis and intervention, as husbands and wives struggle with the child's behavioral difficulties and the seemingly constant turmoil, their interactions appear to be at cross-purposes and out of balance.

Further compounding this distress are the family histories of children with AD/HD. According to Dr. Barkley, the family histories often reveal other stressors in addition to the child's AD/HD. He reports that psychiatric disorders are more common among parents of children with AD/HD, with the most common disorder being AD/HD in the parent. Marital disputes exist with a higher incidence in families where AD/HD is present. Divorce is twice as common. Sixty percent of all mothers suffer from low self-esteem. About one-fourth of the mothers become clinically depressed and require professional intervention. Fifteen percent of the fathers evidence alcohol or other substance abuse problems.

The family disruption does not stop with marital discord. Dr. C. Keith Conners describes the effect this disorder has on the siblings of the child with AD/HD as "profound." He notes that siblings suffer because AD/HD is so disruptive to family life, adding: "Frequently, younger siblings feel terrorized by this child who does not know his limits and will actively avoid any contact with the child with AD/HD. Older siblings are usually more distant and don't spend much time around the sibling with AD/HD because they are embarrassed by his or her behavior."

Younger sister Heather Flood told me she often felt her parents were not fair and always gave her brother far more attention. Diana Stevenson, an older sibling I spoke with, said that whenever she had to go out to dinner with the family she worried someone would say, "Look at the loony tune and his family. They're probably all like him."

Dr. William McMahon of Primary Children's Medical Center notes that siblings of children with AD/HD commonly place the blame for all their arguments and fights on the child with AD/HD. Some siblings do so with such skill they appear perfect. Dr. McMahon follows one family in particular where the younger sister of the child with AD/HD frequently sets her brother up so that the parents do not realize that she has caused the trouble. Ordinarily, when they play, she ends up screaming and the boy gets punished for upsetting her.

Melanie Hartsgrove, the mother of Sandy, a child with AD/HD, said, "Sandy became the family scapegoat. Whenever he and his sister had a fight, Sandy got blamed because I expected him to be the bad child. His sister instigated a lot of the trouble, but because Sandy is louder and can't cover up as well, he got in trouble."

Psychologist Sam Goldstein stresses that the siblings of a child with AD/HD need to be part of the treatment system. In counseling, Dr. Goldstein strives to make the siblings either positive or at least neutral toward the child with AD/HD. He recalled one case where both siblings, because they had such legitimate complaints about their brother's behavior, practically convinced him that the family would be better off if the child with AD/HD moved away.

In homes where great difficulties exist between siblings, therapists often deal with the problem using behavior management techniques for the siblings as well as the child with AD/HD. In the case cited by Dr. Goldstein, to get the siblings to stop picking on the child with AD/HD and vice versa, he used superordinate goals. For example, the entire family would be treated to a trip to the amusement park provided the parents did not hear one word about any fights or arguments between siblings.

Certainly, problems between siblings occur in most families. But when AD/HD is present, the conflicts are perhaps more frequent, more intense, and more destructive. To restore family peace, parents must acquire behavior management techniques. We must be trained to make rules clear, to set consequences, to institute those consequences properly, and to reward good behavior. A parent without these skills can usually slide by when AD/HD is not present. But a child with AD/HD finds every loophole a parent might leave open. Behavior management is simply one of those essential ingredients to order a disordered environment.

Though many parents find such rigidity a drudge, happy side effects do arise from good behavior management. Instead of losing both patience and face because the child does not obey, parents have the option to step out of the line of fire. They can apply a consequence immediately for their child's misbehavior and thereby place the responsibility for the child's actions where it belongs, on the child and not on the parent. That includes making siblings accountable for their behavior as well.

Couples also need to make extra efforts to enjoy life and each other. Husbands and wives can easily become overfocused on the child with special needs to the exclusion of nurturing their mutual interests. Of course, parents often discover that even when they make attempts to spend private, quality time with each other, their efforts are sometimes thwarted because babysitters also find children with AD/HD hard to manage.

Liz Sacca once hired the daughter of a town councilman to watch her child with AD/HD and his brothers. When she arrived home later that night, Liz found the sitter in a heap in the middle of the floor, crying because long after she put the children to bed, the child with AD/HD managed to wake his brothers and engage them in a game of toss with Mom's precious knickknacks. Other mothers, like Betty Garver, never hired babysitters because they worried that a sitter might underestimate their daredevil child with AD/HD.

Finding and keeping babysitters can be especially tricky in situations where AD/HD runs the household. Through the use of behavior management, parents usually meet the challenge of getting AD/HD-related difficulties under control, which results in an abscence of chaos. Quiet, peaceful moments do tend to reappear as do the babysitters who in the past proved unwilling to set foot through your door a second time.

In addition to spending time nurturing the marriage, the parent who is home with the child needs some special time each day to recharge. The time alone does not have to involve an exotic activity. Some mothers get renewed by taking walks. Others, like Laurie Maxwell, find peace in the bathtub. Whatever, we need to develop a healthy respect for the extra energy required to parent a child with special needs and to not push ourselves to the max. Time-out for quiet time is sage advice.

Summary

Signs and Symptoms During Preschool Stage

- Often become highly visible
- Difficulties arise at home, in school, with peers
- Preschool parents and teachers commonly report these difficulties:
  - following directions
  - staying on task
  - immaturity
  - easily frustrated
  - temper tantrums
  - aggressive and destructive behavior
  - non-compliance
  - noisiness

Social Interactions

- Social rejection often occurs
- Parental involvement in encouraging prosocial behavior advised:
  — invite child to be a playmate
  — devise a structured play situation
  — limit the length of play period
  — pay positive attention to appropriate social behavior
  — repeat process frequently with same playmate
- Professional involvement in social skills training
  — intervention experimental but promising
  — group techniques must also be utilized in natural settings

Ineffective Parenting Techniques

- Administering consequences inconsistently
- Noncontingent punishment
- Talk-reason approach
- Excessive repetition of commands
- Making idle threats
- Good cop/bad cop

Effects of Ineffective Techniques

- Increase likelihood of oppositional behaviors
- Reinforce negative behaviors
- Develop a cyclical pattern of negative interactions

Effective Parenting Techniques

- Limit amount and types of demands
- Follow through with immediate consequences
- Provide lots of rewards, i.e., CATCH THE CHILD BEING GOOD
- Make the child accountable for his/her behaviors

Effects on Family Members

- Mothers often become depressed and develop poor self-esteem
- Feelings of guilt develop
- Marital discord
- Siblings become fearful or distant
- Conflicts with siblings more frequent and more intense
- Siblings blame child with AD/HD for sibling behavior
- Finding babysitters proves difficult
- Couples must structure special time to be alone

CHAPTER FIVE

Diagnosis

The fall when David turned five, his dad and I decided not to launch his public school career. We both felt our son behaved in too immature a fashion to succeed in that environment. Instead we placed him in the private kindergarten offered by his nursery school with the idea he could then begin the public school's kindergarten program the following year.

Where previously David's blue eyes had caught the nursery school staff's attention, his black-and-white world now cast him in a different light. David did not see shades of gray. He related to everything and everybody in either/or, good-or-bad, yes-or-no terms. These same teachers who once assured me David just needed to mature, now asked me why he lagged behind.

By now, I realized David's nature had been extreme since day one and would more than likely remain as such. Halfheartedly I joked with his teachers about the way his life would unfold. "David," I told them, "will either be a Rhodes scholar or an eighth-grade dropout, but he will never know mediocrity."

When the school's director administered some standardized tests in October, David's results bore witness to my comments. In most of the areas tested, such as listening comprehension and math concepts, David scored in the normal to above-normal ranges, but he performed quite poorly in the tests which measured simultaneous processing (the ability to discern parts from the whole) and visible discrimination. This score disparity led the director to believe our son had a learning disability. She suggested the school district's child study team evaluate David to find out "why this very capable child could not perform."

Though the evaluation promised some long-awaited answers, I felt threatened with the idea that David might not be able to survive on the basis of his intelligence. All along I had told myself David's intellectual capabilities would compensate for his interpersonal difficulties. Now even that idea seemed unrealistic. His father and I agreed to have our son evaluated by the child study team, though we did not have the vaguest concept of what such an evaluation entailed. Next, we learned the form and function of child study teams fall under the rubric of special education.

Talk about a week! First I had to accept that David might have a problem. Well, I saw enough to know that something was amiss for this wonderful child who really had a good heart and mind though a difficult manner. But then to be told he might need special education! That seemed absurd. Clearly, this child had a lot of capability. True, he had a really hard time getting that capability in sync with his performance, but why should that require anything special, I wondered. Contributing to my confusion was the perception I had, albeit from the Dark Ages, that special education was a place where children with the most severe disabilities were sent to learn life skills.

I now know that special education is the opportunity given to all children with disabilities that allows them the chance to become an integral part of society by providing them with a meaningful education. With great wisdom and compassion, Congress passed the law providing special education in 1975. Then the law was named the Education of the Handicapped Act (EHA). This law, which was renamed the Individuals with Disabilities Education Act (IDEA) in 1991, has integrity. It ensures an appropriate education to children with disabilities. The law also provides additional funds to states and local school districts to assist them in the provision of special education. The IDEA is the educational bill of rights for children with disabilities and their parents.

Every law has a set of rules and regulations created to implement its intent. For IDEA, those rules and regulations are called Public Law 94-142. PL 94-142 mandates the establishment of child study teams in every school district. These child study teams must evaluate any child known to have or suspected of having a disability to determine whether or not that disability adversely affects the child's educational performance. Based on the evaluation results, if warranted, the district must develop an individual educational program for that child designed to meet his or her unique and special learning needs.

Each state, in accordance with the federal law, developed its own statutes to implement the rules and regulations governing the IDEA. Minimally, every school district in every state must have a multidisciplinary team trained to perform educational evaluations. At least one person on that team must know about the disability for which the child is being evaluated. Otherwise, these teams might miss some valuable clues about how the child's disability might interfere with education. (Please see Appendix B for more information about this very important law.)

In the state where I live, the child study team is comprised of a school psychologist, a school social worker, and an LDT-C, an acronym for Learning Disabilities Teacher Consultant, which is a teacher trained in the identification of and special teaching methods for children with disabilities. Other professionals (e.g., pediatric neurologist, speech/language pathologist, physical/occupational therapist) can be invited to submit consultative reports to assist the child study team in its deliberations.

For six months, from October of 1984 through February of 1985, David's father and I learned the nuts and bolts of a child study team evaluation. The evaluation process involved classroom observations wherein the LDT-C and the school psychologist visited David's classroom to observe how he performed academically as well as how he interacted with the teacher and his peers. These team members also spoke with David's teachers to gather their comments and observations about our son that might assist the child study team in determining the nature of David's difficulties. The team members also spoke with David to determine what he thought and felt about himself. The social worker spoke with me for the purpose of gathering a social and medical history, as well as any factors I could think of which might contribute to his difficulties.

The LDT-C and the school psychologist also administered a battery of educational tests to determine David's intelligence, to assess areas where he did not perform to his ability, and to identify his learning strengths and weaknesses. They also sent David to outside medical consultants to rule out any physical causes for his difficulties.

When the team's social worker came to interview me about our family, I felt at ease. I wanted help for David and so I naively answered her every question, though I could not understand what our son's relationship with his grandfathers had to do with his academic performance. I also responded in great detail to the social worker's queries about our marriage, our family relationships, and our social histories. By the time I finished my description, she knew everything there was to know about our family.

In January, the team leader sent us a letter in which she requested we take David for a neurologic examination. I thought of neurologists as heavy-duty doctors who only treated people with gross neurologic illnesses or injuries. When I asked the school's director if she knew why the team wanted this consultation, she too expressed confusion and concern.

The fact that a hospital housed the neurologist's office added to my fear. My imagination conjured up visions of mad-professor-type laboratories where men in white coats hooked people up to masses of electrodes. When young David and I arrived for the exam, I soon saw that the office contained the usual equipment found in any doctor's examining room. But not all my fears subsided. I worried about what conclusions David drew to explain the reasons why he had become the subject of so much scrutiny these days.

When the doctor arrived, I grew very tense. This neurologist made no attempt to warm up to his little patient. Instead, he got right into the business at hand. The exam took thirty minutes. After he took a detailed medical history of David, the doctor questioned me about my son's personality characteristics and home behavior, and asked if I could think of any recent family stressors, such as a divorce, that might account for his difficult behavior. But I could unhappily report to the doctor that David, now five years old, had showed such difficult tendencies since infancy.

After speaking with me, the doctor gave David a physical examination. He next asked David to walk, skip, and touch his finger to his nose as fast as he could. David copied geometric designs, drew a crude picture of a person, attempted to complete two-step commands. He functioned poorly on all these tests and could not repeat words in a sequence. The data gathered from these tests and exercises allowed the neurologist to inferentially determine how David's brain regulated his behavior. Some of these tasks, such as sequencing and drawing, provided data about David's motor behavior. They also provided the doctor with insight into our son's ability to attend to task and allowed him to determine whether impulsivity prevented David from taking a careful and studied approach. Once all the tests were concluded, the neurologist turned to me and said, "David has Attention Deficit Disorder with Hyperactivity." Though he explained what the term meant, I still did not fully understand David's problem.

When the doctor then proceeded to describe David as negative, aggressive, and developing a poor self-image, I became very confused. I never viewed David as someone with a poor self-image. He always seemed so much in control, so much the master of his deeds, so selfish in his demands of everyone's attention, I felt certain David regarded himself too highly, that he thought no one else deserved as much as he.

"Not so," the doctor said. He then told me David showed some features of anhedonia, which meant he did not derive pleasure or satisfaction from things and so might not respond to the reward systems generally used with children who have AD/HD. The full impact of this consultation took effect and my head began to spin.

Once I collected my thoughts, I pushed the neurologist for the prognosis for a child like David. In a clinical, matter-of-fact voice, he said, "Your son is likely to abuse drugs or alcohol. He could become psychotic or schizophrenic. Treatment might help him." I tried to feel strong, but tears rolled down my cheeks for what seemed like a very long time.

Suddenly, I became aware of David's presence. The entire time the doctor and I spoke, David had been in the room to hear every word. Though he probably did not understand such terms as "anhedonic," "schizophrenic," and "psychotic," I'm sure he could not help but pick up the vibes. I became furious with myself and the doctor for our insensitivity and stupidity. I left the room abruptly. Once outside the office, I tried to explain to David that he need not worry, that everything would turn out fine. David yanked my arm by way of a reply.

I felt nauseated the entire ride home. So many thoughts raced through my head. Did I tell the doctor too much about David's history? Did I color his thinking? Did I exaggerate and make David's problems sound worse than they were? Did I cause David's problems? What did the doctor mean by "anhedonic"? David enjoyed himself from time to time. That evening I told David's dad about the meeting. He dismissed the neurologist's prognoses. I decided to wait for the child study team's findings.

When we met with the child study team two weeks later, each member handed us a typed report. In addition to my husband, myself, and the child study team members, all of young David's teachers and the school's director attended this meeting. The social worker presented her report first. I quickly discovered that what I understood to be our private conversation had become my own personal book of revelations. Very little of what she wrote pertained to David's school situation. I learned after the fact to reveal to child-study-team personnel only the family information I wanted to see in print.

The next report came from the Learning Disabilities Teacher Consultant. The LDT-C had spoken with David's teachers and observed him during class. She performed an educational and psychological evaluation and administered a battery of tests to determine his IQ, his learning characteristics, and his academic performance. Her less-than-stellar findings dashed my hopes that David did poorly in school because he found the work too mundane for his genius ability.

His teachers told the LDT-C that David behaved in a distractible and impulsive manner. With regard to social behavior he functioned on a two-to-three-year-old level. When she observed David's classroom performance, though he could follow directions, she saw how David could not remember to raise his hand or wait to be called on. He could not keep his place on a worksheet, nor could he form numerals with ease.

David approached the testing experience with the LDT-C willingly. However, when the tasks became difficult for him, David shut down and could not be redirected to complete the activity. When asked to throw a bean bag at a target, he became frustrated and wildly threw it around the room. She surmised, "In order to protect his self-image and decrease any embarrassment, David manipulates activities so that he appears successful." This sentence gave me great pause. I always thought "manipulative" implied shrewd or devious. Since David always overstated every thought and action, I never dreamed he could cast a smoke screen.

In this report I also discovered the word "perseveration." This behavior is somewhat akin to a phonograph needle stuck in the groove of a broken record. As used in David's case, perseveration meant that during testing, he circled the first choice on an entire page of multiple-choice questions, which left an accurate appraisal of his ability to the whim of the wheel.

The school psychologist's report upset us the most. In general, she described David's behavior as immature for a five-and-a-half-year-old and said he repeated words, made nonsense statements, and engaged in baby talk when she asked him questions about himself. Though David behaved this way with us too, we did not know he acted similarly in school. One teacher told the school psychologist that David showed no sense of humor and that he demanded perfection from himself and the other kids. The school psychologist assessed David's drawings of a tree, house, and people as angular and distorted and she also saw signs that suggested neurological impairment. Before I could absorb what any of this meant, the school psychologist drew our attention to the next page of her report.

I have no idea how my face looked when I read the part which described David's behavior during the testing. But David Sr.'s pallor turned to a putrid shade of green. We read how David lost his compliant manner and suddenly began to climb on the tester's lap. In his highest-pitched voice he made obscene comments to this school psychologist, who interpreted David's behavior as an attempt to avoid the work, to test his limits, and to get a reaction from the examiner. I sort of raised my eyes to check my husband's reaction, but quickly lowered them when I noticed the blank stares on the faces of all the people in the room.

The final paragraph of this report gave me a rare glimpse into the secret world of David's mind. The psychologist wrote, "The examiner tried reading incomplete sentences to David and asked him to verbally complete them. David could not attend to this activity for very long or very well. Two sentences he did complete were 'I wish I could stop . . . being bad,' and 'I worry about . . . strangers.' His comments about what he drew also suggested angry feelings. For example, he described his male person figure as liking to shoot people because he's a bad person when people bother him."

Though others had said David had a poor self-image, until I actually read his words, I had no concept of the darkness that enveloped his world. By the age of five, David no longer possessed a child's capacity to herald in each day of life as though it were a huge gift-wrapped package waiting to be opened. He had lost the joy of childhood and so had I.

With the reports finished, the team leader wanted David's dad and I to sign a form that would make David eligible for special education services. We were stunned to discover on the consent form a label which characterized David as "Neurologically Impaired." My husband and I jumped to the conclusion that this label implied our son had brain damage. His teachers were so alarmed they advised us not to sign the consent form. In actuality, we all had been mistaken.

The team leader cleared our misconception when she explained that this label meant a child had a neurologically based problem which impaired learning. Since the services for David at this stage proved to be minimal, we decided not to accept them. Besides, David Sr. still had reservations about the entire process.

The school psychologist made attempts to bolster our spirits. She seemed to understand that when parents first learn their child is less than perfect, that their child has a disability, the experience proves saddening, scary, disappointing, discouraging, humiliating, and guilt-rendering. She suggested we seek private counseling and recommended a psychologist whose practice mainly dealt with children who had Attention-deficit/Hyperactivity Disorder. Finally, we had met someone who could help us.

The diagnosis of Attention-deficit/Hyperactivity Disorder is made on the basis of the child's observable behavioral difficulties. Though AD/HD is a hidden disability, the problems caused by the disorder are quite visible. Children with AD/HD will evidence academic, social and emotional difficulties. Usually what draws attention to the child's problems with inattention, disinhibition, impulsivity, and hyperactivity are the outcomes of these characteristics, e.g., not completing tasks, losing things necessary for tasks, disorganization, poor planning, and difficulty waiting. Unfortunately, when a child has such difficulties, rather than recognizing these difficulties as arising from a neurobiological disorder, the untrained observer often blames the child.

Recent public awareness about AD/HD has aided in the earlier identification of children who suffer with this disorder. But caution is advised. AD/HD has the potential to create lifelong problems. Children should not be considered to have AD/HD without undergoing a proper evaluation.

When a child is experiencing difficulties which suggest that he or she might have AD/HD, parents can take one of two basic paths for evaluation. They can request the school to initiate an evaluation or seek the services of an outside professional or clinic. By law, schools are required to evaluate any child suspected of having a disability which is adversely affecting educational (i.e., social and academic) performance to determine if the child needs special education. Often, when a child experiences difficulties, the school initiates the evaluation process. Schools are not in the business of providing medical diagnoses. Schools perform an educational assessment. They are concerned with determining whether or not a child meets the eligibility requirements for special education. Thus, they gear their evaluations to determining how the disability affects the child's educational performance, academically and socially.

School evaluations do not determine the extent of difficulties at home or the need for medication, although, when indicated, districts may send the child to an outside licensed practitioner who would look at these factors as well. A school district is only required to send the child for a medical evaluation by a licensed practitioner if it believes such an evaluation is necessary to determine special education eligibility or if it is a requirement of state law. As mentioned in Chapter 3, practitioners licensed to make medical diagnoses include clinical psychologists, pediatric neurologists, child psychiatrists, pediatricians, and clinical social workers.

Whether to go the private-practitioner route or through the school depends upon individual circumstances and need. When choosing a private practitioner parents who suspect their child has AD/HD are at a unique advantage because they can use the services of someone they know to be trained in the assessment and treatment of the disorder. Thus, they avoid the misinformation and wrong diagnoses that can hamper efforts to get help. The practitioner who manages the diagnostic procedure will often refer the child to other specialists for the necessary assessment in their areas of expertise. For instance, a clinical psychologist might refer a child to a pediatric neurologist for a medical assessment to rule out other neurological problems or to prescribe any indicated medication. Similarly, a pediatrician might refer to a clinical child psychologist to administer neuropsychiatric tests.

The process of diagnosis is much like solving a puzzle wherein the diagnostician must look at the child from many different angles. In all instances, the evaluator must make a differential diagnosis. AD/HD-like behaviors can result from a number of different factors including psychosocial stressors such as parental divorce, death, or sexual abuse, or from other neuropsychological or physical problems. To make the correct diagnosis, the practitioner has to look at all the factors, differentiate the symptoms, rule out other reasons for the child's problems, and also consider the possibility that the child has more than one disorder. Of course, AD/HD can exist along with psychosocial stressors and other disabilities. A good assessment would not automatically rule out AD/HD because these other factors are present.

An issue I believe to be of concern for most parents is the type of diagnostic evaluation performed. We need to be informed consumers. Though not all clinicians will assess AD/HD in exactly the same way, there are recommended guidelines that clinicians should follow. A thorough diagnostic evaluation uses multiple sources of information about the child in home, school, and community settings and also has the following components: clinical interviews with parents, child, and teachers to provide relevant information regarding developmental, social, and academic history and to address present-day concerns; medical history and examination; child observations; behavior rating scales; and psychoeducational tests.

When assessing for the disorder, practitioners look to establish a pattern of inattentive and/or uninhibited, hyperactive behaviors exhibited by the child over a period of at least six months and prior to age seven.

With regard to making a differential diagnosis, psychiatrist Paul Wender says, "A good history is always the most important aspect of any psychiatric evaluation." He suggests the history be obtained from the parents and other people, such as teachers or grandparents, who deal with the child on a frequent basis. In fact, Dr. Wender places great stock in the information supplied by teachers since they observe the child's performance in the major developmental tasks of the school-age child, namely, academic performance and social interactions.

The history reported by parents also provides valuable clues about the nature of the child's problems. Many parents, however, are not aware of the importance of their observations. For example, when a pediatric neurologist based a diagnosis of Tom Sacca on a half-hour examination and his mother's depiction of him, Liz Sacca felt skeptical. "I wondered how good the diagnosis could be. Everyone else thought Tommy climbed on mannequins in store windows and never listened to me because I was a bad mother." In Tommy's case, the telltale signs of AD/HD proved so obvious, they could have been outlined with neon lights. Nonetheless, a thorough assessment would use more than one source of information.

In addition to the child's developmental history which is attained during the parental interview, current practice recommends the taking of a family history as well. The family histories of children with AD/HD often reveal incidence of AD/HD in other family members, learning disabilities, alcoholism, maternal depression, maternal feelings of low self-esteem, and the family pattern of reaction to stress. Dr. Russell Barkley notes 50 percent of the parents of children with AD/HD in his clinic need some form of therapy to treat their problems. In fact, he reports that nationally 30 percent of all fathers and 20 percent of all mothers require treatment as adults for their AD/HD. This family information proves useful for devising a treatment plan as it alerts the practitioner to potential sources of strength and conflict.

Another aspect of the diagnostic process is the interview with the child. This interview allows the examiner to observe the child's behavior first hand. Dr. C. Keith Conners cautions examiners about the child with AD/HD who in the first office visit will frequently behave like a model child. He calls such exemplary behavior "the novelty effect." "On the third visit that same kid will dismantle my desk if I let him," he explains. I also suggest parents follow Paula Anderson's example. When she brought her daughter to see a clinical psychologist, instead of trying to control or manage Maggie's behavior, she let Maggie do whatever she pleased. This way the examiner saw the child's typical behavior.

Though Maggie's out-of-control behavior caught the examiner's attention, girls do not generally exhibit this type of behavior to the extent that boys with AD/HD do. Thus, girls go underidentified and consequently underdiagnosed. As Dr. Conners notes, "One has to be a really deviant little girl for someone to take her seriously."

Dr. Sally Shaywitz of Yale University Medical School believes the reason AD/HD often goes unrecognized in girls might reflect a bias in referral. "ADD with hyperactivity is so widely accepted as a predominantly boy's disorder that there may be a failure to even consider the possibility of AD/HD in girls and consequently a failure to identify all but the most severely affected girls," she said.

A pediatric examination is also warranted as part of the diagnostic procedure. The purpose of this examination is to rule out the presence of other physical problems that might create AD/HD-like symptoms. In some instances, vision and hearing checks may also be indicated. Oftentimes many clinicians, pediatricians included, will refer children with AD/HD to a pediatric neurologist for a neurological examination. During this exam the neurologist rules out any gross neurologic problems, for instance, epilepsy. Pediatric neurologist Dr. Bennett Shaywitz reports in 99 percent of the cases, the results of these exams are normal.

As part of the neurological assessment, the pediatric neurologist also looks for "soft signs." Soft neurologic signs do not relate to any particular area of the central nervous system. Instead, soft neurologic signs are signs which are behaviorally associated with central nervous system dysfunction. Unlike paralysis, cerebral palsy, or epilepsy, which give hard evidence of neurologic dysfunction, soft signs are implied rather than definitive. For example, poor motor coordination is a soft sign. Dr. Bennett Shaywitz explained that though soft signs prove a little more common in children with AD/HD, they are not diagnostic of the disorder. Many children without AD/HD present soft signs as well.

Unless a doctor finds evidence of a more serious neurological problem, Dr. Bennett Shaywitz advises against the use of sophisticated and costly medical tests such as EEGs, MRIs, and PET scans because they are not diagnostic of AD/HD. Of course, these technologies are quite useful for their designed purposes. Electroencephalograms (EEGs) measure the brain's electrical activity and have great value in detecting seizure activity. Magnetic Resonance Imaging (MRI) is an X-ray based on the brain's magnetic fields that gives a picture of the brain's anatomy. Since AD/HD is not an anatomical problem, MRIs are of no diagnostic value for AD/HD.

PET scans (positron emission tomography) have been used with excellent results for AD/HD research purposes. Dr. Alan Zametkin explains that this technology is "a technique for measuring brain metabolism using a form of sugar or glucose that is labeled with a small amount of radioactivity." He emphasizes that PET scans are not biological tests for determining the presence of AD/HD, but rather one way to try to find out where the mechanisms for controlling attention are in the central nervous system. In fact, subjects in Dr. Zametkin's study at the National Institute of Mental Health have been diagnosed with AD/HD prior to being selected for his research. To date, this technology cannot be used to diagnose the AD/HD disorder.

Perhaps the most widely used instrument to determine the presence or absence of AD/HD behaviors and the degree to which these exist are behavior rating scales. Usually parents and teachers are asked to complete these, which vary in purpose. For instance, some scales have items to measure a number of childhood behavioral problems. Other scales specifically describe only AD/HD-type behaviors. The principle behind them proves to be much the same. Basically, the parent rates the child in terms of frequency of occurrence of certain behaviors, such as these which appear on the Conners Parent Symptom Questionnaire: cries easily or often; doesn't get along well with brothers and sisters; restless in the "squirmy" sense; problems with sleep (can't fall asleep; up too early; up in the night). Dr. C. Keith Conners, author of this questionnaire, explained that the investigator gets a good indication that a child has AD/HD when the parents or teachers continually check those items which indicate a restless, inattentive, easily frustrated, and impulsive pattern to the child's behavior.

As part of the routine examination many evaluators also administer a battery of psychological tests. Some of these tests measure the child's social and emotional adjustment. Other instruments determine whether or not a child has another disability that impairs learning. One such instrument is an IQ test. Though intelligence tests do not diagnose AD/HD, they tell the evaluator whether or not the child can work to his or her potential. Dr. Conners says such tests and formal examinations also allow the diagnostician to observe the child during a structured intellectual exercise and thus make note of the child's degree of frustration and ability to stay on task.

Many experts believe that a complete psychoeducational battery of tests should be given as routine procedure when diagnosing AD/HD. Besides offering corroborative evidence, these tests provide a valuable safeguard. As reported by Dr. Sally Shaywitz, research studies of children diagnosed with AD/HD reveal a significant incidence of learning disabilities which have gone undetected in these children because the appropriate in-depth educational evaluations had not been done. When this happens, unfortunately, special instructional needs go unnoticed. She believes the behavioral problems evidenced by these children, especially the excessive motor activity, catch everyone's attention to the exclusion of the appropriate educational evaluation. Dr. Shaywitz agrees that a complete psychoeducational battery should be done as part of the routine diagnostic procedure.

As part of a differential diagnosis, the evaluator is determining whether the child has difficulties in addition to AD/HD. In all probability, such will be the case. For example, research indicates that approximately 25 percent of all children with AD/HD also have learning disabilities.

While this percentage is significant, a Yale University study which used an epidemiological sample found that 10 percent of the children with AD/HD had learning disabilities. According to co-investigator Dr. Sally Shaywitz, this 10-percent figure has added significance because the children studied came from nonclinic populations, which means the disorder's severity among the population ranges from quite mild to severe. Children used in studies from clinic populations tended to have more severe forms of AD/HD and thus a higher probability of having co-existing problems such as learning disabilities. (As used here, the term "learning disabilities" applies to specific disabilities such as dyslexia, rather than the difficulty with educational performance experienced by nearly all children with AD/HD as a pervasive element of the AD/HD disorder.)

Two other disorders which have a strong likelihood of co-occurring with AD/HD are Oppositional Defiant Disorder (ODD) and Conduct Disorder (CD). Dr. Barkley estimates that ODD is apparent in approximately 40 to 60 percent of elementary-age children with AD/HD and that between 20 and 30 percent of this group develop Conduct Disorder. As noted by Dr. Paul Wender, "Hyperactive kids tend to be oppositional and have a greater than ordinary risk of being conduct-disordered and learning-disabled. We can identify pure forms of each disorder. One is not the other, but there is a higher probability that each will occur with the other than on a chance basis alone."

Researchers do not know for certain why these disorders co-occur, although environmental factors are considered to play a significant role in the development of ODD and CD. In other words, parents do not cause AD/HD, but if they deal with the AD/HD-related difficulties through negative emotional reactions and power struggles, they may actually contribute to the development of the negative, hostile, aggressive behaviors associated with these other disorders.

Dr. Barkley describes these behavioral disorders as such. AD/HD is a developmental deficiency in several mental characteristics: attention, impulse control, regulation of activity. It is believed the child is biologically predisposed to the disorder and that it arises early in life. Oppositional Defiant Disorder is a group of symptoms characterized as negative temperament, hostile affect, aggression toward others, and repeated intrusion on and violation of the rights of others. Children with ODD evidence a persistent pattern of negative explosive mood, combined with a refusal to obey and aggression toward peers and other people. Conduct Disorder is a repeated pattern of violation of social rules and the rights of others demonstrated by truancy from school, lying, stealing or vandalism of property, sexual promiscuity, cruelty to animals and people, and frequently initiating fights.

Dr. Barkley notes these three disorders sometimes evolve in a developmental fashion with a child evidencing AD/HD first, followed by ODD and then, in later years, CD. His clinic samples demonstrate that children who develop ODD have a very high probability of later developing CD. However, children with AD/HD do not necessarily develop these disorders. Some clinicians maintain ODD and/or CD develop in children from families where parental management can be characterized by excessive punishment and coercive interactions, and consequently, early diagnosis of AD/HD and the multifaceted treatment of symptomatology, including parent training, will hopefully thwart the onset of these other disorders in many cases.

Just as there are disorders that have a strong likelihood of co-occurring with AD/HD, similarly other conditions exist which have symptoms suggestive of AD/HD, such as Central Auditory Processing Disorder, a disorder of perception, sound and language, and Fetal Alcohol Syndrome (FAS). Children with FAS or those with Fetal Alcohol Effect (FAE), for example, are often hyperactive and have short attention spans and poor impulse control. The diagnostic elements previously described would provide enough history and medical information to differentiate between AD/HD and these other conditions, though similar treatments might be used to manage behavioral difficulties.

Once the evaluation process is completed and the AD/HD diagnosis made, education about the disorder and its manifestations proves to be the first step of treatment. By de-mystifying AD/HD and breaking apart myths that we parents often create to explain the child's difficult behavior, parents can change their belief systems. Dr. Barkley, for instance, uses education about AD/HD—its characteristics, its developmental course, and the risks associated with the disorder—to help parents come to view the child as having a disability. "We don't wish to overwhelm parents with grief," he explains. "If I had to choose from all the childhood disabilities one could have, I'd choose this one. AD/HD is by far the least disabling."

Nonetheless, left unrecognized and untreated, this disability has the potential to cause considerable distress for its sufferers. Changing the way we view the child's difficult behavior is an important first step toward achieving a positive outcome. Dr. Barkley has observed that parents who change their perspective expect less from the child and so become less frustrated themselves. Therefore, they do not punish or come down on the child nearly as much.

This change in parenting behavior calls to mind a major principle of behavior management told to me by noted expert Jim Swanson, which is, "Don't shoot the dog!" The diagnosis of AD/HD helps parents to stop blaming the victim for AD/HD-related difficulties. "Don't shoot the dog" also suggests that we parents have to change the way we deal with the child if we want to see a change in the child's behavior.

While diagnosis often brings a sense of relief to parents, it also raises a question. Generally we ask, "What should I tell my child and when?" The explanation Dr. Barkley provides depends on the age of the child. For the older child, he will spend up to an hour on the matter. However, with younger children he suggests a brief explanation. He tells them, "Some kids are good at bike riding, others are not good at art. You have a hard time concentrating on things that are boring and we understand you can't help that."

The AD/HD diagnosis often brings a sense of relief for both parents and child. The clouds of confusion that surround the whys and wherefores of a child's behavior lift with the knowledge that neither the parent nor the child caused the problems. Guilt and blame are replaced by hope and help.

Summary

Special Education and Child Evaluation

- Under federal law, local school districts must have multidisciplinary assessment teams to evaluate children
- Federal law guarantees all children with disabilities the right to a free, appropriate public education
- School systems evaluate children who may need special education services
- Under special education, school systems must develop an individual educational plan

Diagnosis

- Diagnosed on the basis of observable behavioral difficulties: not completing tasks, losing things necessary for tasks, disorganization, poor planning, difficulty waiting
- Requires a proper evaluation by a trained professional
- School districts perform assessments but may use outside medical professionals when necessary for diagnosis
- Requires a differential diagnosis to note or rule out the presence of other disorders

Elements of Diagnostic Evaluation

- Multiple sources of information
- Clinical interviews with parents, child, and teachers
- A thorough medical, social, developmental, and academic history
- Child observations
- Behavior rating scales
- Psychoeducational tests

*Medical Tests **Not** Used for Diagnosis of AD/HD*

- EEG—Electroencephalogram (measures brain's electrical activity) used when evidence of other conditions, e.g., epilepsy, exists.
- MRI—Magnetic Resonance Imaging (X-ray depicting brain's anatomy) used for AD/HD research purposes
- PET scans—Positron Emission Tomography (measures brain metabolism) used for AD/HD research purposes
- Laboratory tests such as blood and urine analysis

Commonly Co-occurring Conditions

- Learning Disabilities—LD
- Oppositional Defiant Disorder—ODD
- Conduct Disorder—CD
- ODD and CD may result from environmental factors

Results of Diagnosis

- Leads to a change in belief system
  - inappropriate behaviors viewed as result of disability rather than a willful choice made by child
- Suggests need to change parenting behavior and educational approach
- Replaces guilt and blame with hope and help

CHAPTER SIX

Management Approaches

Once we had a diagnosis for David, I hoped we would have smoother sailing. But after the first visit with Dr. Burke, our new child psychologist, both David Sr. and I learned that there is no magic cure for AD/HD. In fact, a lot of counseling would be required to restore a smile to David's face. Results from a test administered by the psychologist pointed to David's excessive worry and self-criticism as an indication that our son had become depressed.

Both his dad and I made the assumption that only David would be counseled. However, this child psychologist insisted the entire family be present at the sessions. He explained that a family is a system of reciprocal emotional relationships. Thus, David's behavior affected us and ours affected him in a cyclic and ongoing way.

Before any positive changes could occur, David's dad and I needed to unlearn the ineffective parenting techniques which we had fallen into using. Our inconsistency, criticism, rejection, and physical punishment proved to be the worst possible responses to the behavior of a child with AD/HD. These only served to heighten David's sadness. Like most children with AD/HD, he had no idea why his world had turned out to be such a capricious place.

Neither did I until after an ugly scene erupted between young David and myself. Like Pavlov's dog, David responded to the ring of a bell, only in his case, the ring of the phone sent him into action. During his toddler years, he took this cue as the time to make mischief. As a preschooler, he dropped whatever he might be involved with and demanded my undivided attention. On the occasions I chose to ignore his peskiness, David disconnected the phone plug and left me to hang in mid-sentence.

In his latest strategy to end my conversations, David played mummy and wrapped himself in the cord. As in the past, I ignored this obnoxious behavior, but in order to continue my conversation, I had to exert untold pounds of pressure so the phone receiver would not recoil from my ear. One day I became fed up and reacted impulsively. In an attempt to unravel David, I gave the cord a Herculean tug. I not only sent him reeling to the floor, the cord left a five-inch burn mark across his neck. Whenever anyone asked him about the mark on his neck, young David, who is not prone to go into great detail, simply replied, "My mother pulled a cord around it."

With David's neck still red and raw, we could not help but bring this incident to the psychologist's attention at our next appointment. Though Dr. Burke counseled David about his inappropriate behavior with the phone cord, he made certain both young David and I understood that a neck burn could never be a natural or logical consequence. Instead he suggested time-out as an alternative. Dr. Burke explained, "When David is disruptive, time-out will interrupt him and give everyone a chance to cool down."

In earlier years, our attempts to use time-out failed. After the psychologist walked us through his method, I could see why we had been unsuccessful. He first told my husband and me to select a safe, quiet, boring place to send David when he misbehaved. We had tried to put David in a corner in the kitchen, but he never stayed. Dr. Burke explained in light of all the activity in that room, the kitchen proved the worst possible place for David because most children with AD/HD react to the activity and do not get the essential message that time-out is a punishment for misbehavior.

David's dad and I also thought the length of time our son stayed in time-out should be in direct correlation to how ticked off he made us. But Dr. Burke told us to set a timer for no longer than five minutes. Aside from the fact that this punishment is designed to be a brief consequence for inappropriate behavior, Dr. Burke warned, "If you keep David there too long, he might forget what he did to get sent to time-out in the first place."

Even with such expert advice, I continued to have reservations about this method's success. I figured David would refuse to go to the time-out spot, or leave it before he should, or come back and continue his misbehavior. When I raised these concerns, Dr. Burke told us initially we might have to escort David to time-out and force him to stay there. In those instances where his behavior did not change, David would be sent back to time-out and told he would continue to go back until he complied. Dr. Burke included David in the time-out discussions and when situations warranted this procedure, he did not resist us. However, in the beginning, his dad and I frequently forgot to use time-out as the first resort.

After our third session, the child psychologist requested that David's dad and I note the times our son behaved inappropriately. Our next meeting revealed this startling fact about our assessment of our son's behavior. Both his dad and I did not always know when behavior was inappropriate. For example, though we agreed disrespect should never be tolerated, we sometimes interpreted a disrespectful comment as okay when David couched his remark in truth or humor. Where young David's world proved to be black and white, ours proved to be excessively gray. We did not look at an action for its face value.

The behavior modification charts Dr. Burke taught us to design and implement soon improved our inconsistent approach to managing our son's behavior. As a starting point, he asked us to select the three behaviors which bothered us most from our rather extensive list. We settled on David's horrible behavior during mealtimes, his refusal to obey us, and his nasty treatment of his brother. When the psychologist asked what behavior we would like David to have, I found the question simplistic. Of course, I answered, "I want him to be nice and to behave well."

"Does David know what behave well means?" he replied.

I always said to young David, "You'd better behave." I assumed he understood what I wanted perfectly well. But Dr. Burke explained that behaviors need to be specifically stated because such broad terms as "behave well" are not clear to the child. That made sense, so I suggested on David's chart we put, "Does not hit brother."

Dr. Burke agreed this sort of behavior should be discouraged. However, he explained, since we really wanted to encourage David's use of appropriate behavior, these behaviors should be phrased in positive terms. He suggested we write, "Treats other family members in a polite, respectful, gentle fashion, i.e., no hitting, yelling, or running away." Also, because of the pervasive daylong nature of this behavior, he suggested we pick a manageable time period to focus on initially, like two hours in the afternoon.

"This time limit is not to say that polite, respectful behavior is not important at the other times too. As we get positive results, we'll gradually extend the time period to require such behavior all day," Dr. Burke explained. The other two behaviors we targeted for reward were, "Cooperates with the morning routine: washes and dresses self, eats neatly, ready on time, no yelling" and "Is well-mannered at evening dinner table: comes on time, sits and eats meals without complaint or hassle."

Ever mindful that I had two children close in age, I wondered how David would react to Jonathan's free-agent status. Until Dr. Burke suggested we also use a chart for Jonathan, the thought had not occurred to me that a child need not have a problem to benefit from good parenting techniques. After all, my husband and I wanted to encourage these behaviors in both children.

With our list of target behaviors, Dr. Burke showed us how to construct the chart. He drew a rectangle on a piece of paper and then divided the rectangle horizontally into one large section and seven smaller but equal-sized sections, and then vertically into four equal-sized sections so that the rectangle ultimately resembled a grid. In the first and largest horizontal section, Dr. Burke listed the target behaviors separately one below the other. At the top of each of the next seven sections, he wrote the days of the week Sunday through Saturday one after the other. In the remaining bottom section below the list of behaviors, he wrote "total daily score." (Appendix C has a sample of this type of chart.)

When children are young—preschool through kindergarten—it is often best to use a "star" or "sticker" chart. One star is given if the behavior is done spontaneously by the child or immediately upon first request. No stars are given for noncompliance or if constant or repetitive commands are given.

Later, when the boys were older, Dr. Burke rated each behavior on a numerical scale of three (excellent), two (good), one (needs improvement), and zero (poor). Throughout a given day, David received feedback about his behavior by earning or losing points toward the total daily score. This way, appropriate behavior was reinforced immediately. On the other hand, when David behaved inappropriately in one of the three target areas, he lost a point in conjunction with being sent to time-out. Then at the end of each day, we sat down with David and watched while he tallied the scores for each behavior and then the total daily score. Thus, the chart became a visual record for David to concretely see where he met with success or failure.

Dr. Burke had also established score ranges to denote excellent, good, and poor behavior days with consequences positive and negative set ahead of time for each outcome. The positive consequences came in the form of rewards. In selecting rewards, Dr. Burke made sure we understood one of the cornerstones of behavior modification, specifically, "a reward is only successful if it has meaning for the child." Since both boys bargained for additional time before they went to bed, we made extended bedtime something they could earn. Normally, they went to bed at seven-thirty, so we decided for a good behavior day, they earned this regular privilege. For an excellent behavior day, the child was allowed to stay downstairs with us until 8:00 P.M. Similarly, on a poor behavior day, the child went to bed a half-hour before the regular time as a predictable consequence of lack of cooperation and effort during the day.

Beyond that we also sweetened the pie with a daily monetary reward of twenty-five cents for an excellent day, ten cents for a good day, and nothing for a poor day. In addition, at the end of a good week, each boy could receive a bonus such as a pack of baseball cards or a trip to Dairy Queen, and for an excellent week a video rental or special time with Mom or Dad.

Dr. Burke began each counseling session by studying the weekly charts. Rather than criticize David for the bad days, he offered his condolences and said, "Gee, Chief, sorry you had a problem here." With our child psychologist as the purveyor of this system, David soon saw we took both the charts and time-out seriously. Eventually David learned not to blame us for his low scores and accepted the responsibility for his behavior. We learned that David often behaved quite well. Throughout the months we added new behavior patterns and dropped others that no longer proved problematic. We never concentrated on more than five types of behavior at a time.

Over the course of the summer of 1985, life in our home improved measurably. David was nearing six years of age and Jonathan had just turned four. I attributed this change to the home management techniques we now employed and the child care program both boys attended for six hours a day. Initially I opposed the idea of sending the boys to a summer program, but Dr. Burke emphasized the importance of structure in David's day and advised us not to expect him to make good, orderly use of free time.

When fall arrived, we moved again. After I enrolled David in the public school kindergarten in this new town, I agonized about whether to tell his teacher he had AD/HD. Even though David evidenced problems in nursery school, I still viewed his behavior difficulties as primarily a home management problem and conned myself into believing he would not meet difficulty in school. Besides, I worried that David might be stigmatized as that "pain-in-the-neck kid" if I drew attention to his problems. Despite the child psychologist's recommendation, I decided this situation could be best handled in the privacy of our home.

By mid-October, David's dad and I noticed a change for the worse in our oldest son's behavior. His frustration level lowered and he angered quickly whenever any task presented a slight challenge. He had difficulty keeping himself in control. He talked incessantly, dolphinized, screamed, and hollered. When he began to constantly clear his throat, we rationalized that his change in behavior had been prompted by some form of allergy.

Though we still went to the child psychologist and used the behavior charts, nothing could stop the course of his behavior or the chain reaction that ensued as a result. Since I no longer worked outside the home, I spent every afternoon with David. By evening, after a full five hours of his argumentative, negative, angry, nasty ways, my nerves rattled. I too slipped back to the argue, yell, holler, and scream mode.

Dr. Burke felt certain the source of David's frustration grew out of the demands the school made on him. But I could not understand how a mere two-and-a-half-hour program could create this much distress. Besides, whenever I casually asked his teacher how well he was doing, she never gave a negative report.

However, when the long-awaited first report card arrived home, our six-year-old son's performance seemed totally lackluster. David earned "satisfactory" as a mark in most areas, but "work habits" and "social development" had been checked "needs improvement." Under "comments" the teacher wrote, "David must work on following directions given once. Criticism of peers continues to be a problem. Good knowledge of beginning sounds.'' At the parent/teacher conference, I learned David seldom participated in class activities and apparently "tuned out." During free play, he stayed by himself.

Not all the teacher's comments proved negative. She drew my attention to David's picture of a house. Though I saw a crude structure, the kindergarten teacher said in all her years of teaching five-and-six-year-old children, David was the first student to include a basement on the house drawing, which she thought indicated he was a divergent thinker. She assured me David was a bright child who would do well when he "clicked in."

By mid-November our quasi-docile home environment deteriorated into a bad dream. The child psychologist suggested David needed medication to help treat his AD/HD symptoms. The pediatric neurologist, who a few months earlier had assessed David's symptoms to be mild, now witnessed the change in behavior firsthand. David could not contain himself during any part of the examination. The doctor rated our son's Attention-deficit/Hyperactivity Disorder as severe.

In addition, the neurologist said David's constant lip-licking and throat-clearing represented involuntary motor actions called tics. This information surprised David's father and me. We figured scarlet, cracked lips to be a sign of cold weather. Because of the tics, the doctor, following common practice in those years, did not prescribe the medication usually used to treat AD/HD. The neurologist informed us about alternative medications, and though he did not want to prescribe them at this point in time, he suggested we consider their eventual use if needed.

Three weeks later, the neurologist placed David on one of these medications. Unfortunately, the alternative medication did not produce the desired results, and within a couple of months, from a medication-intervention standpoint, we were back to square one.

During this entire time, we continued to use behavior modification and went as a family to the sessions with the child psychologist. He continued to teach us about the disorder. How we came to understand the extent to which this disorder affected David and the family proved much like the process of peeling an onion. We needed to get through layer upon layer to reach the center.

We first had to learn that children with AD/HD need a calm, quiet, predictable atmosphere. Changes in the routine prompt changes in behavior. As a family, we continually went on spur-of-the-moment outings or undertook major home projects. We seldom thought to keep these things to a minimum or to prepare David for any necessary changes.

We constantly subjected David to large-group activities despite the fact such situations sent him into a frenzy. We thought "the more the merrier," but for David too many people meant an unhappy time. We missed this point over and over again in our desire for normalcy. We wanted David to be like all the other children. When he balked about playing soccer or going to birthday parties, we forced him to participate, until the child psychologist raised our level of awareness. He advised us to "avoid large-group actvities as much as possible. David will do better in one-to-one situations that are short in duration, structured, and well-organized."

During the course of these sessions, David's dad frequently identified similarities between young David's behaviors and his own. When Dr. Burke said things like, "David prefers to play with younger children because he may be a more desirable playmate to them and can be more in control of events," David Sr. responded, "So did I." Eventually Dad realized he had been very much like his son—not a problem child, but rather a child with a problem.

By the end of January 1986, David's classroom difficulties escalated. The kindergarten teacher said he tried on many occasions to take charge of the class and became verbally aggressive with peers. When he did not meet with instant success in a task, he became extremely upset. During playtime he wandered around the room and withdrew from all social involvement.

The child psychologist spoke with the teacher and observed David in class. He instituted a behavior modification program. A month later, the teacher reported an improvement in David's attitude and effort. At home, his behavior seemed to deteriorate.

Lately, the thought had crossed my mind that David would be better off if I left home. When Dr. Burke asked, "Why do you think he behaves his worst with you?" I could only surmise that something about me brought the worst out in my son. But the psychologist offered another possibility. He thought David stored all his frustration until he came home from school because he trusted my commitment to him and felt safe enough to act on his feelings. Though intellectually his explanation made sense, emotionally I felt like my guts were on a platter.

The child psychologist, who still held hopes that David could take psychostimulant medication, prodded us to see another pediatric neurologist highly regarded for his work with AD/HD. Though this doctor charged $350 for an evaluation, David Sr. and I had grown accustomed to the fact that answers for David were an expensive proposition, and we made the appointment.

The waiting room of the specialist's office contained a jungle gym, a slide, and a slew of toys. Six-and-a-half-year-old David became so excited at these prospects, his voice level went beyond dolphinizing. As he attacked each new toy he yelled to his five-year-old brother to come and play, but these days Jonathan withdrew from that kind of heavy-handed activity. Instead of joining his brother, he sat next to his dad and quietly read a book. When the time finally arrived for David to be examined, his activity level had reached the fevered pitch we knew so well.

As the nurse ushered us into the doctor's office, she looked rather tentative. The doctor introduced himself and told us as long as David could be controlled, he would prefer to examine him without us. We no sooner got halfway back to the waiting room when we heard young David make a pronouncement. "I'm the boss of this office," he said. I thought for certain a summons would follow, but we did not see either David or the doctor for over an hour.

Much to our surprise, when the neurologist finally delivered our son, he remarked about the good manner in which David behaved. Before he brought us into the office, he said to David, "Please wait here while I talk to your mom and dad."

David quietly replied, "Oh yes, I'll wait here."

I often joked that a lobotomy might do David some good and wondered what the doctor had done.

Once inside the office, the doctor told us David's waiting room behavior had been the worst his nurse ever observed. Thus, the doctor thought he would have a difficult time with David's exam. Though initially David had been highly distractible, his ability to concentrate "improved remarkably during the individualized attention." This evaluation did not reveal any new information, but at this physician's urging, we tried David on another medication primarily used to control tics.

In early May, the doctor saw him in a follow-up examination. Though his vocal tics had stopped, David's hyperactivity and impulsivity showed no improvement. The doctor increased the medication but no positive result occurred, so he stopped the medication in June. David ended the school year with improvement noted in that environment. The teacher commented on the final report card, "David's effort in reading, although sporadic, is much improved. His interaction with peers has improved but continues to be difficult for David. I look forward to hearing of his continued success in the first grade." We headed into the summer with David's behavior somewhat under control.

Presently, AD/HD has no known cure, no quick fix, no magic treatment. Yet these facts need not be discouraging. Much can be done to minimize the effects of the disorder on the child's life. With the exception of medical management, interventions used with AD/HD are designed to manipulate the environment so the child experiences competence and success.

Typically, the effective management of AD/HD requires what health care professionals call "the multimodal treatment approach." The nucleus of the multimodal approach consists of four major components: education about the disorder designed to develop an awareness of and an appreciation for AD/HD and its related difficulties; parent training designed to help parents alter the environmental conditions, including the use of behavior management techniques as described in earlier chapters; an appropriate educational program (to be discussed in Chapters 8 and 9); and, when indicated, medication. Individual or family psychotherapy sometimes proves necessary as well.

Which of these strategies are used and the extent to which they are employed depends, of course, on the severity of the child's symptoms. Jim Hopkins, for instance, evidenced difficulty mainly in school, so his treatment primarily addressed that problem. Maggie Anderson needed both home and school management, but no medication, whereas my son needed all the treatment modalities.

Dr. C. Keith Conners underscores the wisdom of using multiple treatment approaches. "One aspect of treatment is not enough. The parenting behavior is not going to diminish the vigor of the abnormal biological system in the child. On the other hand, diminishing the vigor of the abnormal biology with medication is not going to teach the kid the rules of the game or his ABCs," he explains.

AD/HD management requires a wide network of caregivers.

Parents, significant others, educators, and medical and mental health professionals must become equal partners invested in insuring that the child has a positive outcome. Of course, as children mature, they too should become part of this treatment partnership. Common sense and experience teach that treatment efforts are more successful when children buy into their treatment programs instead of viewing interventions as something being done to them.

Given that no single approach can accommodate the needs of most children with AD/HD, generally when a comprehensive treatment program begins, it requires a professional to act as a case manager. As mentioned in earlier chapters, this professional might be a child psychologist, child psychiatrist, pediatric neurologist, pediatrician, or social worker. In selecting a case manager, parents are advised to use a professional well-trained in the treatment of children with AD/HD and knowledgeable about the biological, social, environmental, and educational aspects of the disorder. Parents would also do well to select someone who is readily available and helpful to them and the child in whatever way possible. As parents acquire knowledge and become adept at dealing with AD/HD, they eventually assume the role of case manager.

Since most aspects of the multimodal approach have been or will be described in other chapters, this section focuses predominantly on the complicated issues of medication and unproven treatments. Before doing so, a brief review of the other recommended treatment modalities is provided.

To begin treatment, the parents, the child with AD/HD, the grandparents, and other people significant in the child's life should be educated about the disorder. To this end, the practitioner responsible for the child's treatment will explain the disorder's symptoms, manifestations, developmental course, and prognosis. Many parents are also helped through involvement with AD/HD parent support groups. These groups contribute to the ongoing education and awareness process by offering presentations on various aspects of the disorder, including management suggestions. When engaged in the heat of the child's difficulties, we parents can easily lose sight of the fact that the child is in trouble and not the cause of trouble. Support groups often focus our thinking on problem-solving approaches.

A second component of the multimodal treatment approach which enjoys widespread acceptance for its effectiveness is parent training in behavior management. Herein, parents learn how to modify their parenting behavior to accommodate the child's AD/HD-related needs. In addition to developing techniques such as giving commands clearly, following through with appropriate consequences, and limiting the types and amounts of demands made, many parents also find they must modify the home environment. Colleen Paterson recognized her daughter's need for structure and routine. Thus Colleen scheduled an activity for Allison every day after school. Her dinner, homework, bath, and bed times occurred around the same time each evening. Colleen also learned not to make her structure so rigid that she pushed her daughter to a point of frustration, so she frequently allowed Allison to take a five-minute break during homework time if she was finding the work difficult.

Most children with AD/HD also need a modified school environment. AD/HD symptoms usually have such a negative effect on the child's ability to succeed in the educational environment that they must be understood in a special way. Chapters 8 and 9 go into detail about the way AD/HD affects educational performance and about methods to address the individual child's needs. At a minimum, however, Dr. Barkley suggests teachers make the following accommodations: reposition the child's desk to monitor the child closely; use effective rewards and less punishment; and reduce the length of assignments and the amount of written work.

Despite recommendations to use multiple types of interventions to manage AD/HD, medication as a treatment has captured considerable attention. For many children, medication has produced significant positive results. But medication has also come under fire by critics who think it is prescribed too liberally or used as a "silver bullet" by parents and teachers who desire calmer, quieter children. Such opinions are best left to open debate. The following pages present recommended guidelines for the cautious and responsible use of medication therapy, along with information about what medications are used and why.

Parents often find the decision to employ medication therapy a hard one to make. Unlike an antibiotic for an ear infection, the medication used to treat AD/HD must be taken on a long-term basis, because medical treatment does not cure the disorder. Instead, it makes the child's AD/HD symptoms more manageable.

Only a physician can prescribe medication. However, often a nonphysician with primary responsibility for the child's treatment program, such as a psychologist, will advise the use of medication. When making a determination about if and when to use medication as a form of treatment for a child with AD/HD, psychologist Sam Goldstein says most practitioners follow this basic guideline: Medical treatment is recommended when other interventions do not produce the hoped-for results.

However, in cases where the child's behavior is out of control, medication may be started before any other treatments. Dr. Russell Barkley reports that at least 60 percent of children with AD/HD need medication in addition to other interventions. Parents must thoroughly discuss the use of medication with their child's doctor before deciding for or against its use.

Dr. Bennett Shaywitz cautions parents about the use of medication as a sole treatment. In fact, he will not prescribe medication unless a child has an optimal educational program and unless the parents understand the implications of the AD/HD diagnosis. Said Dr. Shaywitz, "AD/HD is a chronic problem which the child will have throughout life. You just don't write a prescription for medication without making changes in the child's school and home situations. Besides, without the right kind of support, the medication probably won't work."

No predictive test exists to determine if a child will benefit from medication. Dr. Paul Wender says one can think about a trial of medication for children with AD/HD in much the same way a physician prescribes medication for a patient with hypertension. In actuality, no one knows for certain if the blood pressure medication will lower the patient's blood pressure, but the physician knows the medicine has been researched extensively and proven safe and effective for this purpose, and therefore recommends that the patient try the medication to see if it helps. However, Dr. Wender cautions that as with all prescription drugs, physicians must weigh the cost-benefit issue and determine if the advantages of treatment outweigh the disadvantages.

Once a child is determined to be a candidate for medical intervention, the physician must choose which medicine, in what dose, and under what circumstances it should be administered. Dr. Charles Popper, editor of the *Journal of Child and Adolescent Psychopharmacology,* explains that several major classes of medications are used in the treatment of AD/HD: psychostimulants, tricyclic antidepressants, and catapres.

In most cases, psychostimulant medicines prove to be the first choice. The most commonly used stimulant medications are methylphenidate (trade name Ritalin), d-amphetamine (trade name Dexedrine), and magnesium pemoline (trade name Cylert).

On deciding which stimulant to use, Dr. Wender says, "The rule is anybody might get better on anything, and that for a given, the only way to tell whether methylphenidate or d-amphetamine is better for a child is to try both. However, if the child responds to the first medicine tried, then that's great."

"Stimulant medications have been demonstrated as most effective for attentional problems, and also useful for decreasing impulsivity and hyperactivity," notes Dr. Popper. He reports that these medications also have positive effects on aggression, oppositionality, frustration tolerance, endurance in working on boring tasks, and increased sociability, adding, "They have been demonstrated to improve the behavior of peers and parents." This statement reflects the positive effect the medications have on the child's ability to inhibit "nuisance" behaviors which provoke others.

Of course, all medications have side effects. Those occurring from stimulants are generally mild. The most commonly reported side effects are loss of appetite, stomachaches, difficulty falling asleep, increased irritability, and perhaps teariness. Dr. Popper also adds "rebound" to the list. He explains that this phenomenon, which occurs in some patients when the medication wears off, actually results in the patient's behavior becoming more difficult than before the drug was taken. This effect goes away with the next dose. Stimulants have also been reported to inhibit growth. According to Dr. Popper, "The height/growth impairment is so mild, I don't know that it bears mentioning."

For children who cannot take stimulants, antidepressants generally become second choice. Numerous preparations fall into this category, but the most commonly used for the treatment of AD/HD are desipramine (trade name Norpramin) and imipramine (trade name Tofranil). Dr. Popper reports that these drugs are effective for all three symptoms of AD/HD, but with regard to the attention difficulties, they seem less effective than stimulants. He describes the most common side effects as dry mouth, mild constipation, sedation, and sometimes increased excitability.

Cardiovascular effects have also been reported with these medications. "The fact that there are cardiac effects in and of itself does not mean these drugs are dangerous," says Dr. Popper, adding, "Drugs like caffeine in Coca-Cola and chocolate also have cardiac effects." These medications require closer monitoring than stimulants. Typical practice, as described by Dr. Popper, would include using an electrocardiogram, probably once a year and also during periods when the dose is being adjusted.

Another widely used medication, catapres (trade name Clonidine), happens to be by itself in its class of medications. This drug, primarily used as a blood pressure medication, has also demonstrated positive effects on impulsivity and hyperactivity, and secondarily on attention. Its most common side effect is drowsiness. Dr. Popper notes that some children at the beginning of treatment tend to get worse, but that effect goes away. Other side effects include what Dr. Popper calls "the nuisance effects" such as headaches and stomachaches. He explains that there are some cardiovascular and blood pressure effects with catapres which do not require electrocardiogram monitoring, but do require routine blood pressure checks.

Parents should always ask the prescribing physician to explain why one medication is chosen over another, what effects are desired, and what side effects might arise. Because stimulant medications, particularly Ritalin, receive so much public attention, the following pages address some of the issues surrounding this class of medications and Ritalin in particular.

No one knows for certain why stimulant medication helps children with AD/HD. Nor does anyone know why some children with AD/HD are not helped by these medications. According to Dr. Popper, "There have been abnormalities in three major neurotransmitter systems that have been theorized to be associated with hyperactivity and impulsivity." Those neurotransmitters are dopamine, norepinephrine, and serotonin.

One theory regarding the neurological basis of the disorder is that children with AD/HD produce too little of the neurotransmitter dopamine. Consequently, in children with AD/HD, the areas of the brain responsible for impulse control, regulation of motor behavior, and concentration are not aroused to the extent they need to be in order to function efficiently. Thus, even hyperactive children with AD/HD, though their motor movements appear to be traveling upward of 100 mph, are actually not functioning to capacity.

Dr. Gabor Barabas, a pediatric neurologist, explains that neurotransmitters are chemicals in the brain involved in the regulation of brain cell function. In order for the brain to regulate behavior efficiently, an appropriate balance of neurotransmitters is required. The exact manner in which stimulant medications work is not known. However, researchers think stimulant medication might enable the child with AD/HD to produce more dopamine so the child's brain cells have the necessary balance of neurotransmitters. As a result, the abnormal biology is altered to a more normal state and the child with AD/HD, with or without hyperactivity, is better able to concentrate, to control impulses, and to regulate motor behavior.

Ritalin, the medication most widely used in the treatment of AD/HD, has been prescribed for over fifty years. This medication has also been one of the most widely studied medicines given to children. In 1988, in a report to Congress, the Food and Drug Administration wrote, "We continue to believe that Ritalin is a safe and effective drug if used as recommended in the approval labeling suggested by the FDA in the treatment of AD/HD."

Ritalin is prescribed more than the other stimulants because of the relatively low-cost/high-benefit results of the medication. By low-cost, I mean that the use of Ritalin in properly diagnosed children with AD/HD seldom results in any serious side effects.

When a patient begins any stimulant medication, the physician starts with the smallest dose possible. The dose is then titrated, meaning raised in small increments until the desired clinical effect is achieved. This practice is also followed with the other medications used to treat AD/HD.

Ritalin happens to be a short-acting medication; thus, its therapeutic effects wear off in a matter of hours. The child's AD/HD symptoms then reappear like clockwork. Since Ritalin is usually in and out of the body within three to four hours, children will often take a morning and afternoon dose and some will even require a late-afternoon or early-evening dose. Some children take a longer-lasting, sustained-release form of Ritalin which lasts approximately eight hours.

When initially placing the child on medication, the prescribing physician will often monitor the child's therapeutic response frequently. Once the proper response is achieved, the physician will usually examine the child twice a year, though frequently the doctor will have phone contact with parents prior to renewing monthly prescriptions. Such practice ensures safety and efficacy. Parents who are concerned the dosage is either too high or too low need to discuss their concerns with the prescribing physician or in some cases seek a second opinion. Many physicians will also take the child off medication once or twice a year to reevaluate the need for its uses.

After a child is determined to be a candidate for treatment with medication, the prescribing physician must determine the circumstances under which a child needs it. Most physicians agree that children with AD/HD who need medication will require this form of treatment during school hours, where they encounter the greatest demands for performance in those areas in which they are significantly compromised, i.e., paying attention, thinking before acting, and sitting still. However, some practitioners believe all children with AD/HD should have drug holidays, and therefore do not prescribe medication for after school, weekends, or summers. Yet children with AD/HD can have the same difficulties in the home and with friends as they do in school, and some do benefit significantly from continuous treatment. The decision with regard to the circumstances under which a child needs medication as an intervention must be made on the basis of each individual child's symptoms not, as Dr. Goldstein points out, in an arbitrary fashion, "based on old wives' tales."

When faced with the decision to use stimulant medication, particularly Ritalin, many parents receive input from "well-intentioned" friends, relatives, neighbors, and, in some cases, total strangers. Some of these people are misguided and wonder why medication is given to children "who obviously just need more discipline." Others are misinformed and think the medication has dangerous side effects.

Either before the child goes on medication or even afterward, most parents hear comments similar to these: Do you really think your child needs drugs? Gee, he doesn't seem that bad. If you give your child drugs, won't she become a drug abuser? Couldn't you provide more activity and tire him out instead?

Some parents have even been accused of giving their child medication to make the family's life easier. Many parents wrestle with the notion that if they were better parents, they could control the child's behavior.

Such misguidance and misinformation does little to help the child with AD/HD or the parent. I believe as parents of children with AD/HD, we need to be aware of all the treatment options available and to have correct information about those options so we can make intelligent and informed choices. We all need to know that medication is not administered to make a bad child into a good child or a poor student into a better student. AD/HD is a biologically based condition. Consequently, the medication used in its treatment is given because it effectively alters the abnormal biology into a more normal state.

In fact, for the child in need of medical intervention, such therapy is often the kindest help. Nineteen-year-old John Brett told me when he began medication in sixth grade his life turned around. The years he spent off medication between eight and tenth grade he called "a living hell." John was taken off medication for those years because of two common misconceptions: the first being AD/HD symptoms disappear with puberty, and the second being the medications used to treat AD/HD no longer work after the child reaches puberty because of physiologic changes in the body.

Current research demonstrates the effective use of medication for the treatment of AD/HD in both adolescents and adults. At the age of fifteen, John Brett went back on medication after home circumstances and his AD/HD symptoms proved so intolerable he entertained thoughts of suicide. Today, his attitude is optimistic and he asked me to tell every person with AD/HD, "If you put your effort into something, you can get what you want out of it."

The use of stimulant medication with children with AD/HD tends to be more effective when parents and the child with AD/HD understand the basis for it. With consideration given to the age and sophistication of the child, Dr. Paul Wender will frequently explain the AD/HD medical treatment in this fashion. "Not being able to sit still or concentrate happens because there are chemicals in the brain. Some people make too much of them and some people make too little. Maybe you make too little." Dr. Wender then tells how the medicine can help the patient to compensate for the lack of chemicals. However, he emphasizes the point that although the medicine might be very helpful to the child, it is not a mind-controlling drug. The patient still has free will and must exercise his or her autonomy. For instance, the medication will facilitate the child's ability to focus attention while studying for a test, but the child must choose to study. The medicine will help the child control his or her temper, but only if the child wants to. The medicine does not control the child.

Many children are not even aware of the manner in which medication has helped them. According to Dr. Wender, because children with AD/HD characteristically lack insight into their behavior, they will frequently report that medication has had no effect even when he and the child's parents note a big therapeutic change. When Dr. Wender asks the child to account for why he or she has not been to the principal's office in three weeks, or why sleepover and birthday party invitations are pouring in, the child will respond, "Just lucky, I guess." The assessment of the positive effects of medication through the use of behavior rating scales and clinical observation often gives an accurate appraisal of the treatment benefit. In fact, many physicians use behavior rating scales to get a before-medication and after-medication measure to determine efficacy.

Some children resist taking medication. When this situation arises, each parent, child, and physician must deal with it on a case-by-case basis. Dr. C. Keith Conners finds that a common reason why a child would resist this treatment has to do with the social disapproval demonstrated by the various names other children assign to Ritalin such as "stupid pills," "smart pills," and "spaz pills." For the child with AD/HD, these unfortunate labels become guilt by association. Thus, the child equates not taking the medicine with not having a problem.

Blatant resistance to taking medication is more apt to arise in adolescence when teens are struggling with the developmental task of becoming independent. Perhaps they view medication as a form of dependence rather than as a therapeutic measure taken to address a biological condition.

We parents and also the child's teachers may inadvertently cultivate the notion that medication is a means to control children and adolescents. We want to avoid making statements or asking questions that give too much credit or blame for the child's behavior to medication. Examples of such statements include, "You're not in control. Did you take your pill today?" or "Gee, you're really having a good day. Those pills must be working."

Parents and teachers are advised to consider these guidelines when their child or student must take medication: handle sensitively and discreetly by not giving too much credit or blame to medication or by calling public attention to its use; dispense as prescribed; monitor side effects; communicate frequently with all caregivers, i.e., parents, teachers, and physician.

Under the auspices of a U.S. Education Department–funded center at the University of California, Irvine, center director Dr. James Swanson has reviewed the literature on medical intervention for AD/HD treatment. He cautions parents and teachers not to judge the efficacy of medication according to the effects it has on their lives. "We want to be sure," says Dr. Swanson, "that the child is performing better, not just sitting quiet and still."

Based on his review, Dr. Swanson also offers another caution about medication use to parents and teachers. He notes that an interpretation of the literature suggests that within one year of medical management, approximately 30 percent of children no longer take medication and that approximately 60 percent cease using it after two years. Reasons why remain speculative. Yet these statistics strongly caution against the over-reliance upon medication as the be-all, end-all treatment for AD/HD. Perhaps this therapy is best viewed as a window of opportunity to work with the child to develop compensatory and remedial strategies for coping with AD/HD. To reiterate, reputable experts agree that medication should never be the sole course of treatment.

In addition to the interventions thus far recommended, other therapies and practices have been proposed as beneficial. Some of these, according to Dr. Barkley, have promise but are still in the experimental stages. Social skills training, self-instruction, and self-control training fall into this category. He suggests parents first utilize the proven treatments which offer the greatest results.

A number of purported remedies exist which Dr. Barkley cautions against because they have no validity for the treatment of AD/HD. He mentioned high doses of vitamins; scalp massages given by chiropractors—which, he notes, may have some associated risks; visual perspective and ocular motor training; biofeedback; allergy treatments; and dietary treatments such as sugar restriction and the Feingold diet.

A number of mothers I interviewed told me they tried the Feingold diet, which theoretically eliminates hyperactivity by restricting additives, preservatives, salicylates, and sugar. The only effect this diet produced proved to be the placebo effect, which is typified by Liz Sacca's experience. Initially, Liz thought the diet had some positive result because she expended such a huge effort and the diet proved to be the first action she felt she could take to help her son. Later, she realized her feelings about herself as a mother improved, but her little boy's symptoms did not get better. According to Dr. William McMahon, "Any treatment carries a tremendous placebo effect. But generally, this effect does not last over time."

With regard to dietary treatment, no expert suggests that children be given a lot of additives, sugar, or preservatives. However, people need to realize that these elements do not cause AD/HD and thus their elimination cannot cure the disorder. In addition, Dr. C. Keith Conners, author of *Feeding the Brain: The Effects of Food on Children,* cautions against diets which are unreasonable and exclude a lot of the essentials needed by children. He explained, "We found on the Feingold diet kids developed vitamin C deficiencies because they missed all the vitamins that come in fruits."

A common misconception among some parents and professionals is that allergies cause AD/HD symptoms. Dr. Russell Barkley warns parents about the "visit to the clinical ecologist who does the huge three-day workup of allergies." He says no evidence supports the treatment of allergies as a significant part of the treatment of AD/HD, though allergy treatment may help a child's allergies. According to Dr. C. Keith Conners, about 25 percent of all children have some form of allergy. However, the incidence of allergy is slightly higher among children with AD/HD. He says, "There is evidence to suggest that kids with AD/HD have less functional immune systems and therefore have more allergies. However, it is very unlikely that allergy causes the disorder."

An equally controversial treatment for AD/HD happens to be biofeedback. According to Dr. Barkley, brain studies of children and adults with AD/HD indicate that the frontal lobe areas seem to be underactive or underreactive. Proponents of biofeedback believe that people with AD/HD can be trained through this method to increase electrical activity in these brain areas and thereby decrease AD/HD symptomatology. To date, insufficient evidence exists to substantiate these claims by biofeedback proponents. Though this approach seems harmless, it requires substantial financial expenditures, and its use in lieu of proven treatments, such as behavior modification or medication, may prove to be very costly to the well-being of the child and adults who need proven, effective interventions. As consumers, parents are advised to rely on scientifically validated treatment methods.

Understandably, parents hope for an end to the difficulties created by AD/HD, for the sake of both the child and the family. With luck and continued medical advances, this hope may become reality. But wishful thinking and quick fixes should not replace the courage needed to face AD/HD problems responsibly by using the multimodal method of intervention. We parents need to be empowered with information so that we do not fall prey, either financially or emotionally, to unproven, controversial treatments. An excellent source of information along these lines is the "Guide to Controversial Treatments" published by CH.A.D.D. (Please see Appendix A for its address.)

We can take heart in the meantime because the symptoms of AD/HD prove to be highly responsive to treatment. Child psychiatrist William McMahon strongly believes that the larger the system of people involved in the treatment of this disorder, the more likely the treatment will be effective. In the behavioral training program employed by his clinic, a price break is given if Mom and Dad come as a couple because experience demonstrates that when both parents are trained, attempts to manage the child's behavior have more success. Clinicians often come upon situations where one of the parents does not accept that the child has AD/HD or may accept the diagnosis, but minimize its seriousness. In these cases, the clinician tries, at the very least, to neutralize the parent.

Sometimes involving both parents in the treatment of the child's AD/HD is not always possible, particularly in single-parent homes. However, other people involved with the child can become part of the system. For example, in both single-parent and two-parent homes, Dr. McMahon often uses grandparents as part of the system because their presence and contributions frequently prove to be a great reinforcer to the child.

In our case, our psychologist proved to be an extremely important part of the treatment complex, though we do not need to see him regularly these days. As Paula Anderson said, "I'm comforted by the fact that I can call him whenever a problem comes up that I don't know how to handle." When the various treatments take effect, fewer and fewer circumstances arise that parents cannot handle.

Summary

Management of AD/HD

- Presently no cure exists, but symptoms can be managed
- Requires involvement of all family members
- Need to unlearn ineffective parenting techniques, such as inconsistency, criticism, rejection, physical punishment
- Requires use of behavior charts
- Major goal is to increase child's self-esteem and competence

Multimodal Management Approach

- Consists of four major components
  — education about the disorder
  — parent training in behavior management techniques
  — appropriate educational program
  — medication, when indicated
    also:
  — possibly individual/family counseling
  — requires a wide network of caregivers, including parents, educators, medical and mental health professionals, and the child

Medical Management

- Generally recommended when other interventions do not meet hoped-for results
- Should *never* be sole course of treatment
- No test exists to predict which patients will benefit from its use
- Benefits must outweigh disadvantages
- Discuss thoroughly with physician

Commonly Used Medications

- Psychostimulants (Ritalin, Dexedrine, Cylert)
  — usually first choice of physicians
  — effective for attentional problems, impulsivity, and hyperactivity
  — offer positive effects on aggression, endurance in tasks

    — mild side effects *may* occur which include decreased appetite, stomachaches, difficulty falling asleep, rebound
- Tricyclic antidepressants (Norpramin, Tofranil)
  - usually second choice when stimulants contraindicated
  - effective on all three core symptoms
  - mild side effects include dry mouth, constipation, sedation, sometimes increased excitability
  - cardiovascular effects have been reported (usually mild)
  - require electrocardiogram annually
- Catapres (Clonidine)
  - usually second or third choice
  - positive effects on impulsivity and hyperactivity
  - mild side effects, most common drowsiness

Psychostimulants/Ritalin

- Used over fifty years, most widely studied medicine given to children
- Seldom results in serious side effects
- Short-acting medication; symptoms reappear when dose wears off
- Usually administered two to three times a day
- Effective in children, adolescents, and adults

Considerations

- Avoid giving too much credit or blame for behavior to medicine
- Handle sensitively and discreetly
- Dispense as prescribed
- Monitor side effects
- Communicate with physician frequently

*Therapies **Not** Proven to Be of Use*

- Megavitamins
- Chiropractic scalp massages
- Visual perspective and ocular motor training
- Biofeedback
- Allergy treatments
- Dietary management, including Feingold

CHAPTER SEVEN

Self-Esteem

An odd occurrence happened in our home for the second summer in a row. Life improved. Without the stress of the school environment, David's symptoms became reasonably manageable. Sure, both his dad and I felt as though the effort required to keep David within limits often felt like pedaling a bike uphill, but we coped fairly well, as did Jonathan. Though David constantly lorded over his younger brother, fortunately Jonathan had a very calm, quiet disposition and seldom balked when David insisted on running our youngest son's life. Provided Jon did not get hurt, we ignored most of David's actions.

During this summer of 1986, David even developed friendships with a couple of the neighborhood children. Interestingly, Jonathan gravitated to a little boy who behaved much like his brother, while David became best friends with a little girl who proved as mellow as Jonathan. With the other children as suitable distractions, David no longer demanded my constant attention.

Even the two-week visit by David Sr.'s seventeen-year-old son, Mark, did not upset the status quo as it had in the past. Though young David adored his older brother, until this summer he could not handle the change in routine. Within a matter of hours after Mark arrived, David's voice grew intolerably loud and he became frenetic and overly emotional. As a consequence, the tension level for the entire family increased, thereby decreasing any chance of a pleasant visit for Mark. But this July 1986, we knew how to keep a lid on David's behavior, and Mark finally enjoyed a happier atmosphere along with the constant attention enthusiastically showered on him by his younger brothers.

When September rolled around, I felt ambivalent about the arrival of school. For years, I anxiously anticipated the peace and quiet I would have once David attended a full-day program. Now I wondered if the school pressures might once again mean a change for the worse in my son's behavior. Over the summer, the child psychologist tried to alert both his dad and me to the potential risks for David in the primary grades. Until the final hour drew close, we both chose to bask in the sunlight of David's improved disposition. When our son charged through the door at the end of the first day of first grade with a smile stretched from ear to ear, both the psychologist's concerns and my own seemed foolish. David had a wonderful teacher who wrote ''I love you'' on every paper. In turn, he fell in love too.

During these happy days, David nicknamed me ''Kitten.'' Though I prefer dogs, David loves felines of any type. When he called me ''Kitten'' I accepted this name as a demonstration of his love, as a sign I had gotten my seven-year-old son back. This nickname and the stuffed animals he brought to my pillow each night served as booster shots to help me throughout the bad days.

In mid-September when I brought David for a follow-up visit to the pediatric neurologist, he proved to be a mere shadow of the former wild fellow this doctor had seen a few months before. While we sat in the waiting room, David picked up a copy of *Marvin K. Mooney Will You Please Go Now* and began to read aloud. He finished the story while the neurologist and I stood by in total amazement. David had never read an entire book nor sat still in a doctor's office. In a report to the child psychologist, the doctor wrote, ''David is neurologically stable at this time. He is doing well in school and I noted a significant improvement in his attentional problems from previous examinations.''

I should not have been fooled by David's apparently reformed behavior. Just as the return of the swallows to Capistrano heralded in the spring season and the promise of happier days in our home, the arrival of David's birthday at the beginning of fall meant a change for the worse in his behavior. This year when he turned seven, the only difference from previous years was that the change caught me off guard. Our son's dark side subtly crept into our lives.

I first noticed David's mood had become transformed into a negative frame of mind when he began to take issue with my driving.

He insisted I tell him where we were going, what roads I planned to take. Heaven help me on the occasions I made a last-minute decision to take a different route without first informing him. David would carry on as though I had violated a sacred oath.

To make matters worse, my car had a speedometer like a digital clock which read out the exact rate of speed in brightly illuminated numbers. Whenever we drove anywhere, David eagle-eyed the speedometer and yelled at me if the number exceeded the posted speed limit. I had no idea why this child turned out to be so inflexible. To David, driving at 37 mph in a 35 mph zone meant speeding. No matter how many times I tried to explain that a slight variation could be acceptable, this boy would not listen to my explanation, and I in turn caught his full wrath and fury.

One day, I gave up trying to explain myself to him and yelled, "I am the boss, not you." I then proceeded to warn my son about the terrible fate his life would meet if he did not learn to mind his business. I did not hear a peep about my driving until a week later when David arrived home after school. With a shaky voice but nonetheless firm resolve, he announced, "Now you're in trouble. I stopped the police car and told him that you speed all the time." I could not believe he turned his own mother in to the authorities.

Here stood proof that once David set his mind to an idea, he never let up. The child psychologist explained to us how our son's propensity to get stuck on a topic, his inability to adjust easily to change, his short attention span, his impulsive behavior, and his poor social skills could really create a miserable existence for him in school. Again Dr. Burke, the psychologist, urged us to ask David's teacher to initiate a child-study-team evaluation so he could receive an appropriate school program.

After our first experience with this procedure, I felt reluctant to go through an evaluation again. Besides, both my husband and I now felt fearful of "the system" and worried about the repercussions of having David labeled. When we voiced these concerns to the psychologist, he explained that without the proper school recognition and program, David could very likely be tagged as the "kid with the ability who refuses to do the work." He said teachers might come to view David's failure to perform as either his voluntary choice or the result of some underlying emotional difficulties.

Dr. Burke then bluntly added that children with AD/HD label

themselves as bad kids with behavior problems. "Which label would you rather David have?" Dr. Burke asked. Well, we knew we would rather have our son understood as a child with special needs which made certain aspects of learning and socialization difficult for him. In mid-October I spoke with David's teacher.

When the conference began, I told the first-grade teacher about our home situation and the tremendously hard time David had been through as a result of this disorder. The teacher listened intently to this information and to my concerns that David meet with success in school. Since all of David's papers came home with stickers that read "Super," "Good Going," or "I Love You," I was surprised that she had already recommended David for the school's basic skills program, which did not require an evaluation.

Still, this program did not address my son's other problems. As in kindergarten, David had difficulty paying attention and could not seem to follow directions. Because he rushed, most of his work looked very sloppy. She kindly assured me that David had tried very hard, that many first-graders have similar difficulty, but when I looked around the room at the other children's drawings and papers, I could not help but see that David's work did not measure up to theirs.

Nor were his work habits the only problem. Just as in kindergarten, David bossed his classmates and reprimanded them whenever they made a mistake. The first-grade teacher told me David tended to be a very serious little boy and she felt his intensity interfered with his ability to make and keep friends. "David's a nice little boy. He's just very hard on himself and his classmates," she said.

We ended the conference in agreement that a child-study-team evaluation for David would be warranted. I knew my son had a chronic problem. But now that I realized parental determination could not alleviate his problem and that the results of the child-study-team evaluation might offer him more help, I found the evaluation process palatable.

Meanwhile, after eighteen months of going to the child psychologist, some of the finer points of home management became a part of my repertoire. For instance, David needed to be prepared for all changes in routine, so when Halloween arrived, this seven-year-old had been well rehearsed for the events of the day. In the afternoon, David and his five-year-old brother would participate in a Halloween parade and play at school which parents and grandparents also attended. That evening, the entire family along with two friends would go trick-or-treating.

This first-grade year, David opted to be a witch. Jonathan, now in kindergarten, had grown so accustomed to being David's shadow, he chose entirely of his own accord to be the witch's black cat. For Jon's costume, I found a black sweat suit, whiskers, a tail, and cat's ears. David would don a black robe, a cape, a witch's hat and broom, a ratty brown wig, a wart-covered nose, and green face makeup. I felt so good about their costumes that I could hardly wait for the boys to come home at lunchtime to get ready for the school parade.

At the stroke of twelve noon, David flew through the door and screamed in horror, "Witches are girls. Get me another costume. I'm not being a witch." I felt panic. We did not stock a cache of costumes ready for any whim. David began to lose control and started to yell, scream, and call me names for "being a stupid mother." Even time-out could not get him calmed down.

He did, however, stop his tantrum the moment the idea dawned on him that his little brother could be the witch. "I'll be the cat," he proclaimed. Jonathan, who had been subservient to his big brother's spell for so long, picked this day to take a stand. He would not hear of a change in costume and I supported his decision. Recognizing defeat, David slipped back into his nasty temper.

I felt like a genius when the obvious solution came to my mind about twenty minutes later. I told David he could be a warlock. "What's that?" he yelled. "A male witch," I replied. But David did not buy this brilliant idea and continued his tirade. Only ten minutes remained of the lunch hour and David, who had not even begun to get dressed, started to criticize Jon's costume, at which point I almost sent him to school as the fabled headless horseman.

Fortunately, my mother arrived on the scene and convinced him that Halloween costumes knew no gender. David put on his costume. I applied the final red blotches on his green face and brought him to school, where all his classmates already sat at their desks. When we opened the door, the entire class cackled and shrieked, "Look at the witch." He did look great.

David ran out of the room and ripped the wig off his head and the warty nose from his face. "They're laughing at me," he screamed. Though his teacher and I tried to explain that the kids just thought his costume looked so real, this seven-year-old witch could not make the distinction. He only agreed to rejoin the festivities after I wiped every smudge of green paint from his face.

As I sat in the audience and watched all the little children, including my son Jonathan, enjoy themselves and revel in their costumes, I became overwhelmed with sadness. This celebration proved to be anything but a party for my son. David's disorder still prevented him from being like all the other kids. Once again my denial tricked me. This witch had been there since his first Halloween. I fled the scene because I could not stop crying.

David came home from school no longer dressed in his costume, but relatively calm that afternoon. I, on the other hand, felt stretched to my limit. When the time arrived to get ready for trick-or-treating, I soon discovered this evil spell would not quit. David acted up again and when I snapped and screamed unmercifully at him, Jonathan joined forces with his brother and began to yell about his costume. By the time my friend and her two children arrived to go out trick-or-treating, I felt like an emotional basket case. I had no idea what could have possessed mild-mannered Jonathan to act up that Halloween day. Normally, Jonathan played a very passive role. At times, I could even fool myself into thinking that my younger son took all the family stress in stride. This horrible scene proved to be the precursor for many bad days to follow.

At our next appointment with the child psychologist, I recounted the horrors of Halloween. He explained that the holiday had all the makings for a blowup: too much stimulation, too much change in the routine, too much excitement, and for David in particular, too little self-esteem. The constant negative feedback from his parents and peers, the frustration he felt from not being able to perform to his ability level in the classroom, and his socialization problems commanded a high price. David could in no way handle being the center of all that attention. The psychologist reminded me that scenes like Halloween would become exacerbated if I responded less than matter-of-factly to my son's behavior. As a result of this nightmare, David had experienced yet another blow to his already damaged self-esteem and I again felt like a terrible mother.

For the next couple of months both his dad and I searched for ways to help David feel better about himself. We tried sports like swimming, gymnastics, and basketball at the YMCA but David balked about these activities. He put a great deal of pressure on himself and could not tolerate the fact that he did not do these sports perfectly. Eventually, we did not force him to go. At least three days a week, I encouraged David to have a friend over to our house after school. David bossed these children so much that I felt embarrassed for my son and uncomfortable for them. I just did not know how to help David build friendships. After a couple of months, only one little boy who never challenged David remained on the social scene.

By December, the school work load increased. Now that homework had been introduced, David had spelling words to study and sheets of math problems to do. He could barely control himself long enough to sit still and do this work. The moment a task presented the slightest challenge he fell apart. He would scream for my help and then he would complain about my input. The child psychologist suggested we add to David's chart, "Completes homework on time without argument." Though the chart helped, I began to feel as though the load we had to carry to keep David on track had grown too heavy.

Despite all the behavior management both his dad and I used, we could not get a semblance of normalcy in our home. Our efforts proved to be only a partial solution. In January 1987, both young David and I crashed and burned as a result of the stresses this disorder placed upon us.

The actual circumstance which brought us to our knees began quite innocently. David had a story to write for homework and I tried to help him. He behaved so nastily that I threw up my hands in disgust, which made him extremely angry. The more he mouthed off, the angrier I became. Pretty soon the scene approached near-Halloween proportions. I had the presence of mind to pull out of the fight. However, the next day I insisted he take a note to his teacher in regard to the problems we had with the assignment.

Throughout the entire school year, David's teacher and I communicated by note, so when no reply came home that day or the next, I questioned David. He developed a guilty posture and avoided answering any of my five hundred questions until I grabbed his face, looked him straight in the eyes, and demanded to know what he did with my note to the teacher. By the time he admitted he never delivered it to her, I was in a fury. I ranted and raved so much that David probably thought he committed a violent crime.

I could not get control of myself. Practically every ounce of frustration I had stored over the past seven and a half years gushed out. Later that evening as David changed for bed, I continued to obsess about the note until I ultimately threatened him. I hollered, "Tomorrow you will take another note and that note will tell the teacher what the first note said and that you did not give it to her."

All the color drained from this little boy's face. David covered his ears and began to scream, "I hate myself. I'm going to climb up a tree and touch an electric wire and die." I felt terrible. I lifted him off the floor and while I rocked him back and forth I told him over and over again, "Mommy was wrong to yell at you, David. You're a good boy. I love you very much. You didn't do anything so bad. Forget the note. It's not important. Your teacher always tells me what a good boy you are."

After a while his sobs stopped and he went to bed. Then I fell apart. My son, though still a small child, felt so much misery he wanted to die. I knew he fought hard to fit, to belong, to feel loved. Yet he stood alone, a ringmaster forced to keep the lions of the world at bay lest they swallow him up. Maybe this night, when the lion became his mother, the effort proved too much.

The next day, we had an emergency appointment with the child psychologist. Even though David's emotional state had stabilized that evening, guilt, shame, and fear overwhelmed me. I thought I must be the worst mother ever, but Dr. Burke said I too had become a victim of this disorder. He explained that I had reached the point of emotional overload and suggested I go away for the weekend to calm down and recharge my batteries, which I did. When I returned, I felt better, though still unsettled.

A few days later, we also saw the pediatric neurologist. After I described our family situation of the past few months and the ultimate crisis, the doctor said the time had now arrived to try stimulant medication, specifically Ritalin.

Though the medication did not promise to be a magic cure, for our son, this treatment provided the missing puzzle piece. The medication enabled David to regulate his own behavior, emotions, and impulsive decision-making. His hyperactivity diminished. His attention span and ability to concentrate increased along with an improvement in his organizational skills. Use of the medicine in conjunction with behavior management techniques, family therapy, and the school program

⏤wed David to experience the world as a kinder place where he could be quite successful and well-liked by others.

Three weeks after David began medication, we went on vacation to Mexico. These ten days we spent together turned out to be the most wonderful time we had ever experienced as a family. Mexico requires much adaptation, yet David maintained a positive attitude, and for most of the trip, acted as resident cheerleader. We came home on Valentine's Day, and that evening I found this note on my pillow. "To cat meow. I love you kitty cat. The best cat in the world." How the tide had turned in one short month. Even Jonathan now sought out his older brother as a playmate.

As a family we continued to work in therapy for the rest of this year. David's behavior grew consistently better and so we now addressed some of the bad patterns our family had fallen into over the years as we wrestled with his condition. The most difficult one for us to break proved to be using David as the family scapegoat. Jonathan had subtly become a master puppeteer who knew precisely how to pull his brother's strings. Whenever any disturbance erupted, David got blamed to such an extent he confessed to sins he never committed. We also concentrated our efforts toward raising our little boy's self-esteem.

In order to make this change, our psychologist told us we had to take certain actions. First, his dad and I had to look and listen at all times before we reacted. We had to learn to view a situation through David's eyes. Oddly enough, when we did put ourselves in David's position, many of our perceptions changed. Above all, we needed to learn not to yell or say damaging things to our child. Dr. Burke told us, "Kids with AD/HD really test your patience and so it's understandable that you lose your temper. But you have to understand how hard life is for them too."

We learned in therapy that David could not help himself and did not understand why we got angry with him or yelled at him. The psychologist said we had to step back a bit and not take the child's behavior personally. Even though he acknowledged how difficult such steps could be, he reminded us that since the child cannot stay in control of his or her emotions, the adults had to do so.

"AD/HD must be managed thoughtfully, not emotionally," the child psychologist told us. Eventually we learned that the goal of any encounter is to teach the child what behavior is and is not acceptable. With all honesty, I must add that even today David's dad and I still fall back into old patterns of response. But never do we or our son David slide as far down as in the dark days.

The darkness of David's first-grade year occurred because his self-esteem hit rock bottom. Though not all children with AD/HD experience the loss of self to the extent that they feel despair, still in all, not feeling good about oneself runs rampant in children with this disorder. Given the factors which contribute to the development of self-esteem, that children with AD/HD prove to be at risk for a poor self-image is not surprising.

As explained by private therapist Judy Welch, the development of self-esteem is a lifelong process. Furthermore, our sense of self changes in response to our feelings of self-worth, self-confidence, and self-reliance. Young children do not know how to nourish their sense of self, so they look to others for support, acceptance, and approval. Initially parents nurture their child's self-esteem, then significant others such as teachers, siblings, peers, and coaches play a role in the child's feelings about himself or herself. According to Dr. Welch, teachers play a vital part in the development of self-esteem in children because they are the main providers of feedback in academic areas. This feedback not only communicates ability level; it tells the child how he or she compares to peers.

In the workshops Dr. Welch conducts on self-esteem, she informs parents and teachers about the manner in which a child's self-image can be elevated based on the opinions the child holds of himself or herself. These opinions, she says, are formed by the messages the child gives himself or herself, those received from others, and how the child interprets the messages from others. Children who receive positive feedback develop an inner confidence and can therefore nourish their own sense of self. They grow into happy, well-adjusted adults. Unfortunately, many children with AD/HD often receive largely negative input from family, peers, and teachers. Therefore, they develop an extremely poor sense of self and eventually prove unable to perceive a message as positive when it is intended as such. Children with AD/HD also become patterned to give themselves negative messages.

Dr. Welch defines self-esteem as unconscious, emotional reflection of a child's judgment about himself or herself which is always characterized by the child's actions and attitudes. She notes children with high self-esteem take pride in their accomplishments, act independently, assume responsibility easily, tolerate frustration well, approach new challenges enthusiastically, and feel capable of influencing others. Children with high self-esteem make comments like "I can handle that job," "I made this picture all by myself," "Wow! I'm going to learn long division," and "I really like this story I wrote about dinosaurs."

A child with low self-esteem expresses a defeatist attitude a great deal of the time. He or she avoids anxiety-producing situations, demeans his or her talents, feels others don't value him or her, blames others for his or her weaknesses, is easily influenced by others, becomes defensive and easily frustrated, and feels powerless. The child with low self-esteem might make statements like these: "I'm not going to school today. There's a hard test in math," "Nothing I draw looks any good," "I flunked the test because the teacher didn't give me enough time to study," "I can't find the scissors," "I don't have an atlas, " and "Now I'll never finish my social studies homework."

In the case of Susie White, her mother, Lynn, recognized Susie's lack of self-esteem when she asked all the little girls in her Brownie troop to draw a self-portrait. Susie did not draw a bold picture and use most of the paper like the other little girls. Instead, she drew her self-portrait the size of a pea and in the lower-right-hand corner of the paper so that it was barely discernible. At this point in time, Suzie's AD/HD disorder had not been diagnosed, and she carried the burden of responsibility for her symptoms.

According to Dr. C. Keith Conners, "Being effective is the basis of self-esteem." He says there are a million ways that kids can be effective. For instance, they can dress themselves, play with other children, succeed academically, and experience a sense of accomplishment through sports or the performing arts.

Dr. Conners explained that most children with AD/HD do not have the means to feel effective. Their symptoms usually make everything they attempt a hassle. Even their special talents often go unrecognized or undeveloped because many children with AD/HD prove unable to practice or sustain interest in their individual milieus. Thus, the normal means by which most children receive boosts in self-esteem do not exist for these children.

Based on his clinical experience, Dr. Conners says, "Most people either write off children with AD/HD as miserable little beings who deserve the negative responses they get, or else they ignore these children." Such responses do much harm to the child's self-image. Dr. Conners reports that long-term, follow-up studies of children with AD/HD reveal almost a uniform deficiency in self-esteem. Though the academic and behavioral deficits tend to persist, he says as adults, the low self-esteem becomes a far more serious deficit because success in life is determined by a person's motivation, belief in self, and confidence.

Dr. Welch adds that many children with AD/HD become battered by a steady stream of failure, frustration, and disappointment, resulting in badly bruised egos. The degree to which the child experiences this emotional beating depends on the degree of severity of the condition. For Peter Rothman, every environment represented a struggle. Even his day camp counselors perceived him as uncooperative. Since he had difficulty going from one activity to the next, ten-year-old Peter turned out to be the last child to get to the starting line and the last one to cross over the finish line every day. His mother, Donna, often mistook his uncooperative behavior as obstinancy.

Undiagnosed children with AD/HD often suffer blows to their self-esteem because of the mythology developed to explain why they do not "get with the program." Many parents and teachers, faced with a child who does not comply, often draw the conclusion that the child has control over his or her behavior, but chooses to act in a way contrary to the rules which have been prescribed.

As a result of this "he-could-do-it-if-he-wanted-to" myth, many children with AD/HD become subjected to a great deal of punishment. Dr. Russell Barkley observes that these children do not want to behave the way they do. By the age of eight or ten, many show signs of poor self-esteem because they really want to behave well. After they are punished for misbehavior, they make great promises to change, which of course they cannot keep because, as Dr. Barkley says, "They are at the mercy of their characteristics."

Yet children with AD/HD come into the world with the same desires as all other children. They want to be loved, liked, and accepted, and so like other children, they want to please. For these children, though, the behaviors associated with their disability displease themselves and others. They experience failure so frequently, their self-esteem gradually erodes. This sense of failure is compounded in those cases where parents, unaware of their child's underlying disorder, decide that their son or daughter is out to drive them over the edge. In actuality, a frustrated parent often sends the child with AD/HD's sense of self on a downward spiral.

Parents often find they compromise the very standards of decency they set for themselves. For example, Judy Woodruff's daughter Karen frequently exploded in fits of temper. Like her daughter, Judy always had difficulty with self-control and punished herself for years with the assumption that if she tried harder to be a better person, her problem would go away. One night when Karen displayed a temper outburst, Judy raised her hand to smack her daughter and unintentionally made Karen's nose bleed. After this incident the mother sought help. Evaluations determined they both had AD/HD.

The message here is not that every person who loses his or her temper has AD/HD, but rather that people with the disorder often spend years trying to explain why they cannot stay in control of their behavior. Like Judy Woodruff, in most cases the explanations employ guilt and blame and consequently foster poor self-esteem. Parents who come from this emotional place have few coping mechanisms to deal with the problems resulting from their child's AD/HD symptoms. Unfortunately, a mantle of negativity falls upon the shoulders of the children with this disability.

Furthermore, when parents and teachers do not understand the dynamics of this disorder, they often have unrealistic expectations. Based on her experience as a former teacher and school psychologist, Dr. Welch notes that many parents and teachers get stuck in the belief that if they really push a child, that child will straighten up and do what is asked. Sometimes when the parents and/or teachers push, the child does perform well, which gives rise to the opinion that if a child with AD/HD does something once, he or she should be able to perform accordingly at all times.

By the way, the child with AD/HD oftentimes proves equally as baffled as to why he or she can get it together sometimes but not others. This "he-could-do-it-if-he-tried-hard-enough" myth and the aforementioned "he-could-do-it-if-he-wanted-to" myth are closely related and reinforced by the inconsistent nature of the child's AD/HD symptoms.

Pediatrician Melvin Levine, director of the Clinical Center for Development and Learning at the University of North Carolina at Chapel Hill, believes inconsistency to be the biggest problem of children with attention problems. Many people act as though the inconsistency of the child's behavior indicates that the child with AD/HD really does have control over his or her actions because occasionally the child does meet expectations without special help.

Why anyone would respond with disbelief and surprise that AD/HD symptoms manifest inconsistently boggles the mind. As Dr. Levine points out, many chronic conditions in medicine are inconsistent in their manifestation. For instance, people with asthma do not wheeze all the time, and people with arthritis may have swollen joints one day and not the next.

But the misunderstandings about the inconsistent nature of AD/HD symptoms take a toll on the child's self-esteem. Instead of allowing the child with AD/HD to feel effective for the times he or she does perform well, these myths and expectations give the child the message that he or she is incompetent.

Unfortunately, the most consistent aspect of the disorder proves to be the fact that most children with AD/HD receive this "incompetency message" regularly. In fact, this message is so consistent, the child often incorporates it into his or her own belief system. Sometimes the incompetency message is delivered overtly by negative feedback and punishment. Other times, parents in particular, though they do not realize it, develop a demoralizing pattern of response to the child with AD/HD. And the negative messages they send to their son or daughter become gradually ingrained within the child.

Dr. William McMahon reports that parents of children with AD/HD frequently fall into a condescending pattern of response to the child which in turn reaffirms the incompetency message. In his practice, for instance, Dr. McMahon has noted some parents who identify the child with AD/HD as a social and emotional cripple and overprotect him or her because they feel responsible for the youngster's every move. In other situations, the parents cut the child a very wide swath and everyone walks on eggshells around him or her. These responses not only deprive the child of normal consequences for his or her actions, but such condescending treatment sets the child apart from everyone else. Children with AD/HD often feel they do not fit in.

Fortunately for children with AD/HD, self-esteem changes when the child's circumstances improve. According to Dr. Welch, the most effective remediation of poor self-esteem is to change the child's belief system in himself or herself. In order to effect a positive change, significant others, particularly parents and teachers, need to alter their belief system about the child. When the parent, teacher, and the child with AD/HD acquire knowledge about the disorder, they all have a basis upon which to begin a change in their point of view.

To change their belief system, parents and teachers must dispel the myth that the child with AD/HD is willfully noncompliant. Once parents and teachers come to view the child as a person with a disability in need of special help, they feel less angry about the child's behavior. As a result, their stress level decreases and their capability to help the child increases. Attention-deficit/Hyperactivity Disorder affects everyone the child interacts with to some degree or another; therefore, everyone must learn to cope with the disorder. Parents need to make changes in their approach to the child with AD/HD if they want to nurture the child's sense of self.

Behavior management, of course, proves to be the most beneficial method of changing parenting behavior. These methods, described in earlier chapters, also help parents to cope better with frustrations created by this disorder. Teachers as well often find behavior management tools have an important place in the classroom. Many parents and teachers tend to view effective management techniques primarily as the use of behavior charts and explicit rules followed by predictable consequences. Once these techniques are employed, most parents especially find they cannot live without them. But though these techniques certainly lessen the amount and type of punishment used, and in addition enable the child to take responsibility for his or her behavior, they do not in and of themselves promote good self-esteem.

According to Dr. C. Keith Conners, the goal of all interventions is to make the child feel good about his or her abilities and to feel effective. To do this, he says, those involved with the child "need to catch the child being good." Throughout the course of most days, children behave appropriately in many instances for which parents can show approval: for instance, when the child remembers to do his chores or to bring home all the necessary homework materials. The child might share a toy or perhaps politely ask for a snack.

None of these appropriate behaviors are above and beyond the call of duty. They are examples of everyday expectations. But even though we expect a child to behave a certain way as a matter of course, we still need to reward the child with AD/HD for meeting expectations. Praise becomes the greatest sculpting tool a parent or teacher has to help the child carve a positive self-image.

Of course, praise needs to be valid. Furthermore, parents and teachers need to know that for a child with a poor self-image, even deserved praise may initially be viewed as contrived. Sometimes the child may even act out to try and prove that the praise was not warranted. Though such a response might evoke an angry reaction from the adult, we need to remember that under these circumstances, the child is coming from a place of low regard. This child truly needs a lot of positive feedback to turn that horrible self-image around.

In younger children, Dr. Conners says blunt forms of praise, such as "Excellent job" or "That's wonderful," work surprisingly well. However, he finds older kids to be sensitive to such blunt statements and so praise must be subtly delivered in statements such as "It looks like you put a lot of work into this."

At the conferences she gives on self-esteem, Dr. Welch tells parents and teachers to check the child's self-esteem bank account to make sure there are more assets than debits. She advises parents and teachers to monitor the number of withdrawals they make through negative feedback and to make numerous daily deposits of praise, encouragement, recognition, and positive attention. To this end, Dr. Welch made a list of phrases parents and teachers can use called "52 Ways to Say 'Good for You.' " Among those included are: "I appreciate your help," "That's a good point," "That's certainly one way of looking at it," "Good thinking," and "Nice going." By the adult's using a variety of expressions, the child knows the praiseworthy behavior really received consideration.

Dr. Welch maintains that realistic expectations on the part of parents, teachers, and the child with AD/HD provide the backbone upon which a child can gain self-respect. Thus, the child's strengths and weaknesses need to be determined. In her clinical experience, she has found the more information parents, teachers, and the child with AD/HD know about the disorder, the greater their sensitivity to the child's strengths and weaknesses. Knowledge is like the white plaster cast worn by a child with a broken arm. The cast conveys the message "I can't write with this hand, but maybe I can type with the other one." Once everyone understands the child's problems, they can revise their expectations, look for constructive ways to overcome the child's difficulties, and not make unreasonable demands on the child's limitations, just as they would not demand a child write with a broken arm.

In addition to providing a great sense of relief, knowledge about the disorder affords the child and the significant others the opportunity to maximize the strengths and compensate for the difficulties. For instance, often the diagnostic evaluation provides teachers with information about the child's learning characteristics. The teacher can use this knowledge to formulate judgments about how long the child can work on a task, how much homework the child can handle, and how the child processes instructions.

Instead of a haphazard existence, parents as well can plan around the child's strengths and weaknesses. When Paula Anderson and her husband learned their daughter Maggie had no control over her ability to sit still, they stopped expecting her to remain quiet for an hour while the family ate dinner at a restaurant. Even children with AD/HD can compensate for their difficulties. For example, ten-year-old John Golding learned to ask his teacher if he could go to a study carrel in the back of the classroom when he needed to have peace and quiet.

In John's classroom, his peers also have been taught ways to help assist him with class projects. Dr. Welch stresses the important effect peers and siblings have on the way the child with AD/HD feels about himself or herself. Thus, peers and siblings should be encouraged to participate in the boosting of the child's self-esteem by giving positive feedback and not criticism.

Dr. Welch believes children with AD/HD, their parents, and their teachers need to look beyond the problems associated with the disorder to its positive aspects. Children with AD/HD have many assets they can play to the hilt, but often they need the help of parents and teachers to tap their natural resources. Many successful adults with AD/HD note that they have learned to channel their energy, drive, and creativity into a productive end.

Parents and teachers can encourage the child with AD/HD to develop a special interest. Children feel good about themselves when they find something they can master. Dr. Paul Wender notes that children with AD/HD often perform superbly well when given a task of high interest to them. For instance, he notes boys with AD/HD tend to be interested in dinosaurs, or in earthquakes, tidal waves, or other miscellaneous catastrophies, and will read voraciously on those subjects.

In addition to nurturing the child's special interests, parents and teachers can build opportunities for success in the child's environment. Children feel good about themselves when they feel effective, competent. They develop confidence when they receive positive feedback, meet with success, and successfully fulfill their responsibilities. Since children with AD/HD often have difficulty taking and meeting responsibility, parents and teachers need to structure the situations where the child can succeed. For example, since John Golding turned seven, he has had the responsibility of feeding the family pets. Lack of organization poses a problem for John, so his mother puts the food he will need on the kitchen table every morning before breakfast. John proudly reported to me that not one pet, not even a goldfish, has died under his care.

There are a hundred different ways parents can build opportunities for their child to experience success. The following are some suggestions which many parents have found to work well. I have arbitrarily divided these suggestions into four categories: special jobs, special interests, play, and extracurricular activities. Some of these ideas may work well for your child. Others might be totally disastrous. When selecting or devising strategies to build his or her success, the individual child's age, strengths, weaknesses, and interests must be taken into account. At times even the best-laid plans fail. In such instances, don't be discouraged and don't assume that you or your child is at fault. These suggestions, many of which apply to either boys or girls, are intended to be catalysts to spark your imagination.

Special jobs can be a cross between chores and fun and provide an excellent way to develop a sense of responsibility. When presenting a child with the opportunity to do such a task, perhaps we all would do well to recall the example of Tom Sawyer. Because Tom made the whitewashing of Aunt Polly's fence appear to be so much fun, the other kids became so eager and highly motivated, they even paid money to be allowed to do his task. Special jobs can involve such daily tasks as setting or clearing the table at mealtime, saying grace, emptying the trash, feeding the pets, or making school lunches. On a weekly basis, the child can put away groceries, plan and/or prepare a meal, water plants, and/or sort objects for recycling. The child can also be responsible for the decorating of the home for the different holidays and for helping plan and map out a family outing. He or she can also be the family historian by taking family photos and/or placing photos in albums.

Children usually love to be helpers. They can be encouraged to assist in special home projects such as building a bookshelf or training a pet. Whenever I wallpapered a room, my children participated by taking the scraps and wallpapering a cardboard box.

Children tend to be naturally curious and often develop *special interests*. The parent can help the child build self-esteem by encouraging him or her to become expert in an area of interest. Many children like to start collections of any number of items such as dinosaurs, sports team memorabilia, stamps, dolls, rocks, or seashells. For a child interested in birds, the parent can help the child build a bird feeder and be responsible for keeping it stocked. Solar-system enthusiasts would enjoy a trip to a planetarium and a telescope to study the night skies. Other children might like to plant flowers and tend gardens.

Parents can also foster good feelings in the child by playing with the child. Dr. Russell Barkley explains that *play* can take two forms: directive or nondirective. He describes directive play as the developmental skills type in which the parent tries to teach the child something through the use of a game or construction kit like Legos. Dr. Barkley said, "Directive play basically involves a lot of teaching and this type of play with children with AD/HD just gets parents in trouble."

Instead he advises the use of nondirective play. Herein the child is given full control over what the parent and child will play. The parent also follows the commands given by the child. Rather than acting as the leader, the parent's job is observing, commenting, describing the child's play, and periodically giving positive feedback.

I accidentally fell into nondirective play with my children when they acquired a Nintendo set and I, of course, could not get past the first board on Super Mario Brothers. Whether playing Monopoly, checkers, chess, or cards, the parent does well to structure the game so the child can win.

Extracurricular activities frequently reported as successful and of high interest to children with AD/HD include team sports such as basketball, soccer, hockey, football, and baseball. Parents can play a crucial role in helping the child develop self-confidence by practicing the skills needed for these sports with him or her. For instance, throw the child balls he or she can catch. Some children might prefer to participate in sports that require little to no interactions with peers such as swimming, skiing, weightlifting, track and field, martial arts, or gymnastics. The performing arts, such as children's theater groups or dance classes, offer yet a third type of alternative. Regardless of which activity the child selects, parents need to support the child by attending practices, contests, and performances.

When first developing extracurricular activities, use prudence. Concentrate on activities the child selects, perhaps with the parents' guidance, rather than force the child to do something in which he or she has little interest. Chances are, under forced circumstances, the child will do poorly, and that of course defeats the very intent, which is to increase success and thereby build self-esteem.

John Brett, a teenager with AD/HD, said to me, "I think when you have AD/HD, you need an outlet." He advised parents to find something their child with AD/HD can do that makes him or her feel positive. For John, weightlifting boosted both his physical strength and his sense of self. He says when he lifts weights, he also develops his ability to concentrate, because he knows if his mind wanders, he could seriously hurt himself. John also asked me to tell parents that even if their child is failing every class, they should not take away the outlet, which often proves to be the only thing in the child's life that makes him or her feel good. Otherwise, says John, "He'll get more screwed up."

Children with AD/HD do not have to be beaten down as a result of their disorder. Dr. Welch says, "We can help resurrect a new self-image in our children with feelings of pride, security, and a sense of I-can-do-it-ness through encouragement and praise." In order to ensure a positive outcome for the child with AD/HD, Dr. Conners offers this advice:

"Parents need to view AD/HD as a chronic disorder. Good things and difficult things about the child will come and go. So you better develop your own sense of equanimity and not give up on the kid, because he will make it eventually, unless the toll along the way proves too high."

Through a concerted effort to boost self-esteem in the child with AD/HD, the miserable effects of the condition can be thwarted. Remember, these children are not the children who *can't* or *won't*. They *can* and *do,* but *can* and *do* come harder to them. To succeed, which means to feel competent, they need our special interest and help.

Summary

Self-esteem

- Provides motivation
- Foundation for positive adjustment
- Root of competency

How Self-esteem Develops

- Changes throughout life
- Initially nurtured by parents and then by significant others
- Based on opinions child has of self formed by:
  — messages given to self
  — messages received from others
  — how messages from others are interpreted
- Poor self-esteem results from negative feedback
- Sense of self characterized by child's attitudes and actions

Factors Leading to Poor Self-esteem

- Belief that child is deliberately noncompliant
- Myths that suggest child could do it if he tried hard enough or if he/she really wanted
- Inconsistency of behavior and performance
- Sending child messages suggesting incompetency

Factors That Improve Self-esteem

- Coming to view child as having special needs
- Changes in approach and feedback given to child
- Behavior management
- Changing expectations
- Emphasizing strengths
- Structure environment to build success experience
  — create special jobs that child can successfully accomplish
  — encourage special interests and hobbies
  — use nondirective play
  — develop participation in extracurricular activities
  — practice recreational skills with child
- Allow the child to choose the areas of interest

CHAPTER EIGHT

The Elementary School Years and Advocating for Your Child

In May of 1987, I met with our school's child study team to learn the results of the evaluation requested the previous fall. Since David's dad and I had already been through this process two years earlier when David had been diagnosed, I thought the conference would be quite easy to handle intellectually as well as emotionally. Yet the formality of the proceedings caught me off guard, and I felt tense and upset with the dehumanizing nature of this meeting. Except for his teacher, no one spoke about my son David, a first-grader, as a living, breathing soul. Instead, he became a summary of test results.

As a result of the child-study-team evaluation, David would indeed be eligible for special education services. The evaluation highlighted his difficulty performing to his ability level. Though David's grades were A's and B's, the child study team expressed concern about the *way* our child performed his tasks. Rarely did he use a careful, planned approach. Usually, he did complete his work on time, but at a very high price. David seemingly worked doubly hard to keep on task, which left little energy to cope with frustration. Adding to all the difficulty was his awareness that intellectually he had a brilliance which proved very hard to manifest in day-to-day tasks. That aspect whittled away at his self-esteem.

Even with all our knowledge about AD/HD, his dad and I still had a hard time thinking of our son as a child with special education needs. True understanding of AD/HD as a serious disorder negatively impacting on all aspects of our son's life took a very long time to register.

A few days after the conference where we learned the results of the special education evaluation, the postman delivered a copy of each child-study-team member's written report about David. Of all the reports, the social worker's interview with my then seven-and-a-half-year-old proved to be the most revealing. She wrote, "David describes himself as American. When pressed to describe himself as a person, he says he is nice. David likes that he has a new puppy, Molly, and that he takes care of her well. He states that he is happy most of the time. David does not like the way his brain makes him get into trouble. It tells him to do bad things and when he does them, he gets into trouble. David also doesn't like that his brain does not think too well. He hardly ever gets a 100 on his spelling test. David likes to play games or build things. He does not like to run or do work. David's three wishes were: one, have all the money in the world; two, own this world; three, could have magic."

Based on David's comments, the social worker drew the following conclusions. "David spoke of his brain in the third person, as though it were separate and apart from him, but very much in control. David did not see that he could alter his perceptions or the work of his brain either by studying harder or concentrating on his behavior. David appears to behave in a certain manner and relinquish blame for his behavior to causes other than himself."

I always knew my son to be very intelligent, but until I read this report, I did not realize his intuitive abilities. In actuality, David described to the social worker, and consequently anyone who read her report, the neurological manifestations of his AD/HD disability. He talked about his brain in the third person because he, more than anyone else, knew how little control he had over his behavior. Though he desired to succeed, to be accepted, to have his intentions properly executed, David could not will his brain to do what he wanted. Before the necessary treatment interventions, most times David had only limited power to regulate his behavior, while at other times regulating the functioning of his brain proved to be a force beyond his control.

At the end of the school year, I received one final note from my son's teacher. "Dear Mary," she wrote. "Wasn't David great today in the play? I'm so proud of him. In fact, his overall behavior has changed in school. His attitude is very positive lately, and several times he has complimented some of his classmates (a real first!). The gym teacher has also noticed the change—and the smiles! I'm just delighted for him. I hope you are experiencing this 'new David' at home, too." Thanks to the behavioral interventions and medication we used to manage our son's disorder, our entire family did reap the benefits of David's improved condition.

I do not mean to imply that all our problems ended. David still needed to learn how to behave appropriately. For instance, one summer evening, he threw a stick into the air which accidentally landed on his brother's head. Jonathan landed in the emergency room. I fully intended to be lenient and forgive David for his mistake, but he did not show any remorse for the consequences of his impulsive behavior. Instead, he bounded in the door and screamed at the top of his lungs, "It was his fault! I told the stupid Jon to move and he didn't do what I said. You should punish him."

Maybe my tightly clenched jaw and glowering eyes persuaded this boy to change his tack. Whatever the reason, David, a survivor, realized this occasion did not lend itself to "the best defense is a good offense" approach. He did not even talk when I sent him to his room for the day, and I felt particularly pleased that my temper did not flare and make things worse.

However, I continued to be disturbed by the thought that maybe David's impulsive behavior would someday push him across the line which separated the horizon and the end of the world. Unlike in his toddler days, I could not watch him like a hawk every minute to keep him from going too far. At our next session with the child psychologist, I decided to bring up this stick incident with the hope that perhaps the psychologist could drill into David's head the realization that impulsive acts can lead to serious consequences. I still had not fully accepted that David often had no control over his impulsive acts.

After I recounted the details of that afternoon, the child psychologist commended me because I gave David an immediate consequence for his action and did not get angry with him. But rather than lecture David about the evils of impulsivity, he asked, "Did you expect the stick to hit your brother?"

"No," replied David in a very soft voice.

The psychologist then queried, "What could you have done differently?" Dead silence.

After fifteen seconds or so I offered, "You could have looked around first to make sure nobody would be in the way."

I did not realize the extent of my poor judgment until the psychologist immediately told David he should never throw sticks or rocks or anything for that matter. I missed the point that this child with AD/HD could not readily or thoughtfully control his impulses, and thus needed strict limits. "No" for David actually proved to be much kinder than expecting him to use appropriate judgment.

That summer between first and second grade, David attended day camp. Since social interactions remained difficult, he continued to be isolated from his peers. Though he did participate in team activities, David spent most of his free time with his twenty-year-old group counselor. Until the winter came, neither my husband nor I realized how the camp experience had benefited our son. David, now eight years old, signed up for swimming and tennis at the YMCA. Such initiative and participation had never before been part of David's style, and in the past, when we forced him into sports activities, our efforts resulted in disaster. For example, we pushed him to play tee ball. During the first game of the season, our pride and joy sat in the middle of the field and proceeded to repeatedly yell, "This is boring." He did not play ball after that morning, and his dad and I no longer made emphatic suggestions purportedly for our son's own good.

When school resumed in September, David left the house each morning eager to begin his day. He returned a happy spirit. One of the first papers to come home showed a rocket blasting toward space. Underneath, David wrote, "When I grow up I want to be an astronaut. I want to do that because it is fun." He neatly formed each letter and spelled all words correctly. I felt such joy to see my son happy. Finally he had shed the difficult skin that bound him like a tightly wrapped coil ready to spring at the slightest jar.

Second grade obviously agreed with David. In addition to the care and concern of his morning and afternoon teachers, our son also had the support of the program designed specifically for him thanks to the infinite wisdom and mercy of special education. When the school year began, David received supplemental help in the school's resource room for two half-hour periods a week. But by mid-October, both his teachers noted the difficulties following directions presented for David every day. If a worksheet had multiple directions, David generally read and followed only the first directive. Though he understood the concepts being taught, his inability to follow directions seriously affected his performance.

Disorganization proved to be an equally formidable opponent. The inside of David's desk looked as though a family of ferrets had taken up residence. Whenever the teachers asked the class to take out a workbook or hand in a homework paper, our son could not find what he needed amid the varied assortment of crumpled papers and books. When he had more than one worksheet to do independently in class, David often forgot to do them all. Sometimes he brought the wrong materials home for homework. Other times he forgot his assignments altogether.

Since I made a habit of communicating with David's teachers on a regular basis, I learned about his school difficulties and frustrations very early in the year. Both second-grade teachers and I agreed that the special education program designed for David at the end of first grade needed some adjustments. We spoke with the person assigned to manage David's program. She devised a solution where each morning a teacher's aide came to my son's classroom to help him along with four other children identified with similar difficulties. The teacher went over the directions for the day's work, answered any questions the children had, and made a daily schedule for each child to follow. As the child completed a task, he or she crossed it off the schedule list.

At midday, the aide followed the same routine for the afternoon session. At the end of the day, she returned to the classroom and checked each child's backpack to make sure that all the necessary materials went home. If the children evidenced difficulty in any area of instruction, she also gave them tutorial help during the day. The program worked wonderfully and gave David the necessary support. Because the other children were involved as well, David felt "unspecial," which for his self-esteem proved to be quite important. David wanted very much to fit in with the gang.

In addition to this support, David's resource-room teacher devised some creative interventions geared to help him meet success in the regular classroom environment. For instance, David showed an interest in the computer, so the teacher developed tutorial computer games for his use at home. Not only did she make game disks for each week's spelling words, but the second-grade teachers told her what tests they would administer and she made study-guide games as well.

Both David's second-grade teachers also played an important role in his academic and emotional development. They took a special interest in him and communicated with me on a regular basis. Yet even with such care, occasionally unanticipated glitches arose. The worst one proved to be the creative writing project the afternoon teacher assigned in honor of Thanksgiving. She asked each child to "imagine you are a turkey and you have just found out you are going to be Thanksgiving dinner. How do you feel and what are you going to do about it?"

When David's turkey-shaped booklet came home with the smiley sticker pasted on the bird's plumage, I couldn't wait to read his response. Before I even opened the cover, I assumed he probably created a scenario where the turkey escaped by some ingenious method. And so I joyously dove into his "Turkey Talk" where upon David wrote, "I just found out I'm going to be Thanksgiving dinner. I think I know what to do. I will bite the farmer. And I'll stab him in the head and put him in a cage and fry him over a fire. And I'll injure his wife . . ." His story line followed this violent tack. As I read on, I wondered what possessed my little boy to such extreme anger.

As luck goes, the next day his father and I were scheduled to meet with David's teachers at the annual fall teacher's conference. As soon as we sat down, I said, "That was some story David wrote." The afternoon teacher called it "quite descriptive" and she said because of the violence, she showed David's story to the guidance counselor.

"What did she think of it?" I said, swallowing rather hard.

In reply, the teacher whispered, "The counselor thought it was, um, a little much, unusually violent, quite intense." With that comment, everyone fell silent.

Long pauses have always made me uncomfortable. After fifteen seconds or so, I found the silence so loud, I slipped into my "crack a joke" mode and, in an attempt to lighten the moment, rhetorically asked, "Gee, do you think Edgar Allan Poe started out this way?" Everyone sort of smiled. A moment or so later, David's morning teacher said she had discussed different Thanksgiving rituals with the class the morning before they wrote their turkey stories. One little girl enthusiastically gave a detailed account of her mother's experience growing up on a farm and how each Thanksgiving her grandfather slaughtered a turkey for dinner. Much to the great disgust and horror of the other children, this classmate described the bloody scene as a headless turkey ran around after it had been decapitated. The teacher reported that eight-year-old David had been quite upset by this information.

Now the violent nature of David's story did not seem quite as inappropriate. In fact, it made great sense to me. This child cried for days when a goldfish died. On occasion, he still mourns the loss of two stuffed animals he left in a taxicab when he was six. He even said to his brother, Jonathan, who had been asking for a hamster. "Why would you want a hamster? It will just die and you'll be sad." I could now understand how my son got caught up in the emotion of the moment as he sat at his desk writing about how he would avoid the evil farmer's butcher knife.

The remaining months of second grade proved to be a happier time for all of us. David's teachers called me every Friday to report about the events of the week. They informed me about any special projects that might be scheduled so I could monitor their completion and thereby avoid the 8:00 bedtime "what do you mean you have a book report due tomorrow?" crisis.

These second-grade teachers also recognized David's lack of self-esteem and made efforts to boost his opinion of himself. Since he loved science, they tried to encourage him in every way. One night one of his teachers even called our home to tell David to go outside and look at the sky because Venus would soon pass in front of the moon. That phone call went a great distance to let David know how highly his teacher regarded him.

Besides the genuine and special interest they showed David, the teachers also had regard for my input. When I called one day because David walked out the door in the morning knowing all the answers for his social studies test and came home in the afternoon with a failing grade, the teacher thought he might have encountered difficulty with the process of selecting multiple-choice answers and offered to retest him. He scored 100. The teachers understood that the mechanics of writing often interfered with David's ability to get spelling words down on the paper correctly, so each week after he had taken the written test, they asked him to orally spell the words he misspelled. Orally, he usually spelled all the words correctly. David received an A for the year. I think these teachers would tell you that the special efforts they made for David took planning and sensitivity, but they did not take a great deal of time.

I admired these teachers because they openly evaluated their methods and found ways to make the school environment successful for my son. They accommodated his special learning characteristics and worked to develop his positive qualities. The teachers never chastised him for his poor social skills or his demands on the other kids. Instead, they complimented him when he behaved in a polite and courteous fashion. They understood his need for structure and so they made his day as predictable as possible. They even gave him special jobs to do. When the final report card came home from school that June of 1988, David received four A's and two B's, and "Outstanding" for effort. But more important, young David came home smiling.

Due to the early diagnosis of my son's Attention-deficit/ Hyperactivity Disorder, I knew the nature of his developmental disability at the outset of his public-school career. I had been alerted to the potential difficulties David might face in school as a result of his AD/HD symptoms. With this knowledge, steps could be taken to protect my son from succumbing to years of demoralizing academic failure. Many children, however, are not diagnosed until third grade. By then, they have established a pattern of poor school performance. Others, even less fortunate, go undiagnosed well into the later elementary, junior high, or senior high school years, in the meantime having experienced a steady stream of academic failure, low self-esteem, and poor social interactions.

For those who would take AD/HD lightly, educational outcomes for children with this disability suggest cause for alarm. Results of long-term, follow-up studies provide the following data: 30 percent are retained in a grade at least once, with many retained more than once; 46 percent are suspended; 35 percent never complete high school; only 5 percent complete college.

With no wish to create fear or desperation, I share this staggering picture of serious academic failure to underscore the point that left undiagnosed and without appropriate educational interventions, we cannot expect these children and youth to succeed against the odds. Data show they fail.

In general, AD/HD affects education by interfering with performance. Many children and youth with the disorder characteristically experience academic and social problems. Frequently they are described as having difficulty with following rules, doing what is asked, working independently, completing tasks, disorganization, excessive activity and vocalization, frequent interrupting, low frustration tolerance, and waiting. Persistence of effort also proves hard to maintain.

Such characteristics account for the reason children and youth with AD/HD are at high risk for at best poor school performance marked by underachievement and at worst for academic failure. Unlike their peers without disabilities, the education available to all Americans is much harder to come by for children and youth whose AD/HD interferes with paying attention, organizing, thinking before acting, and inhibiting activity.

Not all children and youth with AD/HD experience educational difficulties to the same degree. Furthermore, as indicated in Chapter 1, the diagnostic criteria now distinguish between types of AD/HD. The inattentive type has difficulty with tasks requiring attention; the hyperactive/impulsive type generally does not have difficulty with attention, but is prone to uninhibited behavior; and the combined type exhibits inattentive, hyperactive-impulsive behavior. Dr. Russell Barkley notes that most elementary-age children will fall into the combined type of AD/HD. Beyond the preschool years, the hyperactive/impulsive type absent difficulty with attention usually does not occur often.

The type of AD/HD a child has predicts the nature of his or her school difficulties. Those students with the inattentive type tend to have difficulties with selective and focused attention. Often their academic difficulties arise because they do not seem to understand where to direct their attention and are usually very disorganized. Starting tasks and following directions may be especially difficult. They might also be somewhat restless and squirmy, but not "motor driven," as Dr. Barkley would say. These children have been described as "absent-minded professor" types.

Those with the combined type of AD/HD or the hyperactive/impulsive type are the children Dr. Barkley describes as "managed by the moment." Usually, they have difficulty sustaining attention and thinking before acting. Disorganization proves common. Their uninhibited pattern of behavior and lack of persistence prove quite frustrating to parents and teachers because these children seem to understand the requirements and yet they do not perform accordingly. Understandably, this behavior is often perceived as a choice made by the child to be noncompliant. In actuality, these children behave in a way that comes naturally to them. They do not have the option of choice. As Dr. Barkley explains, their difficulty is not in knowing the skill, but in controlling impulses and using the skill effectively. Additionally, the children with AD/HD: Combined Type may also have difficulty with selective and focused attention.

AD/HD is a performance disability which interferes with learning. Let's think about some typical school performance requirements. Students are usually expected to be on task, which means they start, stay with and finish work in a specified amount of time with a reasonable degree of accuracy. Students are asked to follow directions, to organize multistep tasks, to go from one activity to another in an orderly manner, and to produce work at consistently normal levels. Additionally, they are expected to have socially appropriate interactions with others.

To meet these typical school requirements, students with AD/HD need to pay attention, plan, and stay in control of activity and impulse. Understandably, these children and youth will have difficulties performing when requirements demand skill and proficiency in precisely those areas where they are compromised. Though excessive activity creates disruption, difficulties with attention and impulse control seem to have a more profound effect on educational performance.

Dr. Ron Reeve, associate professor of education at the University of Virginia, explains that the attentional process is comprised of a subset of skills. When we pay attention, we focus, select, sustain, resist distractions, and shift attention. When trying to pinpoint academic difficulty, each area of the attentional process requires evaluation. Generally, the inattentive subtype of AD/HD results in the child not paying full attention to the important features of a task, whereas hyperactivity and impulsivity often interfere with sustaining attention and completing tasks.

Children with any of the three subtypes may have difficulty resisting distractions, though for quite different reasons. The inattentive type is apt to be pulled off task by a distraction and then not be able to reorient to the important information. On the other hand, those with the hyperactive-impulsive pattern are drawn toward distractions, especially when they are engaged in activities that are boring and repetitive.

Like attention, impulsivity can also be separated into domains: cognitive and behavioral. Dr. Barkley explains that cognitive impulsivity refers to difficulty in stopping, thinking, and reasoning through a situation. Behavorial impulsivity is the inability to wait or delay making a response. Both cognitive and behavioral impulsivity often result in a similar outcome: poor planning or approach to task. Children with AD/HD are behaviorally impulsive. They often know how to make a plan, but they are not programmed to wait. Thus, they have difficulty delaying a response, so rarely do they use a plan. Instead, they just act first.

"AD/HD is not a problem of knowing what to do. It is a problem of doing what you know," observes Dr. Barkley in reference to these children with the uninhibited-hyperactive pattern of behavior. When children "know better," we tend to blame and punish them for their actions. That is why I think it is important to be aware of two theories currently receiving considerable attention about why children with AD/HD behave as they do.

One theory, put forth by Dr. Barkley, has to do with motivation. He says, "Knowing what to do is a strategy problem. Doing what you know is a motivational problem." He believes that children with AD/HD have a motivational problem which he thinks is neurologically based. Consequently, they have difficulty sustaining attention, particularly when doing tasks that are boring and repetitive. They also seem to need immediate reward and pleasure. A motivational basis for the disorder might possibly explain why these children perform better when lots of encouragement and incentive are provided.

Complementing the theory that AD/HD has a motivational basis is the work of Dr. Sydney Zentall, an AD/HD researcher and professor of special education at Purdue University. In order to become motivated, people need stimulation in varying amounts. Dr. Zentall believes that "people who need more stimulation, do more to create it." Based on her research, she finds that children with AD/HD are seekers of stimulation with an attentional bias to find what is novel or salient in the environment and in tasks. Unfortunately, the salient (most interesting) information is not necessarily the relevant information, so children with AD/HD may miss what is important in a task.

Dr. Zentall observes that most academic problems are produced by tasks with little novelty, i.e, tasks requiring repetition, rehearsal, and practice. These tasks which are basically detail-oriented and change very little do not sustain attention. She reports that studies show that difficulty sustaining attention results in more errors and messier work on later performance, and increased activity from morning to afternoon and from the beginning of a task to its end. Additionally, behavioral problems increase during repetitive, nonstimulating activities.

Children with the impulsive-hyperactive behavior pattern experience added academic and social problems arising from their difficulty waiting. Academic performance problems reflected by poor productivity and accuracy generally arise when the child has to organize, follow directions, or plan because these situations require the child to wait prior to responding.

To increase task performance and decrease impulsive responding, Dr. Zentall suggests the following: add novelty to the end of tasks; delete repetition within tasks, e.g., by using flip cards or working with peers; shorten tasks; develop routines for work completion; give the child something motoric to do while waiting to respond.

Children with AD/HD have been characterized as learn-by-doing, trial-and-error learners. Dr. Zentall says they will work at something stimulating, active, and novel, and will work to get away from something boring or repetitious. Both her theory and Dr. Barkley's make the point that children with AD/HD can perform, but to do so, they require more enriching activities, clear rules and structure, and lots of rewards and motivation to encourage their use of plans and on-task performance.

Given the lack of awareness about AD/HD, these children who do not "get with the program" have not traditionally gotten what they need to be successful. Instead, as Dr. Melvin Levine points out, the inconsistency of their symptoms and the unevenness of their development add to their woes. Often teachers and parents view the child with AD/HD as just not trying hard enough. After all, they rationalize, if Susie can remember to bring her book to class one day, she should be able to remember every day. If Johnny can do well in math and spelling, he should be able to do well in social studies. If Susie and Johnny did not have a disability, these assumptions might be correct.

Because children with AD/HD tend to be disorganized, not only do they forget to bring the necessary materials to and from school, they also lack a systematic approach to tasks. Dr. Zentall notes that they do not readily establish routines. They may have difficulty following sequences in four- or five-step processes. Though AD/HD primarily affects the student's performance, as Dr. Richard Zakreski explains, "Children who have difficulty paying attention, organizing, and concentrating will not learn reliably and efficiently." Research shows that these students do not acquire learning strategies on their own.

Beyond the primary grades, new tasks build on previous skills and become more complex. Dr. Zakreski observes that children with AD/HD have difficulty with complex behaviors like study skills. He explains that most children acquire study skills when, as younger children, they either are shown techniques by teachers or parents or they develop techniques on their own. Children with AD/HD, however, when exposed to the same models and patterns as their classmates do not acquire these skills without very concrete and deliberate instruction. Since study skills are seldom taught in this manner, when asked to read a chapter independently or study material for a test, children with AD/HD frequently have no idea where to begin or what information is salient.

In fact, even the manner in which children with AD/HD process information often interferes with their performance. Dr. Reeve observes that there is a tendency to "scatter-shoot" information. Characteristically, the students can provide a lot of details but have difficulty explaining how the information interrelates.

Inefficient information processing also explains why many children with AD/HD will leave for school in the morning knowing all the answers for a test and return home in the afternoon with a failing grade. According to Dr. C. Keith Conners, "We often see a distinction between what the child with AD/HD knows and what he or she can produce." Dr. Conners explains that when taking a test, the student has to focus on, select, concentrate on, and mentally organize the material to produce what he or she knows. Because many children with AD/HD have difficulty with these skills, Dr. Conners notes that teachers often think the child has a short-term memory problem because it appears that the information stored is very fragile and only available for a short time.

Dr. Conners believes the problem is more a function of the AD/HD interfering with the child's ability to focus on the material as it is being retrieved. While this same child will be disorganized on the playground as well, Dr. Conners says this characteristic will not be apparent in that setting. "But in school, the structure is much tighter and reveals the extent to which he or she is unable to adapt to that structure. Under the proper circumstances, perhaps a Platonic dialogue between the teacher and student, the child with AD/HD would be able to reveal what he or she knows," he concludes.

Similarly, children with this disorder have been known to "jump out of their seats" to answer a question in class or to share information. Then when asked to wait or to first raise a hand, by the time they get called on, they have forgotten what they had to say, which, of course, frustrates them, the teacher, and perhaps the other students as well.

The expectation for responsibility and self-control also proves troublesome. As children advance to the upper grades, they are required to work independently to a large degree, generally with little incentive or immediate reward. Students may be asked to read an entire chapter and be responsible for knowing and understanding the content in that chapter, often without teacher involvement. Because their minds wander, Dr. Zakreski explains, children with AD/HD do not assimilate the reading material in a cohesive manner. Instead they must continually redirect themselves to task and try to pick up the thread of where they left off. As a result, continuity is lost and they do not learn the material efficiently. Often they find these tasks so tedious and frustrating that they may eventually avoid them.

Handwriting also happens to be another very common problem for children and youth with this disability. Many parents I spoke with reported that teachers frequently complained about their child's messy work. In fact, poor handwriting often compromises the child's performance. For example, numbers illegibly formed or not arranged carefully will lead to math computation errors.

According to Dr. Levine, approximately four different causes can result in handwriting difficulties experienced by these children. First, impulsivity prevents some children from taking special care. Second, to write well, children need to have coordination between the flow of ideas and the flow of motor movements, and in some children, the flow of their ideas is too rapid for their fingers to keep pace. A third possible reason would be that handwriting is very much a memory task. The children have to simultaneously remember letter formation, punctuation, grammar, capitalization, vocabulary, directions, and ideas. Finally, some of these children have fine motor dyspraxia, which results in difficulty knowing which muscles to use and in what particular order to employ them to form letters.

Dr. Levine wisely explains, "It is important to pinpoint which particular pathway of writing difficulty is affecting the child, because it will have bearing on which remediation is used."

So far the learning problems I have been describing are problems that arise primarily from the symptomatology associated with AD/HD. These difficulties result in academic productivity problems and in information-processing problems, the latter being particularly germane to older schoolchildren required to perform more complex tasks. Clearly, these problems create much difficulty for many children with AD/HD in traditional school settings. Educational interventions will be addressed in the next chapter.

In addition to educational performance problems arising from AD/HD-related difficulties, children with AD/HD can have other disabilities that also affect their education. Among the more commonly co-occurring disabilities are specific learning disabilities, which are estimated to affect between 11 and 30 percent of all children with AD/HD. In the past, with so little known about the disorder, AD/HD had been viewed as a subtype of learning disability. Today, most experts agree that AD/HD is a distinct disorder. Thus, when assessing school-related difficulties, evaluators should determine the presence or absence of both conditions.

Clearly, most children with AD/HD will need some type of modified educational program. The Professional Group for Attention and Related Disorders (PGARD) estimates that approximately 50 percent of the children with AD/HD can be educated within the regular education program provided their teachers are trained to recognize and make appropriate modifications for their AD/HD-related difficulties. Examples of appropriate interventions include adjusting curricula, altering classroom organization and management, using teaching techniques that incorporate behavioral management techniques, and increased parent/teacher communication.

Beyond that, the other 50 percent of children with AD/HD will require some level of special education intervention. PGARD estimates that 35 to 40 percent of these children will still spend the majority of their day in regular education settings, and will additionally require combined services likely to include support personnel and supplementary or resource-room programs. Finally, the remaining 10 percent will probably require self-contained classrooms, generally because they have a severe degree of the disorder and other disabilities as well.

Unfortunately this ideal array of services has generally eluded many children with AD/HD. Dr. Barkley aptly observes, ''The majority of children with this disability fall through the cracks in the current educational system.'' As many parents know all too well, he explains, no adequate educational program presently exists to thoroughly and efficiently deal with AD/HD-related difficulties. In fact, until our recent advocacy efforts on the national level, many states and local districts did not understand their obligations to address the needs of children with AD/HD in public school settings. Rather, many teachers and administrators had little if any knowledge about this disability. Consequently, these children often were perceived as the cause of their own distress.

Though recent U.S. Education Department policy has clarified the state and local obligations to serve children with AD/HD, most school districts are still playing catch-up. Establishing the rights of children with AD/HD to an appropriate public education has at least given parents some degree of clout. Previously, cases existed where parents asking for help had been told that AD/HD was not considered a disability, and according to Dr. Barkley, ''Many parents had to shop around for the best school district or the best teacher they could find willing to be flexible enough to use some of the interventions which work for these children.'' Fortunately, many teachers and school districts have been and are willing to help the student with AD/HD. Nonetheless, our children's right to a free and appropriate public education should not be relegated to the luck of the draw.

As parents, we play an invaluable role in obtaining the best education possible for our children. Because we have a vested interest in our child's well-being and know that child better than anybody else, we are his or her best advocates. In fact, studies indicate that students with disabilities who make the most progress in school have very involved parents.

Being involved with our child's school program is not an easy job. Not only does it require time, effort, and energy, but many of us feel intimidated by school personnel. We often don't think we know what we are talking about. Even when we do, we sometimes worry that if we make requests on behalf of our child, the school personnel will come to view the child as that pain-in-the-neck kid with the pain-in-the-neck parent. Some of us fear our efforts to acquire help for the child will backfire, and instead, our child may be made to suffer because we are ''bugging'' school personnel. Because we have rights guaranteed under the law, should our worst fears come true, such situations can be dealt with fairly.

But I am convinced for the most part that administrators and teachers really do have the child's best interests at heart. Being an educator is hard work. That is not to say that there are not unreasonable teachers and administrators, just as there are unreasonable parents. For instance, I know of one parent who wanted to sue the school district because she felt it should provide her child with after-school social activities in addition to the program the school had in place during school hours, which did address his social difficulties.

Effective parent advocacy involves creating partnerships with the school personnel. Though many parents are intimidated by their child's teachers and administrators, these educators often are wary of parents as well. Diplomacy goes a long way in avoiding many disputes. When meeting with school personnel, a good attitude and a courteous demeanor are really important. We want to be problem-solvers and not problem-makers. We must work to ensure that our child receives needed services, and at the same time we need to be certain that we hold realistic expectations for the child. As our child's advocate, we need to be assertive, to ask questions, to question answers that do not make sense to us. Being assertive, however, does not mean being aggressive. Threats and name-calling do not help anybody.

Sometimes we parents of children with AD/HD are just so tired and frustrated, we have a hard time maintaining a calm and collected posture. But we really do serve our child and ourselves most productively when we remain nonconfrontational with the school staff. Though we parents and school personnel may have disagreements with each other, we ought always to agree that we share common ground, specifically, the child's well-being.

Though we often think that the teacher should know how to manage our child in school, we need to remember that few teachers have had any formal training in regard to AD/HD, though thankfully that training is now beginning to occur. Nonetheless, in this present state of affairs, in absence of a diagnosis, often teachers are equally as frustrated and in the dark as we parents are about why the child behaves poorly or does not perform well in school. Thus teachers may make the same false assumptions that we parents might make, that is "He could do it if he wanted to" or "She could do it if she tried hard enough." Even when teachers know the child has this disorder, they too often feel helpless and confused about how to help the child with AD/HD.

Teachers usually make great students. Rather than complain or get angry, try to work with teachers to be a problem-solver. Give them literature to read about AD/HD. Give them any helpful suggestions you may have picked up along the way. (Some suggestions are included in the next chapter.) Since many children with AD/HD are served in the regular education classroom, you could even suggest that your district use one of the teacher in-service days to present a program about AD/HD to the entire staff, not just the special education staff.

Many parents find meeting with school personnel to aid in the selection process of their child's teachers very productive. Parents of children with AD/HD, like Jan Lawes and Barbara Chapman, are often heard to say, "My child had a wonderful teacher who really understood him and he did great last year. This year the teacher is not so willing to help and he's doing a rotten job."

Rather than wait until the school year begins, teacher selection should be made before the end of the previous grade. Children with AD/HD need teachers who are structured and organized but not rigid, who are patient and willing to take a little extra time to understand the nature of the child, and who will use a little extra effort to help the child succeed. Teachers of these students also need to use a lot of encouragement and praise, because, as we know, children with this disability perform better when they are reinforced for appropriate behavior.

Making an appointment with the child's teachers at the beginning of the school year is also a wise move. At this meeting, we parents need to discuss the concerns we have for our child, as well as the child's strengths and weaknesses. We want to encourage teamwork and let the teachers know that we will support their efforts at home. Suggest frequent and open communication throughout the year, but not only to keep abreast of how the child is doing or to determine if further interventions are needed: we also want to keep track of any special assignments or projects looming in the future. A parent who approaches a teacher in a nonthreatening way, who shares information, and who tries to be supportive will be appreciated by most teachers. If your child's teacher resents parental involvement, then the child has not been placed appropriately.

When advocating for your child bear in mind the adage "knowledge is power." The more you know about your rights and your child's rights, the better chance you have to see that your child receives an appropriate educational program designed to meet his or her unique learning needs. Knowing your rights means knowing the laws governing the education of children with disabilities. I have explained what rights these laws provide and how they apply to parents of children with AD/HD and the children themselves in Appendix B.

Finally, parent advocacy also involves keeping thorough records. Many parents maintain a file on their child which contains any communications from the school, copies of communications from you to the school, copies of all reports about your child, copies of all report cards and achievement test scores, and records of any phone calls or meetings including the date, the time, and the names of the person or persons with whom you spoke. I also save all my son's school papers until the end of the school year so I can look them over to identify any problem areas before I attend conferences to plan his program. By keeping good records, should disputes arise, you will have a better chance to protect your rights and your child's rights.

Summary

Effects on Educational Performance

- Educational outcomes present a picture of serious academic underachievement
- Typical problems include difficulty in:
  — starting, staying on, and completing tasks
  — following rules
  — working independently
  — disorganization
  — excessive activity and vocalization
  — frequent interrupting
  — waiting turns or delaying responses
  — low frustration tolerance
  — persistence of effort
  — socialization
  — handwriting

Subtypes and Related Difficulties

- Predominantly inattentive
  - selective and focused attention
  - disorganization
- Combined (inattentive, hyperactive-impulsive)
  - difficulty sustaining attention
  - behavioral impulsivity
  - difficulty delaying responses and waiting

Attention Bias Theory

- Biologically driven to seek out novel, interesting stimuli
- Problems evident in tasks that:
  - lack novelty, e.g., detail-oriented, lacking in variety
  - are too long or too hard
  - require delay in making responses
- Task performance improved by adding novelty to tasks, decreasing length, developing routines for work completion

Providing Educational Services

- Regular education modifications and accommodations:
  - adjusting curriculum
  - altering classroom organization and management
  - incorporating behavior management techniques
  - increasing parent-teacher communication
- Special education services offering a range of placement options and interventions

Parental Involvement and Advocacy

- Better outcomes result when parents are active and involved
- Use diplomacy and assertiveness but not aggression
- Engage in problem-solving, not problem-making
- Provide informative literature
- Participate in placement and teacher selection
- Meet as often as necessary with teaching staff
- Maintain thorough records

CHAPTER NINE

Educational
Interventions

David's first eight years of life were not the carefree wonder years we associate with childhood. Instead, David's wonder years were filled with tension, with negativity, with not fitting in. But as he entered his ninth year, it was as though he emerged from a chrysalis at peace with himself. David's affect had changed and this once unhappy child now smiled most of the time. He acquired an enthusiasm for life and a sense of humor, but most important, he liked himself. This change I attribute to his early diagnosis and treatment, and his incredible resiliency. Though the entire family has had to deal with the effects of this disorder, the struggle is borne by David. He is on the front lines every day.

In July 1988, I brought David to the pediatric neurologist for a follow-up visit. After the doctor examined my son, he sat me down in his office and said, "What a wonderful change. You know, I used to worry about the both of you and wonder how you were ever going to make it. David's symptoms were so severe. You should be very pleased."

Well, I was more than pleased. I felt such gratitude and such relief that my little boy's symptoms had stabilized.

But the relief did not come from a sense that David had been cured. By now I had come to understand that this disorder has no cure. The neurologist also told me that day in his office there would always be new issues to deal with, new problems which would arise. But the doctor knew and I now knew our entire family had the tools to handle them. One of the tools proved to be the AD/HD parent support group a few of us formed with the aid of Dr. Burke, our child psychologist. Through this group we helped and encouraged each other to learn how a family can live comfortably with this disorder most of the time.

By no stretch of the imagination did our family walk off into the sunset, hand in hand, a perfect fifties sitcom family. Coping with AD/HD requires a lot of hard work and constant effort. Nor was AD/HD our only struggle. Shortly after Jonathan, our younger son, entered first grade, we learned he was dyslexic. As a result of his learning disability, Jon too experienced frustration in school. At times, he acted out behaviorally. Often he said to me, "I'm stupid" or "No one likes me."

Clearly, six-year-old Jonathan needed to have his self-esteem bolstered. His dad and I had to find some avenue where Jonathan could excel which was totally separate from any activity in which David participated. We enrolled him in tennis lessons. At the first lesson, the instructor said, "Put the racket in your right hand, put your left hand over your right, put your left foot forward, then pivot on your right heel and swing the racket."

By the time Jon finished following these commands, he looked like a Haitian contortionist. I did not insist he take another lesson. Instead of tennis, Jon, this dyslexic child who wrote all his letters and words backwards and upside down, decided to write and illustrate stories. By the end of first grade, he had a portfolio. Through the help of special education, he also read on grade level.

In addition to his academic struggles, Jonathan also needed to assert himself in the family. For years he had watched David command center stage. He accepted his supporting role so passively, it appeared he adapted quite well. In fact, Jon behaved so responsibly, he often seemed like the older brother rather than the young sibling. But between first and second grade, Jonathan no longer would accept the role of peacemaker. When David tried to monopolize toys, games, Jon's friends, and/or family members, Jonathan began to fight back. And because of his survival instincts, he has emerged into his own person.

In September 1988, David entered third grade. I assumed his school experience would be as wonderful as the previous year's. But in our district, third graders move to a different school. The teachers in this new school did not know David. They hadn't watched him struggle and grow during his primary school years. Nor did they know his capabilities. They did not know me either. So not only did I have to introduce the teachers to my son, the child with AD/HD, I had to introduce them to his mother, the woman who watches her kid like a hawk.

As in previous years, I had to make appointments with his teachers to explain the disabling effects of AD/HD on my son's performance and to highlight his strengths as well as his weaknesses. Despite the fact that I hate this task, experience has taught me that good and frequent communication between home and school is a necessity. For the most part, David's teachers have been wonderfully supportive.

This third-grade year, however, such communication proved to be crucial. Children in our district change classes in third grade. They are grouped by ability in math and reading. David had four teachers. Despite the fact that his second-grade teachers had great faith in my son's ability, his grouping was determined by the placement tests the third-grade teachers gave in early September. Though David's body was present, his mind had not yet fully reported to school. Thus, he did not perform well and was placed in groups below his ability level. David came home from school angry because, as he said, "I did this stuff last year." With David's teacher advocating on his behalf, the school staff willingly rethought the situation, and David was placed in groups more in keeping with his capabilities.

No fault lies here. Finding the appropriate placement for David is not an easy task. My son's ability is not just a measure of his scores on intelligence or achievement tests. AD/HD is a performance deficit. As a child with AD/HD, David juggles many balls. In his school program he must be presented with material commensurate with his ability, but not challenged to the point where he experiences so much frustration he shuts down or feels bad about himself because of his performance. David is a perfectionist who sets very high goals for himself. Innate ability and the ability to perform are often separated by a very fine line.

In this third-grade year, though the major battle had ended, new skirmishes developed. David did not want me to be so involved with his school. He resented the extra set of books I kept at home for the times he forgot his homework materials. He did not want the teachers to make any modifications in his program. He just wanted to be like all the other kids. Yet some of the kids called him "loudmouth," and ultimately David did not always feel that he fit in. His dad and I made special efforts to help David develop some friendships. By the middle of the school year, we often had a house full of boys.

David's confidence eventually grew to the point that he became less guarded about sharing his feelings with us. He even told his dad and me about goings-on in school. The day he came home and said, "Mom, I did something in art today that no one has done in eleven years," admittedly I became a little queasy. I managed to muster some strength and asked, "What was that, dear?" To my relief he answered, "I drew a triangle in a triangle." It seemed the art teacher had not encountered too many third-grade students who could draw two-dimensional triangles.

In May 1989, when I went to the parent-teacher conference, I felt certain that David was in good hands. His teachers opened the meeting by telling me, "You have some smart kid there. I wouldn't worry about him. He's going to run a corporation some-day. He just needs to get through school first."

I always worried that David would fall through the cracks, but this comment reassured me that his teachers had taken the time to get to know my child and to appreciate him.

And thanks to the results of his treatment, David made great strides at home too. The scales have tipped, and the days when David cannot control his behavior are few. Sure, new or unantici-pated problems arise. There are times when he does not remember to stop, look, and listen before taking action. For example, we went on vacation to an island where farm animals roam freely. David was swimming when suddenly this huge, black beast on the beach caught his eye. He excitedly charged out of the water toward the animal. Fortunately, David made a great racket which caught my attention, because the beast he was about to throw his arms around turned out to be a bull who did not appreciate this enthusi-astic attention.

But what do bulls know anyway? Both his dad and I have now come to appreciate David's zest for life, his boundless energy, the enthusiasm he brings to tasks which interest him, and the battle he has fought. Though sometimes our son still spins a little, he stays on course, and so do we.

The year I began to write this book, David announced he wanted to be an astronaut. Though I had hoped he would pick a career closer to home, I now felt certain he was not trying to get as far away from me as possible. I even knew he was not playing on my fear of heights and trying to get me riled and scared. When I asked David if he minded if I wrote this story, his eyes lit up and he danced around the room, chanting, "Oh wow. I'm going to be famous."

As the manuscript progressed, David stole glances at bits and pieces of the earlier part of the text, which did not impress him. My description of him ran contrary to his emerging sense of self. David had just begun to feel as though he belonged, to believe he was a pretty terrific kid and worthy of fame. To think that Mom might make him infamous was not his idea of great literature.

Often he came to my desk early in the morning, before I was awake, and penciled comments into the manuscript. Two particularly compelling notations were "Stoopid" and "Why are you writing this junk?" I tried to explain, but David did not seem to understand. When I referred to the infant as "a baby monkey on its mother's back," he scribbled, "You're a monkey on your own back." After that, I quietly sat with nine-year-old David and asked him if he would like me to stop writing this book. He quickly and emphatically told me he did want me to write this book and then added, "But if you only put the good parts." After a two-day pause, he added, "And I want to read it before anybody else does, because I might have to edit it."

David is a gutsy kid, and I could empathize with his defensive instincts. He has had to fight very hard to protect himself in situations which are not always kind. On top of that, I sometimes run too much pass interference. I try to overprotect him, which does not help David to feel effective and competent. When I told him I would rather he not sign up for football because I was afraid he might get hurt, David just sighed and said, "Mom, how do you expect me to make the NFL if I don't practice and play?" Who could argue?

Today, my hope for David and for all children with AD/HD is that the time will come when the world will stop trying to control these children and stop expecting them to fit into environments too small to appreciate or accommodate their special needs. For now, though days and periods come and go when my son spins off course, just as such times come and go for me as well, I know David will land on his feet.

Other children with AD/HD and their families have not been as fortunate as mine has been. "I've never felt successful in school," seventeen-year-old Louisa Christianson told me. Louisa's AD/HD was not diagnosed until she was sixteen. For most of her academic career, Louisa thought she was dumb. She says she is not motivated by much and hates school "because they don't let you take the classes you're good at." Since Louisa is easily distracted, she cannot take a test if the classroom door is open. She says she even gets distracted by her own thoughts.

Louisa is just one of many children with AD/HD whose school experience has been predominately negative. Even children diagnosed at earlier ages often feel like failures because they experience such difficulty in the school environment. Ten-year-old John Golding's classmates call him stupid. One of his teachers told him he was a daydreamer. His art teacher marked him down a grade on a drawing because she felt he did not try hard enough, yet John's classmates all said that his drawing was better than anyone else's picture. John felt he did the best he could. Though that teacher made him angry, John also gets angry with himself because he often knows the correct answers to test questions, but he usually marks the wrong answer box.

Before Gene Conlin's son was diagnosed, he and his wife were advised by the school to take a parenting course. Gene said, "The teacher was convinced that Frank could produce if I exerted my authority as a father and gave him a kick in the pants." The Conlins did take a course and found it helpful, but not for Frank's school performance. When another teacher complained to Gene that his son did not concentrate, did not pay attention, and never finished his work, Gene recalled teachers making similar comments to his parents. He felt overprotective of his son, explaining, "It was so painful to have people yell at me and discipline me all the time. I thought it was so unnecessary and I did not want Frank to go through all that unnecessary pain. I did not want my son to repeat my life because my life was filled with loneliness, self-doubt, negativity, and the feeling that I just did not fit."

Much of Gene Conlin's frustration rose out of an overwhelming sense that as in his life, Frank's teachers did not realize Frank wanted to succeed but could not. Gene Conlin is not unusual. Often parents complain that teachers do not seem to understand or acknowledge their child's AD/HD problems. But, as Dr. Sam Goldstein notes, "It is awfully hard to fault the teacher because he or she is a product of the system that educated him or her.'' Dr. Goldstein points out that regular education teachers, and often special education teachers, do not have any background in basic neurological processes and problem areas such as AD/HD. Many pre-service teacher training programs do not offer instruction about how students learn, why they learn, or why they do not learn.

Furthermore, given the current behavioral expectations found in most public schools, students with AD/HD do not easily fit into the regime, which places a premium on self-control and performance. Many fall short of meeting typical classroom demands. When presented with a student who has no visible disability, who has ability, who performs sometimes but not always, and who appears to choose to misbehave, understandably teachers draw false conclusions. Nonetheless, children and youth with AD/HD should not have to go through school experiencing frustration and failure. Today, enough is known about how to effectively educate children with this disability to make a difference.

Perhaps the first step in changing the way the schools treat these children is for everyone involved to acknowledge and understand that AD/HD happens to be an environmentally dependent disability. Under certain environmental conditions, AD/HD-related difficulties tend to be less problematic. For instance, researchers have long understood that when observing children in a playground setting, children with AD/HD will not readily distinguish themselves as being more active than their peers.

Though AD/HD exists as a constant, ''environmentally dependent'' means that problems do not typically arise until demands are made upon the child to use certain skills in which he or she is deficient. Thus, much of the school-based intervention for this disability will require altering environmental conditions to provide better access to students with AD/HD, rather than attempting to change the students to meet environmental expectations and demands.

Generally, researchers note that these children tend to have less difficulty in educational settings that are structured and predictable, that offer more individualized instruction, that have shorter work periods, a highly motivating, interesting, and interactive curriculum, and that use a lot of positive reinforcement. Conversely, they observe an increase in behavioral difficulties when tasks are difficult, when work is required for an extended period of time, and when there is little direct supervision.

Though the types of interventions recommended below have been demonstrated to be successful, they must be viewed as guidelines. No two children with AD/HD are alike. Similarities exist, but still each child is an individual with strengths and limitations, so what we do to help one child may not be what is indicated for another.

Children with AD/HD need a range of placement options and services in school. As mentioned in the previous chapter, some will do reasonably well in the regular education classroom with only minor modifications needed, while others might require more extensive accommodations and interventions, including special education services.

Regardless of what program is used, ultimately all interventions have the same goal: to build the child's sense of competence and self-esteem. Educators, particularly classroom teachers, play a vital role in the network of caregivers that can enable our children to achieve a positive outcome. Thus, they need to be educated about the disorder and its ramifications in the home, school, and social environments, and especially need to know the characteristics of students with AD/HD, including techniques and strategies for effectively educating them. In absence of a clinical diagnosis, educators also prove a valuable referral source and so they require instruction in methods of identifying children who display AD/HD characteristics. This important training can take place through in-service programs, recertification programs, and college curricula for educators in training.

Placing the student with a teacher who can deal with the child's special needs often makes a major difference in how the child feels about himself or herself. A good teacher for a student with AD/HD is one who not only understands the nature of the disorder, but who appreciates the child's struggles, is willing to change conditions to meet the child's needs, and who welcomes parental involvement.

Equally important is what I call teacher effect. The research literature continually points to positive reinforcement as the best medicine for these students. In general, they will do well with a teacher who has a loving, kind, and supportive attitude, is highly structured, and who recognizes, rewards, and encourages positive behavior. Such a teacher cultivates a safe classroom atmosphere minus all ridicule, responds calmly to inappropriate behavior, uses positive actions and commands that tell the child what is expected, and acts rather than reacts in response to behavior.

Children with AD/HD will be helped to meet expectations when the environment is structured and predictable. Expectations must be specifically stated and understood with frequent positive attention in the form of praise or even tangible rewards given when expectations are met. Here again, the classroom teacher happens to be the critical person to fashion this classroom ecology and to provide the necessary organization for these students, who tend to miss the neutral information inherent in a situation.

Suggestions for structuring the classroom include displaying classroom rules; posting daily schedule and homework assignments in the same place; providing separate and specific places for completed work and uncompleted work; setting aside specific periods for specific tasks; easing transitions between activities; seating the child away from auditory distractions and in close proximity to the teacher and a positive role model or cooperative learning partner.

Similarly, tasks and lessons can also be structured to address AD/HD-related difficulties. For instance, these students tend to be more productive in the morning, so academic subjects should be planned for these hours. Incorporating regularly scheduled and frequent breaks, adjusting the amount of written work, and alternating types of activities help eliminate desk fatigue and maintain interest. Complex tasks with multiple components can be broken down into easily completed parts.

Routines alleviate some of the problems arising from impulsivity and disorganization. Guidelines for the neat arrangement of work on paper, e.g., specifying placement of headings and spacing, structure the student and the task. Other aids include cues that signal time to begin work, to complete work, and to put materials away.

As the above recommendations indicate, students with AD/HD require a considerable amount of teacher involvement. These types of interventions manage AD/HD-related difficulties. They do not cure the disorder. Consequently, when these types of supports are withdrawn, though the child may have developed some compensatory strategies, in all likelihood, academic and behavioral difficulties will increase and may even revert to pre-intervention levels.

As one mother reported, under the guidance of a thoughtful teacher who tried different strategies to help her son, Steven, whose favorite book was *Leo the Late Bloomer,* bloomed. He earned straight A's in second grade. In third grade, he floundered. At the midyear conference, the teacher reported to his mother that almost every day, twenty minutes after she had handed out an assignment, Steven's page was blank. Both the teacher and his mother told Steven that he simply had to do his work. One day after the conference, Steven came home from school teary-eyed and told his mother, "Mommy, I'm trying. I just don't know what to do." Now in fourth grade, Steven is receiving the necessary support, and once again he is achieving.

The challenge faced by most teachers in educating students with AD/HD goes beyond the environmental manipulations briefly described above. As Dr. Ron Reeve explains, instructional theory principles have much to lend toward building successful experiences for these kids. The basic principle of instructional theory applied to reading, for example, says that a child is appropriately placed when he or she can read 90 percent of the words correctly. Conversely, the child is placed at the frustration level when reading fewer than 75 percent of the words correctly. "Children with AD/HD need to experience that 80- to 90-percent level of success," Dr. Reeve maintains.

Children with AD/HD are known to frustrate easily. In addition to modifying the environment, the curricula must be designed with these children's special needs taken into consideration. Too often, though, curriculum modification is viewed as reducing the amount of work required and lowering expectations. This notion reminds me of the old adage, "Give me a fish and I eat for a day. Teach me to fish and I eat for a lifetime." We don't want to inadvertently foster the child's sense of incompetence.

I am not, however, suggesting that reduction in work is necessarily inappropriate. If a child can demonstrate proficiency by solving ten math problems, then he or she probably does not need to spend time completing fifty problems. But modifying curricula also means changing the types of tasks, the approach to tasks, and the methodologies used.

Children with AD/HD tend to be interactive learners. They require a lot of stimulation within tasks. Yet teachers do not have to be stand-up performers to keep these children engaged. Tasks can be made interesting by using color to emphasize key elements or phrases. Lectures can be brief and followed by hands-on activities. Programmed materials requiring correction before the student can proceed to the next activity control impulsive responding and redirect attention. Clearly, curricula can be modified and made more interesting in a myriad of ways. The point here is that children with AD/HD require teachers willing to work outside of the status quo.

So far, the educational adaptations presented could be characterized as "basic good teaching." For children with AD/HD, they are a necessity. But even with the use of such strategies and techniques, some children with this disability have significant impairment and require more intensive levels of help. Some may need special education services such as resource-room programs or aides working as consultants to the regular classroom teacher. In still other cases, behavior management strategies using systemic approaches may be required. Such programs range from the use of behavior modification charts within the regular classroom environment to the presence of a trained behavioral specialist within the regular classroom or within a special classroom.

Many teachers are familiar with using behavior charts. Like parents, some teachers find them intrusive. Still, their use has been demonstrated as effective, thus making them an important tool.

There are many different styles of school charts. But Dr. Richard Zakreski describes a well-designed school charting system as having the following components: The child should know ahead of time what behavior is expected. He or she has the choice to decide to meet or not meet the expectations. Feedback is then provided about how well he or she met expectations. Finally, the child receives consequences, either positive or negative. Usually the consequences are meted out by the parents, but school-based responses can also be used.

Sample school charts are included in Appendix C. The charts not only provide the child with feedback about his or her school performance, they are also an effective way for parents and teachers to work as a team and to communicate frequently.

Besides the valuable feedback charts offer, Dr. Zakreski explains, school charts also serve other useful functions. First, they help the child overcome the characteristic inattentiveness associated with the disorder by providing motivation to attend to task and complete work. Desirable outcomes in the form of rewards which have meaning to the child are tied to work completion. For instance, a primary-grade child who finishes all his or her seatwork on a given day might earn a trip to the park. An elementary-age boy might opt for a pack of baseball cards.

Second, the school chart also helps organize the child. Most of these charts include a space for the child, or teacher if need be, to record homework assignments. The child with or without teacher direction can then use the chart as a guide to gather the necessary homework materials before leaving school at the end of the day. Once at home, the parents review the chart to check the daily progress and that evening's assignments. Since forgetting to bring completed homework back to school happens quite frequently, the child, with the help of the parent if need be, can use the chart to reorganize his or her backpack so the completed work gets back to school.

As explained in Chapter 6, medication often proves to be another valuable intervention for children with AD/HD. In fact, according to Dr. Zakreski, the use of medication has been associated with improved academic performance. This is not to say that all children with AD/HD should be given medication. As explained earlier, this decision must be made by a competent physician on an individual-case basis. However, through altering the child's abnormal biology, often the AD/HD symptoms which interfere with the child's ability to learn are lessened.

Dr. Zakreski believes that before a child with AD/HD takes medication, a chart system should be used for a few weeks to assess what the child is able to do on his own when provided with a program designed to motivate and draw upon the innate desire to achieve. Once this baseline is established, it can be used to guide the decision about whether to use medication. Should medication be warranted, Dr. Zakreski says, "Some type of rating scale such as the Conners Teacher Symptom Questionnaire should be used to document the effects of the medication and what dosages prove most effective."

Though medication can be an enormous benefit to many children with AD/HD, some caution needs to be observed so that the child is not given the wrong message about the medication. First, we do not want the child to develop the belief that the medicine alone is making him or her function appropriately. These children need to know that medication is only a support and that they have control over their behavior. Second, teachers should not publicly ask these children whether they have taken their medication that day. Not only does such an insensitive question single the child out and humiliate him or her, it also verifies to the child that he or she is different from peers and incompetent. Finally, medication ought never to be the sole course of intervention.

One of the nicest aspects of summer vacation for many parents of children with AD/HD is that they do not have to think about homework. Without question, this task has driven many parents and the children themselves to utter desperation. This work requires a considerable degree of self-direction and motivation. It also requires the child to perform after an entire day of trying to energize himself or herself to regulate behavior so as to follow rules, concentrate, and inhibit impulse. It creates so much tension and frustration, Gene Conlin, a father I interviewed, called it "a confrontation." Gene explained, "Every night I used to spend three or four hours yelling at my son until I was red in the face because it took him that long to complete a fifteen-minute homework assignment."

This experience is not unique to the Conlin family. Donna Rothman told me that night after night her son Peter sat in the kitchen chair spinning around while she tried to help him get his work done. She would say, "Peter, pick up your pencil." But Peter would just spin some more. Then she would plead, "Peter, please pick up your pencil and just write the answer down. You just told me the answer. Now write it down." When the interchange reached the yelling point, sometimes Peter would scream back and other times he would be passively defiant. Donna would get to the point where she started to shake. Then she gave up and told Peter to pack up his books. Many days Peter went to school without his work completed.

Fortunately, parent training can help minimize these nightly horror shows. Depending on the child's age and attention span, Dr. Russell Barkley recommends these general guidelines to manage the homework hassle. First, he believes the amount of homework assigned should not be excessive, but rather appropriate to the child's ability to attend to task. Thus, he suggests a meeting with the teacher to reduce the amount of homework and to determine that the homework is legitimate homework and not uncompleted classwork. He explained that the child with AD/HD should not be asked to make up in a few hours at home the work that he or she could not get done during the majority of the school day. In fact, he emphatically states, "Unfinished classwork is the teacher's jurisdiction. It is corrected by changing its management at school, and not by dumping it into the home."

Second, once the homework assignment is of an appropriate length, Dr. Barkley teaches the parent to break the work into smaller units. Thus, the child works for a period of time, takes a break, and then comes back to finish. The units of work time depend again on the age and attention span of the child. A timer is set during the work period so the child knows there is a limit to the amount of time he or she has to complete the task. If the child completes the work on time, he or she is rewarded with tokens (chips, points, stars, etc.) which can be used as currency and applied toward a particular reward, such as a trip for pizza or extra television time. If the child does not finish on time, he or she loses tokens.

During the first few weeks of this homework program, Dr. Barkley says the goal is to increase productivity. Once the child meets this goal by completing homework assignments, the program then focuses on accuracy. At first, the child is rewarded when 70 percent of the homework is done accurately. After that, the accuracy standard is increased in slight increments until the child receives an accuracy rate of 85 percent.

In addition, some children also receive a checklist to keep alongside their homework. This checklist offers a step-by-step procedure for the child to recheck his homework. For instance, the child would be directed to look over the instructions for an assignment, reread the action words, and then check to see that the directions were followed correctly. By the way, in keeping with the positive response to structure and routine by the child with AD/HD, a specific place and time should be established for the homework task.

With adolescents, Dr. Barkley also modifies the homework plan. However, he notes that adolescents have longer attention spans than younger children and therefore can do more homework. Still, the homework needs to be legitimate homework and not unfinished classwork. Timers are also used, set for six periods so the youth can move around in between assignments and not get frustrated or bored. A checklist, individualized for each student, directs him or her to double-check the work and make sure the directions were correctly followed.

Dr. Barkley also suggests that a second set of books be kept at home for middle and senior high school students since their lockers and thinking are usually not terribly organized. Consequently, necessary materials are often left at school. Dr. Barkley acknowledges that most teenagers are not thrilled with these interventions, but as he said, "Our goal is not so much happiness as success." With both younger and older children, parents are asked to check the completed assignments against the assignment sheet to make certain the child has accomplished the assigned tasks.

The systematic approach to homework can work for many parents. But Dr. Barkley cautions, "At least a third of the parents of children with AD/HD are not good at supervising homework. They might be equally as temperamental, impulsive, quick to upset, or perhaps overstressed by other circumstances." In these cases, he suggests parents use a tutor whenever possible. Dr. Barkley notes that tutors can be arranged through direct hiring and that special education teachers generally make good matches. Additionally, many areas of the country have tutorial centers. For children who go to an after-school care program, homework tutoring can sometimes be done there. Finally, Dr. Barkley has even placed children with teachers who stay after school to do paperwork. Though these teachers do not necessarily tutor, the child is at least afforded a structured environment in which to work.

Dr. Barkley also acknowledges that not all teachers will be amenable to modifying the homework program. In those instances, he informs the teacher, "The child is unlikely to get that degree of work done." He then instructs the parents to write a note to the teacher when, in their judgment, the amount of work on a given day is too great. In these cases where the teacher for whatever reason does not believe the homework program should be modified, sometimes the teacher's supervisor needs to be called upon to arbitrate. Sometimes the child needs to be placed in a different classroom. And, said Dr. Barkley, "Sometimes the parents have to move to a better school district."

The idea that a family might need to move to obtain an appropriate education for their child raises *justified anger*. But it also makes me think about one aspect of intervention that frequently gets overlooked. Because children with AD/HD often feel that they do not fit in, unfortunately, many of the things we do to intervene inadvertently reinforce that belief. Some children and youth come to resist efforts to intercede because they view them "as just another way for me to be labeled as a bad kid.'' Interventions designed to change children to "fit in" tend to create that impression.

We need to understand that the child's behavior is but one part of the equation. Antecedents and consequences are the other parts. Antecedents set the stage for behaviors to occur. Consequences provide either the reward or the punishment.

Too often, children and youth with this disability are held accountable for not fitting in, when in actuality, we adults in their lives perpetuate their behavioral difficulties by not changing our behavior, meaning we use the same antecedents and consequences. This phenomenon reminds me of a popular quip which defines insanity as doing the same thing over and over and expecting a different result.

Summary

Providing Environmental Access

- Structured, predictable settings
- More individualized instruction
- Shorter work periods
- Highly motivating, interesting, or interactive curriculum
- Lots of positive reinforcement

Improving Performance

- Requires educator training about the disorder, including:
  — knowledge and manifestations in educational environment
  — methods of identifying children with the disorder
  — characteristics of these students
  — techniques and strategies
- Requires careful teacher selection
  — willing to change conditions to meet child's needs
  — uses a lot of positive reinforcement
  — encourages parental involvement
  — actively involved with students during work periods
  — has patience, humor, and a positive attitude
- Structured learning environment and tasks: specific schedules, routines, tasks that include novelty, hands-on activities, programmed learning materials, etc.

- Use of behavior management techniques
  - provides positive feedback
  - implements preset rules and consequences
  - results in behavior charts that list expected behaviors, provide feedback about student's choices, provide consequences, help organize the student
- Do not rely on medication as only intervention

Handling Homework Hassles

- Make sure homework is legitimate and not uncompleted classwork
- Reduce amount to reasonable expectations
- Provide frequently scheduled breaks
- Provide rewards for completion
- Focus first on productivity then on accuracy
- Provide a checklist for following directions
- Establish a specific place and time to work
- Keep an extra set of books at home
- Use a tutor when necessary

CHAPTER TEN

Adolescence and Adulthood

As my son David enters his second decade of life, I feel hopeful that the early diagnosis and treatment of his AD/HD have paved the way for him to have a near-normal, happy, and well-adjusted life. Yet I would be less than candid if I did not say that problems still exist. As David meets new challenges and faces greater demands, his AD/HD symptoms flare. All problems considered, I firmly believe knowing about this disability and ways to cope with it helps David minimize the stresses and strains of ordinary and extraordinary life events.

Many children with this disability will not be as fortunate. They will go undiagnosed and untreated, and so they will go through life barraged by negative and demoralizing feedback because their behavior, though the outward manifestation of a disability, is seen as a deliberate choice to be difficult, a way to get attention, or whatever. Their lives will be painful and, in too many cases, tragic as well.

Anecdotal reports of people with AD/HD diagnosed as adults bear witness to this outcome. Unlike the children, who lack the insight or verbal ability to tell the world what growing up with this disorder is really like, thanks to public awareness, adults with AD/HD are finally realizing the root of their troubles and are coming forth in record numbers to tell us what happened to them, and how they have suffered, and that they continue to be challenged by this disability.

Many of these adults learned about their AD/HD after having a child diagnosed. Such was the case for David's dad, who did not view young David's behavior as out of the ordinary. To the contrary, David Sr. often commented that our son behaved much better than he had as a child. For many years, David Sr. thought of himself at worst as a "bad seed" and at best as "just not good enough." But never until the diagnosis of our son did Dad realize that he too had been at the mercy of the symptoms of AD/HD.

By the age of ten, David Sr.'s life was darkened by a steady stream of frustration and failure. In elementary school, he could not concentrate, had difficulty following instructions, persisted in doing the first thing that came to his mind, and could seldom sit still. Yet at times he would "ace" a test, which led everyone to believe that he just did not apply himself. Though most adults viewed him as polite, well-mannered, and articulate, problems with peers proved to be a constant source of disappointment.

Academic and social problems stayed with him through adolescence. He continued to show poor judgment and never really thought about the consequences of his actions until he landed in the thick of trouble. Sometimes his impulsive actions were hidden under the guise of just the exuberance of youth. Yet most times he felt remorse and bewilderment about what might have possessed him to behave so poorly. Nonetheless, his difficulties led to harsh consequences. By his teenage years, David Sr.'s sense of self hit an all-time low and he always felt depressed.

In early adulthood David Sr. was still immature. He wanted immediate gratification and often felt bored with life in general. He changed jobs and relationships frequently. Many times his significant others questioned why this nice, capable guy did not live up to his potential. Here is his account of life with AD/HD as he told it to me:

Elementary school is a blur, but I do remember that my parents moved a lot and I never attended the same school for any substantial period of time. I can remember not grasping what was going on in class. As early as kindergarten, I got into trouble for doing things like walking on tables, wandering off during recess, and having problems with the other kids. I remember being unhappy when I had to go to school and I used to stall by not eating my breakfast. School was a fearful place for me. I felt scared by the size of the place and the authoritative teachers who disciplined me because they had to, I guess. I knew I didn't do well and did not like feeling that humiliation. I got left back in kindergarten.

Life at home was not much better. Even as a real young kid I got into a lot of trouble. I actually remember playing with matches and accidentally setting some curtains on fire in my mother's room when I was five. In that same house I also pushed my older sister through a glass door, which cut her wrists and scarred her. I never meant to do any harm. For some reason, I either did not or was not able to operate within the rules. I felt very lonely and very much like an outsider, even in my own family.

My two sisters were successful students and people. I was the boy with a lot of promise who was going to be a late bloomer. In fourth or fifth grade my parents sent me to some special classes after school for reading and writing. I had to spend hours writing on a blackboard to try and improve my penmanship.

In junior high school, my good experiences were few and far between. How afraid I was of the teacher determined whether I pretended to pay attention. With a teacher who cut any slack, I behaved like a real wise guy/troublemaker. Some teachers hated my guts because as soon as they turned their backs I threw something. I usually behaved that way with the teachers who gave me no encouragement.

But I did do well with some teachers. They understood me as being a sharp kid and allowed me to express the things I knew. And I knew a lot. My seventh-grade geography teacher was a jazz buff who always hummed jazz in class. One day he said, "Does anyone know what song that was?" Of the entire class, I was the only kid who knew it. I not only knew that song, I knew as much about jazz as the teacher. From that day on, he and I talked jazz. We developed a rapport and I did pretty well for a couple of marking periods, but I could not sustain the effort.

During the time I did perform well in his class, that teacher realized I had a lot going for me. So I had a good experience with him and with a few other teachers as I went along. But for the most part, I met with alienation, with comments like, "Why aren't you more like your sisters?" "Why don't you try harder?" "You're bright, but you're just lazy."

I have a short attention span. In those days, unless something really interested me, my attention span was horribly short. I knew the batting averages of every baseball player, and every singer and song on the charts. I did not necessarily have an interest in the things other people liked, but still I could sit and study those things that interested me for a long time and understand them. To this day, if anything I don't have a terrific interest in goes on longer than a short period of time, I'm lost. That holds true from cocktail party conversations to lectures. I can tune in with the best of them for the short haul, but I cannot stay with it.

During junior high school, my group of friends and I began to get into trouble. This group I hung around with didn't have any wimps. It didn't have any Rhodes-Scholar types either. We used to let the air out of tires and rip antennas off cars. We even went as far as to break into the houses of people we knew. We'd find a window or door that could be opened and raid the refrigerator. We never took more than a can of Reddi Wip. I never thought about the consequences. It just seemed like fun.

Eventually the police caught up with us. No charges were pressed. But the embarrassment deterred me from ever doing those things again. We lived in a small neighborhood so everyone knew what I had done. My parents moved to another community shortly after that.

In this new school, my problems with studies persisted. Though I was basically a terrible student and a discipline problem, I did develop some friends who were good students and athletes. I wanted to be an athlete too, but I was afraid I would fail and afraid I would succeed. I had no idea what to do with success. I lived a kind of double life that eighth-grade year. In school I hung around with the president of the student council and dressed well. My after-school friends barely made the fringe of acceptability.

During eighth grade, I spent many long periods sitting in classrooms without the vaguest idea of what was going on. Most times, this confusion concerned me. I remember being fearful because I was failing, but did not know what I could do about it. I didn't think I was dumb, but I began to believe that I just did not want to succeed. I spent so much time worrying about why I didn't want to succeed that I became a nervous wreck and very depressed. One marking period my sister forced me to work and I wound up getting very good grades. Of course, this said to all the teachers and my parents, "You can do it if you want to." But without my sister's help, I slipped back into my old ways, and left to my own devices, I just did not get the work done. I had to go to summer school that year.

Around this time, I began lying to my parents a lot. I think in the beginning I lied because it seemed easy to do and my parents never challenged me much. My lies were really exaggerations of how I did in school. As I got older my exaggerations became more elaborate. For example, whenever we moved, I told the new kids what life was like in the previous city. I would tell them I had been a star athlete or that I got into a fight with another kid and inflicted serious damage. That kept the new kids at a distance. And I wanted things that way because I knew that I had lied about how successful I was and I knew damn well that if you hung around me long enough you would find out that my story was not true.

While my classmates didn't like me much, adults and older kids did. I think maybe they saw me as bright and appealing, which are things kids don't necessarily see. When I was fourteen years old I had a job as a batboy for a minor-league baseball club in the town where we lived. The players let me tag along when they went out socially. I loved that. Being a batboy was ironic because I got cut from Little League my first time out.

When I entered ninth grade, even though I had done so poorly in school, people still thought I was college material. In those days, you were either in college prep or dummy classes. So at that point I had mainly college prep courses, but I also had a few dummy courses because I couldn't pass subjects like basic algebra. I hated Monday mornings. They meant school. I only got by in ninth grade because of some benevolent teachers.

After ninth grade, my parents decided to put me in private school. As a requirement for acceptance, I had to start again as a freshman. I bombed out of that second-rate prep school, and then I went back to public high school. That public school had a lot of tough characters, and I had my usual problems, but I was happier in that school than I had ever been anywhere else. I made some friends. My football playing improved to the point that I showed real promise. The teachers did not ask much from me or from any of the students for that matter. Though I didn't do much academically, they passed me. I actually got a few C's and a B or two.

While at this school, I did not set the world on fire, but I was acceptable. Once again, I had a dual life going. My girlfriend went to a prestigious private school, so when she was home, I turned my belt from the side to the front, buttoned my shirt, and went to see her. With my friends I dressed punk. With my coach I was a different way. I just was not the same with anybody.

Meanwhile my father was worried about how I would ever get into college. Somebody suggested to him that I needed to go to this school where they used a lot of discipline, straightened out kids with problems, and got them into college. So I changed schools for the millionth time and went to this place that was just short of being a military school. I had a terrible year there and did not go back.

From there, I went to another second-rate prep school. That environment was not too demanding. I played football and actually made all-state that year. I didn't do any studying, but two months shy of turning twenty, I actually graduated from this place. Still, I had a lot of sleepless nights because I certainly shouldn't have passed. I even went into a couple of final exams and didn't bother to look at the questions. But they passed me, probably because I had been accepted to a college for my football ability. Not too many kids from that school got accepted to college. Needless to say, I was not at all prepared for college and had serious academic problems. I left as soon as football season ended.

I felt very depressed, empty, and afraid, like the jig was up. I had no idea what would happen to me or where I would end up in life. I tried some different things and nothing panned out. I felt more and more frustrated. I considered enlisting in the service, but I knew I didn't really want to do that, so I joined the reserves. For active duty, I played football. I didn't have to go to boot camp so I just slept, ran, and chipped a little paint for the rest of my time. Back then, I thought I had pulled a great coup, but now I wish I had gone through the regular program, because I didn't learn anything that the other guys did.

After active duty, I got a job selling advertising. My boss thought I seemed like a nice, bright guy but so unsure of myself and always uptight. Still, he liked my work and advanced me. My father, however, got a lot of good feedback and I got panicky. I felt so afraid that somebody would ask me to do something I couldn't and that I would fall flat on my face. This fear was terrible. Even though I had a job, a car, I had no confidence and didn't feel good about myself. So I decided to quit and move to the West Coast.

I had a similar experience there. My life was a farce. When I decided to move back east and leave my new job, my boss told me the same thing I'd heard before. "It's too bad you're leaving because it seems like you're at the point where you understand what we want and you're doing a good job." But I never felt a sense of permanence. Instead, I always felt like this good stuff is gonna pass and then what? I always worried about tomorrow.

Then I reached a point where I tired of dodging bullets. All the time I felt my life had no purpose, that it would always be painful, and that I would never be able to keep fooling everybody. I was at the point of totally bagging it when somehow, around the age of thirty, I got into counseling. Some of that helped, though I never felt like I really had a good sense of why I was such a mess.

But I did start to realize that I was succeeding somewhat in life. I think slowing down and maturing helped me to see that I had actually been doing better than I thought. I built on that realization a bit. I have always had a competitive nature and a high energy level. Where at times those traits had been destructive, they turned into positive factors. I had some more success and like anything else, success leads to more success. Even before I had a real sense of myself and knew that I had problems which were not of my own making that caused many things to be difficult for me, I started to get better.

Between the ages of thirty and forty, I made real strides in life. Though I changed jobs a lot, each move meant more responsibility and improved salary. The year I turned thirty-three, I got married, and in addition to my son from my first marriage, I had two more boys. Finally, I felt part of a family.

When my son David started to have his difficulties, I had a hard time believing he had a problem. Maybe one of the manifestations of this condition is not believing it exists or denying it. For as long as I could remember, there was always a lot of noise in my head. But I thought this was normal. I always thought of ten things at a time instead of one and could never focus. But I didn't know that made me different from anyone else. Whenever I got something right, it was always a great relief. You know, "Boy, I got through that," or "I hope I don't have to do that again."

I knew that my son and I had a bond of similarity and that many of the problems he had were like the ones I'd had. But when I had to learn about AD/HD and go to professionals with David, I began to realize that maybe this life of fear and inability to get with the program and do what everybody else was doing might have been caused by some reason other than the fact that I'm a no-good person.

I consider myself fortunate. I have had some success and been able to build on it. I think a lot of people with AD/HD or similar conditions maybe pass the point where they are going to have success and then go downhill. Though I believe I have to work harder than many other people, I also know now that I have an edge. I know my strengths and how to play them. I'm driven less by what others expect of me and more by what I feel is right for me. I'm able to accept the fact that I have pluses and minuses and don't feel defensive about the minuses the way I did most of my life. I am able to bounce back from setbacks a lot faster and without going into a tailspin. Things are pretty good for me today. I feel optimistic.

I realize now that I am a capable person. I have talent. I'm not afraid to take chances or try new things. I've become a very reliable person and I've been able to establish relationships. I feel good about myself as a person and as a parent. So I'm not so sure AD/HD is a handicap for me today. The people I know who have this condition have superior traits. They tend to be bright, energetic people.

What I want to impart to other people and what I try to get across to my son David is that you can channel your energies in a positive way. If you want to be successful and happy, you may have to try harder and delve deeper, but I think ultimately this struggle is a plus because you learn more about yourself. I think most people go through life without really knowing themselves. Learning about my weak points and my blind sides has been positive. Life can be structured around them.

Though I had always been taught that such things could be overcome, I now know that I can't overcome all my weak points, so I'm a lot better off recognizing them and taking steps to minimize their effects. Many people with AD/HD have been very successful in life, despite their problems. What I try to tell my son is that there is no reason to be discouraged about this condition.

Whenever I told people that my son had Attention-deficit/ Hyperactivity Disorder, invariably they asked, "Is this AD/HD something new?" Well, as David's dad's story demonstrates, generations of children with AD/HD have passed through the stages of life never quite knowing why they had so much trouble or why they underachieved. Thanks to more public awareness and more recognition by the medical and mental health communities, children with AD/HD are being diagnosed and offered treatment.

As a result, their parents with AD/HD are also learning for the first time that they were not problem children, but rather children with a problem. In fact, Kevin Murphy, chief of the Adult AD/HD Clinic at the University of Massachusetts Medical Center, reports that the majority of his patients are referred to the clinic after they have brought their children in for evaluation, subsequently learned about AD/HD, and then associated it with difficulties in their own lives.

Sometimes the similarity of presentation of AD/HD difficulties between parent and child is uncanny. Joe Curran, a father I spoke with, has never been diagnosed with AD/HD. But he told me, "When I read the neurologist's and psychologist's reports about my son, all I had to do was change the name of the patient, and they described me as a kid exactly. Then when a note on a report card came home from my son's teacher that matched word-for-word one of my report cards at the same age and the same grade level, I knew my school problems had been related to AD/HD."

At one time AD/HD had been considered to be a self-limited disorder, which meant that like an ill wind it would blow away with puberty. The past two years have brought an explosion of interest in the diagnosis and management of AD/HD in an adult population estimated between five and eight million people. Today, researchers know that approximately one-half to two-thirds of the children with this disorder carry AD/HD symptoms into adolescence and adulthood. Each of these life phases raises its own unique set of challenges, complicated by AD/HD.

Adolescence as a developmental stage poses worrisome aspects to parents regardless of whether their son or daughter has AD/HD. The adolescent quest for independence and freedom often results in experiments, choices, and judgments that can lead to potentially damaging outcomes. Add to that the impulsivity and poor self-control characteristic of the disorder and the combination can be devastating.

Consider the risks associated with the disorder during this developmental stage. According to Dr. Russell Barkley, the incidence of car accidents is three to four times higher for teenagers with AD/HD, so parents might want to postpone the child's acquisition of a driver's license or supervise the use of the car much more than they would do otherwise. Children with AD/HD are likely to begin smoking and using alcohol earlier than their peers. The risk of suicide, though very low among teenagers with AD/HD, is nonetheless higher than that of their peers.

Jean Bramble, a caseworker at Primary Children's Medical Center in Salt Lake City, is also concerned that "raging adolescent hormones combined with the drives to be social and accepted by peers, the use of alcohol, and the characteristic impulsivity are a setup for unplanned pregnancy." She believes parents need to address sex education with vigilance.

These cautions are not meant to cause alarm, but rather to encourage parents to be "overly involved" with their adolescent's comings and goings. Even teens diagnosed and treated during childhood may experience extraordinary adolescent adjustment problems. As explained by Dr. C. Keith Conners, "Kids go through phases of this disorder in which the intensity of it may be more apparent. For example, they often have a terrible time in the early years when they first go to school. They might settle down a little, but then suddenly as they go to junior high school, the rules of the game change and they become disoriented again."

Furthermore, Dr. Conners notes that as physiologic developmental changes occur, where before these children had little sense of self, they now begin to experience internal states. Dr. Conners said, "The adolescents with AD/HD I talk to are full of fear and anxiety, which I believe have been accumulated over time. They find they're in a heck of a mess because in school they have not been able to learn."

Adolescents with AD/HD have good reason to feel so anxious. According to Sam Goldstein, a nationally certified school psychologist, "The American education system is designed with the best interests of the adolescent with AD/HD at the bottom of the line." He cited typical performance expectations of junior and senior high schools that require adolescents to have more internal responsibility, which is lacking in students with AD/HD.

These students experience even more trouble operating within the system because now they have seven teachers and must get from class to class with the appropriate materials. Because they are in a larger system where their teachers are responsible for one hundred–plus children in the course of a day, the undiagnosed adolescent has to be "a real screwup" in order to be identified. By the high school years, Dr. Goldstein reports, 80 percent of kids with histories of AD/HD are behind at least one year in one basic academic subject. Follow-up studies indicate an estimated 10 percent drop out of school. A small percent complete college.

As a result of her difficulties negotiating within the junior high school setting, as an eighth grader Christine McLean did get diagnosed as having AD/HD. Chris is adopted. Her mother, Sally, explained to me that she and her husband did not have any information about their daughter's biological background. Chris's biological mother had also been adopted. When their daughter was younger, the McLeans had no idea why Chris was such an emotional and impulsive little girl. However, Sally McLean reported that Chris's serious school problems did not begin until she got into junior high school. When Chris was faced with the task of getting from class to class and keeping track of her belongings, she fell apart. She also started to "pick the wrong kind of friends," her mother told me.

By the time undiagnosed and/or untreated children with AD/HD reach junior and senior high school, the cumulative effects of the disorder levy a heavy toll. In addition to feelings of depression, they may present with secondary problems such as those associated with Conduct Disorder. Regarding these secondary problems, Dr. Conners finds them hard to dissociate from the primary AD/HD problem. "If you take the history carefully," he remarks, "you'll see the antecedents to [these children's] behavior patterns are the impulsive, restless, inattentive, poor learning style culminating in rebellion and rejection of the things around them."

Dr. Conners believes teenagers with AD/HD are often aggressive because they have developed a lot of anger over their failure to adapt to the home, school, and social environments. Consequently, the adolescents he observes are often "angry, defeated, and demoralized to the point where they openly rebel or get in trouble."

Some adolescents with AD/HD develop a pattern of lying and stealing. Dr. Conners explained that all kids lie occasionally. However, he observes that some kids with AD/HD appear to continually keep lying because they always get themselves in situations where they feel the need to cover up for something they did without thinking. Sometimes, Dr. Conners says, adolescents with AD/HD will also steal something because they are immediately attracted to it, but afterward they realize they were wrong.

Dr. Conners strongly believes that these behaviors in adolescents with AD/HD are very different from an antisocial behavior disorder pattern in which deeds are more calculated and premeditated. He said, "Kids with AD/HD are not sociopaths. They make a lot more mistakes and get into a lot more trouble, but this behavior comes more from an inability to restrain themselves than out of calculated wantonness. Parents need to understand that the kid with AD/HD is not a bad kid."

Small wonder that adolescents with AD/HD are at risk for more serious problems. By the teenage years, as Dr. Goldstein so sympathetically describes, "If you have AD/HD, you are at greater risk because you've gotten a lot more quit it, stop it, cut it out, don't do it, just a lot more negative reinforcement than everybody else."

According to Dr. Paul Wender, "Nobody knows for sure whether early treatment prevents subsequent psychopathology." He believes, however, that parents and practitioners alike have to operate on the assumption that early treatment will prevent subsequent behavior problems and psychological scarring. He says it seems logical that if a child gets treatment, he performs better in school and gets along with parents, siblings, and peers. Thus, Dr. Wender said, "You would expect a good psychological experience, rather than the bad one the child is likely to have without treatment."

The treatment for adolescents with AD/HD is much the same as it is for children. They require a modified school program, behavior management, psychotherapy, and, in the cases indicated, medication. Given the adolescent need for autonomy, a wise practice is to actively involve them in the decision-making process regarding the management of their AD/HD-related difficulties.

A common misconception about stimulant medications is that they are ineffective for adolescents. Dr. Wender reports that stimulant medication is effective for the treatment of AD/HD in adolescents, and in adults for that matter. As is the case for children with AD/HD, the use of stimulant medication with adolescents needs to be carefully monitored.

Dr. Bennett Shaywitz notes that monitoring the clinical effects of medication with college students poses problems. He explains that given the college student's erratic schedule, it is hard to pinpoint the student's target symptoms and when the student should take medication. Furthermore, in the absence of a teacher or parent to report about the medication's effects, the clinical response proves hard to measure. For one patient, Dr. Shaywitz tailor-made a rating scale for which he and his patient selected six areas requiring intervention. The scale rated the effectiveness of medical management in those areas.

Concern has been raised regarding the potential for abuse of stimulants by adolescents, and by adults as well. Both the efficacy of the stimulants and the concern regarding potential abuse was addressed by Columbia University professor Rachel Gittleman-Klein and reported in her paper "Prognosis of Attention Deficit Disorder and Its Management in Adolescence" *(Pediatrics in Review,* January 7, 1987). Dr. Klein writes:

> The only small study in which the effect of methylphenidate (Ritalin) in adolescents has been examined confirms the now common clinical observation that these medications continue to be effective through this age range. The stimulants enable better self-control, do not induce euphoria, and are not known to lead to addictive behavior. To the contrary, the major management problem in adolescents with ADD-H is their reluctance to take the medication and to stay on it; as a result, they are difficult to engage in treatment. Psychiatrists are often resisted because their speciality is often interpreted by the adolescents as indicating that they are "crazy."

By the time many people with AD/HD reach adulthood, their overall functioning shows significant impairment. Dr. Edward Hallowell, a Harvard Medical School faculty member and psychiatrist in private practice, cites the following as typical among the population of adults with AD/HD: a sense of underachievement, even in high acheivers; disorganization; impulsivity either verbally or in action, evidenced by such things as career changes, geographical moves, and spending money excessively or pathological gambling; a tendency to be drawn toward highly stimulating activities whether through dangerous pastimes or high-pressure jobs; a propensity to get involved in many projects simultaneously, often without completion of any; chronic ruminative worrying over nothing in particular; difficulty maintaining relationships; poor self-esteem and feelings of incompetency; problems with accurate self-observation; and a tendency to self-medicate, which leads to substance abuse or dependency.

According to Dr. Hallowell, frequently women present with difficulties somewhat different from those of men. Often they seek treatment for depression, and when upon inquiry, they report disorganization, not being able to complete tasks, and feeling like a "space shot."

Judy Woodruff learned she had AD/HD after her daughter had been diagnosed. With the information came relief. She explains, "From the time I was very young I knew I had something wrong with me, but I always blamed all my problems on my home life. When I saw the same symptoms in my daughter, I realized I was not neurotic and that something else caused my problems. When I learned about AD/HD and that it was a genetic disorder, I felt so relieved to have a label and to know that this problem can be surmounted."

Diagnosis of AD/HD in adults can be complicated. As Dr. Hallowell points out, "So much ADD among adults is out there masquerading as something else." Adults can present symptoms suggestive of other disorders such as depression, dysthymia, anxiety, substance abuse, eating disorder, bipolar or manic-depression, and obsessive-compulsive disorder. As with childhood assessment, clinicians must make a differential diagnosis whereby they attempt to ascertain the presence or absence of other disorders.

Dr. Wender, who pioneered much of the adult research in AD/HD, maintains that identifying the AD/HD disorder in adults is fairly easy provided the practitioner knows that the disorder can exist in adults and that an adult can have more than one disorder. "We certainly see people with combined major biological depression and AD/HD," he explained.

Dr. Murphy as well notes that rarely in his clinic do they see patients who solely have AD/HD, and so an issue in diagnosis is determining whether AD/HD is a problem, and if so, whether it is the primary problem. The most commonly co-occurring conditions he finds are anxiety, depression, and substance abuse. Approximately 60 percent of his adult patients with AD/HD at some time in their life have either had a major depressive episode or dysthymia, a milder form of depression characterized by an overall sense of malaise.

"That these adults feel depressed makes sense," says Dr. Murphy, adding, "Often they've grown up with a history of failures and frustrations in school, work, and social arenas. They have internalized all kinds of negative messages about themselves and their abilities.'' These adults quite often suffer from generalized anxiety about meeting performance expectations also. Substance abuse problems, which commonly co-occur, are thought to arise from the tendency to self-medicate.

The Adult AD/HD Clinic at the University of Massachusetts Medical Center follows a very thorough evaluation process which incorporates many of the same tools used in childhood diagnosis: a careful history; an in-depth, structured interview focusing on various areas of life including the core AD/HD symptoms; questionnaires and rating scales that assess school functioning, work history, and psychological status; reports from others such as parents and spouses; and a structured diagnostic interview that screens for other possible psychiatric difficulties. Typically the diagnostic process takes about three hours, though adults with AD/HD needn't be discouraged. The tasks vary and this helps to sustain attention and concentration.

Presently, the diagnosis and management of adult AD/HD happens to be a new field of service delivery. Thus, many areas of the country lack professionals trained to deal with the disorder in adults, though this situation is changing rapidly. Dr. Murphy advises adults seeking help either to contact a local CH.A.D.D. chapter or to ask the local professionals how much experience they may have with AD/HD, how many patients they treat, what their evaluation methods are, and what the services cost. "If the professional is reluctant to openly discuss what methods are used to arrive at the diagnosis, then I would stay away," he recommends.

While some of the information taken by Dr. Murphy's clinic is for research purposes, the assessment is a comprehensive and thorough one. Most private practitioners will probably not do such an in-depth evaluation as the clinic, but still the components of the University of Massachusetts evaluation serve as a guide to inform clients about the types of assessment instruments the diagnostician may be using.

Prior to the evaluation appointment, forms to be filled out by the patient, his or her parents if possible, and the spouse are sent to the patient. These include behavior rating scales used to establish the existence of the core symptoms both presently and retrospectively. AD/HD does not have an adult onset; therefore the diagnosis cannot be given to an adult unless a childhood history of the disorder can be documented.

It is important to note that discrepancies among informants is not uncommon. Parents, spouses, patients, and significant others may view symptoms differently, especially when rating childhood symptoms. Interestingly, Dr. Murphy has found that when the parents of the adult being assessed are asked both through rating scales and an interview to report upon the existence of the core symptoms in childhood, often the parents rate their adult son or daughter as far less deviant than the patient's self-report does. Dr. Murphy points out how unlike this response is from what happens in child clinics, where, he notes, "Parents primarily complain that the child is a behavior problem in school or a discipline problem at home."

Reasons for the disparity of ratings between adult patients and their parents remain speculative. Nevertheless, examiners should be aware that parents' or others' recollections and responses may not be consistent with the patient's accounts. Dr. Murphy generally finds a much higher correlation between patient and spousal reports. Another source of corroborative information is any objective data the patient might have. For example, school records often reveal a history of childhood-AD/HD-type problems.

Among the forms and questionnaires the patient fills out are an employment history and a social history. These provide information about adaptive functioning and problems potentially related to AD/HD such as frequent job changes, problems at work, difficulties with relationships, temper problems, incidence of speeding tickets and car accidents, and the number of residence changes made since high school. Clients are also given the Michigan Alcohol Screening Test, which assesses for alcohol abuse.

A careful history both of the patient and his or her extended family is taken. The history delves into prior evaluations and diagnoses, psychiatric problems, learning problems, drug or alcohol abuse, and the presence of AD/HD in the patient's immediate and extended family.

Of course, the patient interview proves to be a critical element of the assessment. The interview has two parts. First, the assessor asks a variety of questions to document the presence of AD/HD symptoms. Dr. Murphy frequently finds that when given an open-ended question about why the patient thinks he or she may have the disorder, those who turn out to have it usually provide "a richness of response," graphically describing AD/HD difficulties and the sense of chronic frustration they have experienced in their lives. Moreover, the language these patients use when answering assessment questions is often quite similar. In contrast, he notes that patients with psychiatric difficulties and not AD/HD tend to respond less readily and much less specifically.

For the second part of the interview the assessor uses the Structured Clinical Interview for DSM IIIR (SCID). This is a standardized and structured interview which helps to determine the presence of other psychiatric disorders. Additionally, the patient completes another screening instrument to assess psychological functioning.

Dr. Murphy also does a brief intellectual screening to assess intellectual functioning and administers achievement tests when learning problems are suspected. "We do not have a neuropsychological testing focus at the clinic because we do not believe the diagnosis is made on the basis of test results," explained Dr. Murphy. This is because, to date, no specific test or test battery has been shown to reliably differentiate individuals with AD/HD from those without the disorder. Although testing can add some useful information to the assessment, it is not by itself a valid way to establish the diagnosis.

Once the diagnosis of AD/HD is made, the adult's treatment begins, as it does for children, with education about the disorder. Many patients are also given medication, which of course is never recommended as a sole course of treatment. Generally, the same guiding principles described in Chapter 6 for children apply to adults. However, adults may have unique circumstances, such as a history of substance or alcohol abuse, which warrant additional guidelines for the safe and effective medical management of AD/HD.

To date, no clear-cut consensus exists among practitioners regarding whether or not patients with a history of substance abuse or dependency problems should be given medication. Some will prescribe, others will not. At the University of Massachusetts Adult AD/HD Clinic, Dr. Murphy reports that some patients with episodic substance abuse problems have shown improvement both in their AD/HD symptoms and in their substance abuse problems when given medication. However, if a patient is determined to have a primary substance abuse or substance dependence disorder, then he or she is referred to an appropriate treatment facility to deal with this problem first. In contrast, for those who are episodically abusing or self-medicating and do not have a primary substance abuse problem, medication may be quite helpful. These patients need to be monitored very closely. In fact, Dr. Murphy strongly advises, "If somebody is not prepared to follow up closely when prescribing medication to a substance abuser, then they should not do it."

For adults who have suffered their entire lives from AD/HD-related difficulties, the diagnosis can bring a great deal of relief. "I can't tell you how many successful adults come to my office and just break into tears when they realize they've had AD/HD all their lives," says Dr. Hallowell. "They talk about their struggle of always knowing something was wrong with them and the secret life they've lived trying to cover up," he adds.

Dr. Hallowell, who also has AD/HD, strongly believes the treatment focus has to begin with helping the adults get past their negative feelings and poor self-esteem. "The treatment process," he maintains, "is not just taking medication. It's an education process that creates a reunderstanding of oneself and a restructuring of one's life." In fact, he places medication last on the list of the five phases of treatment he employs in his private practice, because without using other approaches, Dr. Hallowell finds medication alone leads to sooner relapse wherein "the green monster emerges again."

Dr. Hallowell views diagnosis and patient education aimed at changing the patient's belief system as the first two treatment steps. He finds many patients frustrated by their inconsistent performance, a phenomenon dating back to childhood. Because of impulsivity, distractibility, and the inability to focus and finish, Dr. Hallowell says, "They've never been able to harness the engine they've got, so even though they may have achieved a lot, there's always a sense that they could do better."

Generally, these adults seek high-intensity situations as a way of focusing themselves, Dr. Hallowell has observed. He describes one patient who did vertical skiing, which entails being deposited on top of a mountain by a helicopter, pointing the skis downhill, and then basically gliding on sheer ice at speeds upward of 100 mph. The patient told him, "The only time I feel truly focused and relaxed is when I'm vertical skiing." Dr. Hallowell does recommend an aerobic exercise activity at least four times a week or other heart-rate-raising pursuits.

Coaching is a technique used to aid in redefining one's self and in restructuring one's life. Just as implied by the term, coaching involves having someone provide direction, encouragement, and reminders to the adult with AD/HD. Dr. Hallowell finds group therapy with these adults to be a tremendously effective coaching tool wherein group members validate and encourage each other, as well as provide help in defining goals and working toward them.

Many an adult with AD/HD has sunk in the quicksand of details that come from having too many projects started at one time. Here, coaching can be extremely useful for redirecting focus. Dr. Hallowell finds that large organizing principles provide immense structure. "These adults," he explains, "need what Alfred North Whitehead called 'an habitual vision of greatness,' a banner posted in the front of their minds showing what they are working toward."

The fourth treatment element consists of developing an arsenal of organizational tools. These include learning to prioritize, setting deadlines, breaking down large tasks, and using pocket reminders, calendars, notepads, color-coding, rituals, reminders, etc. These organizational techniques can help considerably with improving job-related performance.

Regarding employment, the adult with AD/HD might need other accommodations as well. In the lead article of the January 1993 issue of *CHADDERbox,* published and available through CH.A.D.D. (see Appendix A), Edward Hallowell and Ratey provide fifty tips for management of AD/HD in adults. Some of these tips relate to life in general and others relate specifically to performance management.

As Dr. Murphy notes, many adults are reluctant to seek accommodations from employers because doing so can work against them. The passage of the Americans with Disabilities Act (ADA) in 1990 prohibits discrimination against persons with disabilities regarding employment and accommodations. Thus, this law provides rights and protections to people with disabilities. The act defines a person with a disability as one who has a physical or mental impairment that substantially limits one or more of the major life activities, who has a record of such impairment, or who is regarded as having such impairment. For such individuals, employers, for instance, must provide reasonable accommodations. (See Appendix A for agencies that assist with ADA questions regarding accommodations and employee discrimination.)

Undoubtedly, AD/HD has great potential to create misery in an individual's life. The disorder poses a lifelong challenge. Yet Dr. Hallowell emphasizes that AD/HD has a positive side, which he feels does not receive the attention it deserves. He cites as examples creativity, energy, intuitiveness, and openness with people. These qualities when played out in conjunction with life-management strategies can be the driving force to success. There's the hope. As Dr. Hallowell said to me, "I'm at the point where I would rather have AD/HD than not have it because I think the assets outweigh the liabilities."

Summary

Difficulties in Adolescence

- Developmental challenge for independence combined with impulsivity, poor planning, and attentional problems leads to poor choices and judgments
- Associated risks include:
  — higher incidence of auto accidents
  — propensity to earlier alcohol and substance use/abuse
  — though very minimal incidence, higher suicide rate
  — unplanned pregnancy
  — secondary problems such as Conduct Disorder
- Careful parental supervision required
- Continuation of educational performance problems resulting from
  — increased expectations for self-control and responsibility
  — larger system, more classes, multiple teachers, less task supervision work against AD/HD difficulties
- Higher incidence of grade retention, dropping out, suspension, and expulsion, and less completion of college
- Managed as in childhood (see Chapter 6)

Problems in Adulthood

- Overall functioning can be significantly impaired
  — underachievement in employment
  — more career changes and geographical moves

— disorganization
— engagement in high-stimulus activity often involving risk
— involvement in too many activities at once, often without completion of any
— chronic worrying
— difficulty in interpersonal relationships
— tendency to self-medicate and episodic substance abuse
— higher incidence of substance/alcohol abuse or dependence

Issues and Methods of Diagnosis

- Must have childhood history of the disorder (can be documented retrospectively)
- Commonly co-occurring with symptoms of anxiety, depression, substance abuse, or dysthymia
- Symptom presentation must be differentiated from other psychiatric disorders
- Assessment includes
  — careful history
  — in-depth, structured clinical interview
  — questionnaires and rating scales
  — reports from others, including parents and spouses
  — objective data, including school records and prior psychiatric evaluations

Treatment Approaches

- Education about disorder to change self-concept
- Restructuring methods of operation and situations
- Medication
- Coaching to provide direction, encouragement, and helpful reminders done through group therapy or individual counseling
- Developing organizational tools
- Employee assistance
- ACCENTUATING THE POSITIVE

CHAPTER ELEVEN

In Appreciation of Individuals with AD/HD

Over the last two decades, research has generated a great deal of knowledge to add to the understanding of Attention-deficit/Hyperactivity Disorder. Yet at this point in time, though much is known about the way the disorder manifests and its probable basis, any explanation about its actual neurological basis remains theoretical. Over the course of writing this book, I learned that AD/HD is as multifaceted as a prism. Though general patterns exist, each child is imprinted with environmental circumstances and varying degrees and symptoms of the disorder so that no two children with AD/HD are exactly alike. Still, in speaking with the authorities on the subject, I found some of the analogies they made to describe the "generic" child with AD/HD helpful in conceptualizing the struggle these children, as well as adolescents and adults, face daily.

Dr. Melvin Levine explains the child's deficits in terms of an unskilled pilot who must manage the multitude of controls in an airplane's cockpit with such precision that the plane flies effectively and evenly. He developed a chart called the Concentration Cockpit which has a series of meters and dials depicting the various thought processes and/or behaviors the child with AD/HD must regulate in order to fly straight. Among the wide array of meters the child with AD/HD has to operate efficiently include the selective focus control, the consistency control, the tempo control, the motivational input control, the arousal control, the mood control, the memory control, the social control, and the motor/verbal control. Understandably, a child innately deficient in the skills needed to operate these controls will experience difficulty adapting to the myriad demands placed upon him or her by the environment.

Dr. Russell Barkley views the disorder as an inability to motivate and regulate behavior. He describes the child with AD/HD as a company highly motivated to maximize profits for immediate gain and not so motivated to plan for future development. According to Dr. Barkley, our society has a hard time accepting the notion that an individual's biology rather than one's willpower is in control of one's motivation. Perhaps that is why children with AD/HD are often blamed for their characteristic inability to "get with the program."

Dr. C. Keith Conners says the child with AD/HD is like a company with too many workers managed by an ineffective boss. Because the child with AD/HD suffers from a lack of appropriate energizing ability, he or she cannot arouse himself or herself to the level necessary to effectively order the mind's workers, who need a lot of executive input.

Though each of these analogies is different, a common thread runs through them. Children with AD/HD are not the children who won't. It may be that we do not need to know any more about AD/HD than that. Instead, maybe we need to know how to adjust our attitudes about the disorder, because like everyone else, individuals with AD/HD thrive on love and acceptance given freely, unconditionally, and with no demands attached. Unfortunately, for children, adolescents, and adults with AD/HD, approval, acceptance, and love often come with a price tag.

Psychologist Sam Goldstein believes, "As a society we need to recognize that the demands of the culture actually play favorites with our kid's lives." He pointed out that one hundred years ago, these children who could not sit still and listen to the teacher, who did not fit into the school system, were probably sent out to work the land or roam the frontier. While this alternative may not have been the best, at least a place existed where people with AD/HD could tap their potential.

"But, unlike a hundred years ago," said Dr. Goldstein, "we have no place to send these people. Today, we have no wilderness where they can go and be fur trappers, no farms they can work. We are between frontiers. Yet the demands of the culture are such that these people have a real hard time fitting in. When we do finally open up space, the last frontier, maybe we'll send these people out to be explorers, trappers, and miners on the moon. And some of them will probably want to go. But why? Maybe the kid who wants to be an astronaut is saying, 'Gee, get me the hell out of here. I need a new frontier. I want to go someplace where I won't bump into somebody all the time.' ''

I think we need to ask ourselves if we view the children who do not "fit the mold," the children who cannot "get with the program," as square pegs. Rather then search for their intrinsic value, do we try to force these people into round holes? Maybe AD/HD is not necessarily something gone amuck which needs to be fixed. Many of the traits associated with this condition can be either assets or liabilities.

Consider perseveration. Dr. Goldstein says, "Being perseverative when you're a kid means you're a pain in the neck. Mom tells the child that she will take him or her to the park in half an hour and the child asks every thirty seconds if it is time to go. But being perseverative, which is rooted in the word 'persevere,' is a valuable trait when you find something that interests you and you are willing to stick with it. Maybe a child with AD/HD might someday find a cure for cancer because he or she has extraordinary energy and curiosity and is willing to stay up all night and test a million different hypotheses until the cure is found.''

Admittedly, when my child was first diagnosed, I had no concept that this disorder might have a plus side. Then a parent sent me an article from *Pediatric Clinics of North America* (February 1982) titled "The Unhappy Wanderers: Children with Attention Deficits" by Melvin Levine and Raun Melmed. The authors discussed the potential dividends of AD/HD. They suggested that the highly distractible child with the wandering mind might see things others lacking this trait might never perceive. The wandering mind may represent creativity. The child who is insatiable may become the adult with ambition. The trait of egocentricity may form the foundation of leadership. They also cautioned, "Environmental circumstances, patterns of nurturance, critical life events, and educational experiences can minimize or aggravate the effects of attention deficits. It is likely that the responses of adults have a significant impact on prognosis.''

When I interviewed Dr. Levine for this book, he expressed his dissatisfaction with the AD/HD label given these children. He explained why. "One of the remarkable things about kids with attention deficits is that they have extraordinary strengths and affinities. For that reason, I do not like to take a fully pathological view of them. We need to at least consider the possibility that the word 'deficit' is wrong. Maybe AD/HD is just an alternative way to be wired. I am worried that with the current label of the disorder we may be creating a self-fulfilling prophecy in which these kids feel they have brain damage, which is sort of implicit in the name.''

Dr. Levine acknowledges that applying some type of label to describe these children and adults leads to recognition and help. But he observes, ''So many kids we see with attentional problems are highly entrepreneurial and creative people who have certain foci of interest that are very sophisticated and exciting. Perhaps we need to direct our energies to help the child recognize the existence of these traits. It would be so much better for them to think they just see the world differently from a lot of other people and there are good advantages to that and there are problems created by it. The child needs to see his or her potential value.'' And so does the adult.

Dr. Levine's point of view raises an important consideration. We know that AD/HD presents a unique set of challenges both to the individuals who struggle with its manifestations and to those who care for them. But when does a challenge become a disability? Certainly many people with disabilities lead happy, well-adjusted lives despite, or perhaps in spite of, their struggles. My hope for my child and those individuals with AD/HD I have come to know is that as a society, we come to understand our role in cultivating a playing field where the challenges of AD/HD do not become insurmountable obstacles that break the spirit. In nature there is no right or wrong. There are only consequences. Maybe the label for these individuals should be, ''Handle with care.''

Appendix A

National Organizations for Information, Support, and Advocacy

CH.A.D.D. (CHILDREN AND ADULTS WITH ATTENTION
DEFICIT DISORDERS)
National Headquarters
499 N.W. 70th Avenue
Suite 308
Plantation, Florida 33317
(305) 587-3700
(CH.A.D.D. has local chapters throughout the United States.
Locations, contact names, and phone numbers available through
National Headquarters.)

COUNCIL FOR EXCEPTIONAL CHILDREN
1920 Association Drive
Reston, Virginia 22091
(703) 620-3660

LEARNING DISABILITIES ASSOCIATION
4156 Library Road
Pittsburgh, Pennsylvania 15234
(412) 341-1515

NATIONAL CENTER FOR LEARNING DISABILITIES
99 Park Avenue
New York, New York 10016
(212) 687-7211

NICHCY (NATIONAL INFORMATION CENTER FOR
CHILDREN AND YOUTH WITH DISABILITIES)
P.O. Box 1492
Washington, D.C. 20013
1-800-999-5599

HEATH RESOURCE CENTER
(National Clearinghouse for Post-secondary Education for People
with Disabilities)
1 Dupont Circle N.W.
Washington, D.C. 20036

Disability Rights Advocacy Organizations

BAZELON CENTER FOR MENTAL HEALTH LAW
1101 15th Street N.W.
Suite 1212
Washington, D.C. 20005-5002
(202) 467-5730
(202) 467-4232 TDD

CENTER FOR LAW AND EDUCATION, INC.
955 Massachusetts Avenue
Cambridge, Massachusetts 02139

DREDF (DISABILITIES RIGHTS EDUCATION AND DEFENSE
FUND, INC.)
1616 P Street N.W.
Suite 100
Washington, D.C. 20036

NATIONAL COUNCIL ON DISABILITY
800 Independence Avenue S.W.
Suite 814
Washington, D.C. 20591
(202) 267-3846
(202) 267-3232 TDD

NPND (NATIONAL PARENT NETWORK ON DISABILITY)
1600 Prince Street
Suite 115
Alexandria, Virginia 22314
(703) 684-6763
(NPND has listings of federally funded parent training and
information centers in each state.)

United States Government

For questions about IDEA and PL 94-142:

U.S. Department of Education
Office of Special Education Programs
400 Maryland Avenue S.W.
Washington, D.C. 20202
(202) 205-5507

For questions about Section 504:

U.S. Department of Education
Office for Civil Rights
400 Maryland Avenue S.W.
Washington, D.C. 20202
(202) 732-1635

For questions about Americans with Disabilities Act (ADA)

Regarding discrimination:

EEOC (Equal Employment Opportunity Commission)
1801 L Street N.W.
Washington, D.C. 20507
(800) 669-4000
or see phone book for the EEOC office in your state

Regarding accommodations:

United States Department of Justice
Civil Rights Division
P.O. Box 66118
Washington, D.C. 20035-6118
(800) 669-3362

Appendix B

Education Rights and Protections Under Federal Law

Recent advocacy efforts have resulted in an awareness throughout the education community that AD/HD can adversely affect educational performance to a significant degree. As a result, in September of 1991, the U.S. Department of Education issued a policy clarifying the responsibility under federal law of states and local school districts to address the needs of children with this disability. (A copy of this policy is included at the end of this appendix.)

The U.S. Department of Education policy regarding AD/HD in no way created new law. Nor is the AD/HD policy a mere recommendation. The responsibility of school districts to provide special education and/or related aids and services to children with AD/HD who require them arises from two federal laws passed by Congress in the 1970s and their subsequent amendments. Those laws are IDEA, the Individuals with Disabilities Education Act (formerly the Education of All Handicapped Children Act), and Section 504 of the Rehabilitation Act. Each of these laws entitles children with disabilities to a free and appropriate public education. They also provide rights and protections to the children and their parents in the form of procedural safeguards. Furthermore, the services provided by school districts must be designed to meet each child's individual educational needs.

Each of these laws, IDEA and Section 504, has different requirements and procedures for implementation; however, they are similar in the following respects:

• School systems must have procedures in place to locate, identify, and evaluate any child known to have or suspected to have a disability to determine the child's need for special education and related aids and services.

• Special education and related aids and services must be provided at no additional costs to parents.

• Evaluations must be conducted without undue delay.

• Parents must be provided notice in writing whenever the school district undertakes to identify, evaluate, or change the educational placement of their child; or whenever the school district refuses to identify, evaluate, or change the placement of the child.

• Both schools and parents have the right to due process should disagreements arise between parents (guardians) and schools regarding appropriate educational placements and interventions for a child. Cases are presented before an impartial hearing officer, and that officer makes a determination based on the evidence presented. Due process hearings are not formal court cases, but they are heard by an administrative law judge, whose rulings are enforceable under the law. Parents are entitled to counsel or representation by an individual qualified to speak on behalf of their child's impairment(s).

Prior to due process, or while waiting for a due process hearing, parents and the agency involved may choose to use mediation when disputes arise. If mediation is used and the results are not agreeable to both parties, the parties involved in the dispute are still entitled to due process. Mediation proceedings must be conducted by a mediator who is trained in such techniques and special education laws and procedures and who is not affiliated with either party.

Education advocate Fran Rice explained that the special education and related aids and services provided under IDEA were intended to be very specialized for children with disabilities whose impairments were of such a nature and severity that the child warranted this highly specialized program.

Under IDEA, every child with a disability does not automatically receive special education services. He or she must be found eligible. To be eligible, two criteria must be met. First, the child must have one of eleven categories of impairment listed in the regulations. Important for parents of children with AD/HD to know is that this disability is considered "a health impairment" under the law when it results in limited alertness (inattention). Second, the disability must adversely affect educational performance. Children with AD/HD whose education performance is significantly adversely affected by the disability would be eligible for special education and related services.

When a child with AD/HD is being evaluated for eligibility under IDEA, the school must follow these evaluation procedures, among others:

• The evaluation must be conducted by a multidisciplinary team including at least one member knowledgeable about the disability.

• The evaluation must be comprehensive; no single test measure may be used; tests and other evaluation materials which assess specific areas of need must be used. Ability/achievements tests are not sufficient to find a child eligible or ineligible.

• The team must prepare a written report of all evaluation findings and include determination of eligibility, the basis for the determination, the relevant behavior noted during observation of the child, the relationship between the child's behavior and performance, and educationally relevant medical findings.

• Children found eligible must be re-evaluated every three years.

As mentioned earlier, this disability often co-occurs with other conditions and so children with AD/HD can be found eligible under other categories of impairment as well. Moreover, when other impairments are present, the special education and related aids and services must address all of the child's disability-related needs. If a child has AD/HD and dyslexia, or epilepsy, for example, the special education services must address all of the difficulties arising from each impairment. Children must be evaluated for all known or suspected disabilities. Thus, if a child is already receiving services and the parents or school have reason to believe or know for a fact that the child has another disability and had not been evaluated for that disability previously, the district must re-evaluate to determine the need for additional special education services.

Children found eligible under IDEA must receive an individual educational plan (IEP) designed to address their specific and individual educational needs. The IEP must include information about current levels of functioning, instructional goals and objectives, placement and services decisions, and procedures for evaluating the plan's effectiveness. The plan must be developed with parent participation, which is also required any time the plan is reviewed or revised. Parents are often asked to sign the IEP, but doing so is not a federal requirement.

In discussing the IEP, Fran Rice said, "The IEP is a very important legal document which parents should not enter into lightly." Your child's IEP must center around the effects of your child's diagnosed impairment(s) on any area of education, including social and academic performance. Once in place, the IEP cannot be significantly amended without written parental consent.

Ms. Rice advises parents to learn all they can about their child's impairment(s) before entering into the IEP development. Guidelines for IEP meetings are included at the end of this appendix along with a copy of "The Surefire Four-Step Record Decoder," which offers a step-by-step guide to help parents understand all their child's evaluations and recommendations so they can participate effectively in the IEP process.

Other important rights under IDEA include:

• a continuum of special education services and placements appropriate to the child's individual needs;
• education in the "least restrictive environment."

IDEA and its implementing rules and regulations, Public Law 94-142, are a minimum standard to which all states must comply. Each state has its own law and regulations to implement the federal law. Some states may exceed the requirements set forth in the federal law, but they may not go below these standards outlined above.

Section 504 of the Rehabilitation Act is a civil rights law. It says that a person with a disability cannot be discriminated against on the basis of that disability. As in IDEA, all children with AD/HD are not automatically protected under this law. They must meet the definition of a handicapped individual as set forth in the law. Section 504 defines a "handicapped person" as any person with a physical or mental impairment which substantially limits a major life activity, for example, learning. Depending on the severity of the child's AD/HD, the child may or may not fit within the definition.

Under Section 504, school districts have to evaluate a child when the parent believes his or her child is handicapped because of AD/HD and consequently may need special education or related services. School districts can use the same process as IDEA for evaluation or a separate process. Children with AD/HD who are not eligible under IDEA may qualify under Section 504. If a child is found qualified, the school district must provide special education and related aids and services to the child.

Fran Rice notes that Section 504 protects children in regular and special education. The child is entitled to an individual educational program designed to meet the child's individual educational needs. The IEP can be used for this purpose. Additionally, Section 504 requires the following:

• The quality of services must be equal to that of services provided to students without handicaps; thus the teacher must be trained in the instruction of persons with the handicap in question and appropriate materials and equipment made available.

• The child's education must be provided in the regular education classroom unless it is demonstrated that education in that environment cannot be achieved satisfactorily without the use of supplementary aids and services.

Even with an understanding of the rights and protections guaranteed under both IDEA and Section 504, many parents need the assistance of trained advocates or lawyers to help when schools and parents disagree. Appendix A has a listing of advocacy organizations that can assist in the process. When parents have a complaint under Section 504, they can write or call their regional Office for Civil Rights for assistance. Those addresses and phone numbers are listed at the end of this appendix.

Establishing a Record

When dealing with any agency, including the public schools, your chances are better if you have a written record of all communications with that agency. The following suggestions should increase your chances in getting action and will strengthen your positions when confrontations arise.

WHAT SHOULD BE IN A RECORD
1. *All* letters *from* you to the school district and other agencies about your concern.
2. *All* letters to you from the school district and other agencies about your concern.
3. *All* reports from the school, doctors, other agencies, and others including: report cards, parent-teacher conference reports, diagnostic reports, minutes or reports of meetings with persons involved with your concerns, IEP recommendations, etc.
4. *A log of telephone calls* giving the dates and time and length of the call, who initiated the call, who participated in the call (i.e., sometimes calls are transferred to more than one person or are conference calls), a summary of the conversations (i.e., who said what, what conclusions were reached or what action was promised, etc.).

HOW TO DEVELOP AND KEEP A RECORD
The following are suggestions for establishing and maintaining a record of contacts with the schools or other agencies.
1. Purchase a three-ring notebook, pocket folder or small

file. This will be the one location where you will keep all information related to the record.

2. Organize the record in whatever way helps you to locate the information quickly. (It is suggested you use reverse chronological order with latest information on top.)
3. Place all written reports, minutes of meetings, letters, etc., in the record. (See 3 above.)
4. Write down all phone calls (see 4 above). You may want to have the telephone log as a separate section in your record.
5. For meetings and phone calls for which there is no record, ask the school or other agency people to supply a summary of the meeting or call. If you agree with the summary, file it.
6. If you do not agree with the record or summary of a meeting or phone call, put your own interpretation in writing, and send it to the persons who chaired the meeting and wrote the minutes or summary. Ask that person to respond if they disagree with your interpretation.
7. Make your own notes at every meeting. If you have trouble writing notes during the meeting, *use a tape recorder* and transcribe your notes later.
8. Write out a summary of your interpretation of each meeting or phone call. Send your summary to the chairperson and minute taker and ask that person to react to your interpretation if he disagrees with it.
9. Make enough copies of all your correspondence so that you can send copies to all persons related to your concern. Always keep a copy for yourself.
10. Always send copies of your complaint letter to the following people:
    a. Local Superintendent
    b. Local Director of Special Education
    c. School Principal
    d. Local School Board President
11. Notifications of formal action such as requests for a hearing or filing of a complaint should have copies sent by certified mail to all those listed in 10 above.
12. If your initial letter is not answered or responded to, you may wish to follow up by doing any of the following:

a. Make a telephone call to any of the above listed persons

b. Make a direct phone call or in person visit to your local Superintendent of Schools.

13. *Never* let anyone have the master copy of your record except your legal counsel. You may want to have photo copies made and sent to others to help make your point.

By Harold W. Spicknall
Provided to the author from:
Fran Rice
Advocacy Associates of Northern
New England, Montpelier, Vermont

Telephone Log

PERSON I TALKED TO   TELEPHONE   DATE

QUESTION/INFORMATION

FOLLOW-UP:
 • I PROMISED TO —

 • HE/SHE PROMISED TO —

 • ADDITIONAL ACTION NEEDED —
   (i.e. letter documenting phone call,
   others to contact, etc.)

PERSON I TALKED TO   TELEPHONE   DATE

QUESTION/INFORMATION

FOLLOW-UP:
 • I PROMISED TO —

 • HE/SHE PROMISED TO —

 • ADDITIONAL ACTION NEEDED —
   (i.e. letter documenting phone call,
   others to contact, etc.)

Provided to the author by Statewide Parent Advocacy Network SPAN
516 North Avenue East, Westfield, New Jersey 07090

Guidelines for Being an Effective Partcipant in the IEP Process

How Should Parents Prepare for the IEP Conference?

Although parents may not be experts in the area of special education, they are experts on their child's strengths, weaknesses and learning patterns. Therefore, the full participation of parents is important in developing an appropriate IEP. Further, the parents' knowledge of their child will help them in deciding whether a proposed IEP is "appropriate." Parents should not be afraid to ask questions at the IEP conference or to speak up if they disagree with the educators.

If the parents have an IEP for their child from the current or previous school year, they should review each section of that IEP prior to the conference. Do they agree that their child requires special education in each goal area listed? Are the "objectives" or tasks appropriate, or has the child already learned these skills? Should other areas be included? Are all necessary related services being provided and are the type and amount listed sufficient? Do the parents believe the child could spend more time in class with non-handicapped students? If no IEP yet exists, the parents should think about these IEP areas prior to the conference. The checklist below provides other areas for all parents to consider before, during and at the end of the IEP Conference.

IEP Checklist

Before Attending an IEP Conference:

- review all school records, including school district evaluations;
- review the results of any outside evaluation done on the child;

- talk with people who have worked with or evaluated the child;
- identify those areas in which the child needs special attention, including, if appropriate, vocational areas;
- identify and/or review the goals (both long- and short-term) for the child and the type of educational setting the child needs.

During the IEP Conference:

- get an explanation of all evaluation results, terms and recommendations;
- find out how much progress the child made in achieving the goals and objectives in the previous IEP (if one exists), which teaching methods and materials worked and which did not;
- review each aspect of the district's proposals, including current levels and goals, and compare these to the parents' own observation of their child;
- discuss parents' academic and vocational goals for the child and the types of skills they want their child to learn;
- make known any agreement or disagreement with the district's recommendations and ask that any modifications or additions be included in the IEP;
- discuss the type and amount of any related services the child requires;
- discuss the amount of special education and regular education the child requires;
- discuss any modifications to the child's regular education classes that may be necessary.

At the End of the IEP Conference:

- make sure that the type and amount of all related services appear on the IEP;
- make sure that the amount of time the child will participate in regular education appears on the IEP.

Excerpted from *The Right to Special Education in Pennsylvania: A Guide for Parents,* published by The Education Law Center, 225 South 15th Street, Philadelphia, Pennsylvania 19102.

The Surefire Four-Step Record Decoder

STEP I: ORGANIZE
1. After obtaining the *complete set of records* from the school system, separate reports about your child (teacher reports, psychological evaluations, social history, etc.) from the correspondence.
2. Make an extra copy of the records in order to have an original and a working copy you can mark, cut, paste and use in any way that will help you.
3. Arrange each set, reports and extra documents, in chronological order.
4. Secure the pages in a folder with a clip or in a loose leaf notebook.
5. Number each report and make a chronological list that can be added onto as new records are generated.

STEP II. READ

1. Read through the entire record to get overall impressions, tones of the school's view of your child.
2. In the margins of your working copy, mark with a "?" the statements or areas of the reports with which you disagree or do not understand.

STEP III: ANALYZE

1. While re-reading the reports, underline the phrases or sentences, you feel best describe *both* your child's strengths and your child's problems. Put an "S" in the margin opposite a description of your child's learning strengths, a "P" opposite problems.
2. Using a worksheet, place the phrases or sentences about your child's strengths and problems within the categories of Oral Expression, Listening Comprehension, Basic Reading Skills, Reading Comprehension, Mathematical Calculation and Mathematical Reasoning, and Social Perception.
3. After each piece of data put the *source* and *date*. Often you

will find trends beginning to emerge. The same observation, said in similar language, may occur in several reports
over a period of time. You can indicate this by simply
recording additional sources and dates to the original data.

4. List *recommendations* in the last section of the analysis
    sheet that are made by each evaluator; for example, ser-
    vices needed, classroom environment, class size, type of
    school setting, recommendation for further testing, specific
    teaching materials or methods.

STEP IV: EVALUATE

Using the question mark quotations you have made in the margins and your overall sense of the records from your analytical
work with them, evaluate their accuracy against the following
criteria:

ACCURATE—

do these reports and portions of
the records correspond with your
own feelings, perceptions, observations and assessments of your
child?

COMPLETE—

are all the documents required by
the school system for the Eligibility, Individualized Education Plan
(IEP) and Placement decision
available in the file? For example,
medical report, psychological
examination, educational report
and others as required.

JARGON-FREE—

do the reports describe your child
in non-technical terms and/or
language you can understand and
use? In a good report diagnoses
and technical language will be
used and defined within the
report.

CURRENT—   are the dates on the records recent enough to give a report of your child's present behavior and functioning?

CONSISTENT—   are the reports contradictory? Is there consistency between the descriptions of your child by each evaluator?

UNDERSTANDABLE—   is the language used meaningful, clear and understandable to you? Example of an unclear statement: "She appears to have a psychological learning disability, calling for treatment involving a moderation of the special focus on interpersonal sensitivity she has received so far." "WHAT DOES THAT MEAN?"

OVERALL INTEGRITY—   considering the records as a whole, do they make sense and lead to the given recommendations?

Provided to the author from Fran Rice, Advocacy Associates of Northern New England, Montepelier, VT 05602

Department of Education Office for Civil Rights Regional Civil Rights Offices

Region I
Connecticut, Maine, Massachusetts, New Hampshire, Rhode Island, Vermont

Regional Civil Rights Director
Office for Civil Rights, Region I
U.S. Department of Education
John W. McCormack Post Office and
  Court House-Room 222
Post Office Square
Boston, Massachusetts 02109
(617) 223-1154   TTY   (617) 223-1111

Region II
New Jersey, New York, Puerto Rico, Virgin Islands

Regional Civil Rights Director
Office for Civil Rights, Region II
U.S. Department of Education
26 Federal Plaza, R33-130
New York, New York 10278
(212) 264-5180   TTY   (212) 264-9464

Region III
Delaware, District of Columbia, Maryland, Pennsylvania, Virginia, West Virginia

Regional Civil Rights Director
Office for Civil Rights, Region III
U.S. Department of Education
Gateway Building, 3535 Market Street
Post Office Box 13716
Philadelphia, Pennsylvania 19101
(215) 596-6772   TTY   (215) 596-6794

Region IV
Alabama, Florida, Georgia, Kentucky, Mississippi, North Carolina, South Carolina, Tennessee

Regional Civil Rights Director
Office for Civil Rights, Region IV
U.S. Department of Education
101 Marietta Tower, Room 2702
Atlanta, Georgia 30323
(404) 221-2954   TTY   (404) 221-2010

Region V
Illinois, Indiana, Minnesota, Michigan, Ohio, Wisconsin

Regional Civil Rights Director
Office for Civil Rights, Region V
U.S. Department of Education
300 South Wacker Drive, 8th Floor
Chicago, Illinois 60606
(312) 353-2520   TTY   (312) 353-2540

Region VI
Arkansas, Louisiana, New Mexico, Oklahoma, Texas

Regional Civil Rights Director
Office for Civil Rights, Region VI
U.S. Department of Education
1200 Main Tower Building, Room 1935
Dallas, Texas 75202
(214) 676-3951   TTY   (214) 767-6599

Region VII
Iowa, Kansas, Missouri, Nebraska

Regional Civil Rights Director
Office for Civil Rights, Region VII
U.S. Department of Education
324 E. 11th Street, 24th Floor
Kansas City, Missouri 64106
(816) 374-2223   TTY   (816) 374-7264

Region VIII

Colorado, Montana, North Dakota, South Dakota, Utah, Wyoming

Regional Civil Rights Director
Office for Civil Rights, Region VIII
U.S. Department of Education
Federal Office Building
1961 Stout Street, Room 1185
Denver, Colorado 80294
(303) 884-5695   TTY   (303) 844-3417

Region IX

Arizona, California, Hawaii, Nevada, Guam, Trust Territory
of the Pacific Islands, American Samoa

Regional Civil Rights Director
Office for Civil Rights, Region IX
U.S. Department of Education
1275 Market Street, 14th Floor
San Francisco, California 94103
(415) 556-9894   TTY   (415) 556-1933

Region X

Alaska, Idaho, Oregon, Washington

Regional Civil Rights Director
Office for Civil Rights, Region X
U.S. Department of Education
2901 3rd Avenue, Mail Stop 106
Seattle, Washington 98121
(206) 442-1636   TTY   (206) 442-4542

Parents may obtain copies of PL94-142 and Section 504 of the RHA by writing their Congressperson or by ordering them from the U.S. Department of Education, Office of Special Education, Washington, D.C. 20202

U.S. Department of Education Policy on ADD

UNITED STATES DEPARTMENT OF EDUCATION
OFFICE OF SPECIAL EDUCATION AND
REHABILITATIVE SERVICES

THE ASSISTANT SECRETARY

MEMORANDUM

DATE   :   Sep. 16, 1991

TO   : Chief State School Officers

FROM   : Robert R. Davila
              Assistant Secretary
              Office of Special Education
              and Rehabilitative Services

              Michael L. Williams
              Assistant Secretary
              Office for Civil Rights

              John T. MacDonald
              Assistant Secretary
              Office of Elementary
              and Secondary Education

SUBJECT   : Clarification of Policy to Address the Needs of Children
              with Attention Deficit Disorders within General and/or
              Special Education

I. *Introduction*

There is a growing awareness in the education community that attention deficit disorder (ADD) and attention deficit hyperactive disorder (ADHD) can result in significant learning problems for children with those conditions.[1] While estimates of the prevalence of ADD vary widely, we believe that three to five percent of school-aged children may have significant educational problems related to this disorder. Because ADD

---

[1]While we recognize that the disorders ADD and ADHD vary, the term ADD is being used to encompass children with both disorders.

has broad implications for education as a whole, the Department believes it should clarify State and local responsibility under Federal law for addressing the needs of children with ADD in the schools. Ensuring that these students are able to reach their fullest potential is an inherent part of the National education goals and AMERICA 2000. The National goals, and the strategy for achieving them, are based on the assumptions that: (1) all children can learn and benefit from their education; and (2) the educational community must work to improve the learning opportunities for all children.

This memorandum clarifies the circumstances under which children with ADD are eligible for special education services under Part B of the Individuals with Disabilities Education Act (Part B), as well as the Part B requirements for evaluation of such children's unique educational needs. This memorandum will also clarify the responsibility of State and local educational agencies (SEAs and LEAs) to provide special education and related services to eligible children with ADD under Part B. Finally, this memorandum clarifies the responsibilities of LEAs to provide regular or special education and related aids and services to those children with ADD who are not eligible under Part B, but who fall within the definition of "handicapped person" under Section 504 of the Rehabilitation Act of 1973. Because of the overall educational responsibility to provide services for these children, it is important that general and special education coordinate their efforts.

II. *Eligibility for Special Education and Related Services under Part B*

Last year during the reauthorization of the Education of the Handicapped Act (now the Individuals with Disabilities Education Act), Congress gave serious consideration to including ADD in the definition of "children with disabilities" in the statute. The Department took the position that ADD does not need to be added as a separate disability category in the statutory definition since children with ADD who require special education and related services can meet the eligibility criteria for services under Part B. This continues to be the Department's position.

No change with respect to ADD was made by Congress in the statutory definition of "children with disabilities"; however, language was included in Section 102(a) of the Education of the Handicapped Act Amendments of 1990 that required the Secretary to issue a Notice of Inquiry (NOI) soliciting public comment on special education for children with ADD under Part B. In response to the NOI (published November 29, 1990, in the *Federal Register*), the Department received over 2000 written comments, which have been transmitted to the Congress. Our review of these written comments indicates that there is confusion in the field regarding the extent to which children with ADD may be served in special education programs conducted under Part B.

A. *Description of Part B*

Part B requires SEAs and LEAs to make a free appropriate public education (FAPE) available to all eligible children with disabilities and to ensure that the rights and protections of Part B are extended to those children and their parents. 20 U.S.C. 1412(2); 34 CFR §§300.121 and 300.2. Under Part B, FAPE, among other elements, includes the provision of special education and related services, at no cost to parents, in conformity with an individualized education program (IEP). 34 CFR §300.4.

In order to be eligible under Part B, a child must be evaluated in accordance with 34 CFR §§300.530–300.534 as having one or more specified physical or mental impairments, and must be found to require special education and related services by reason of one or more of these impairments.[2] 20 U.S.C. 1401(a)(1); 34 CFR §300.5. SEAs and LEAs must ensure that children with ADD who are determined eligible for services under Part B receive special education and related services designed to meet their unique needs, including special education and related services needs arising from the ADD. A full continuum of placement alternatives, including the regular classroom, must be available for providing special education and related services required in the IEP.

B. *Eligibility for Part B services under the "Other Health Impaired" Category*

The list of chronic or acute health problems included within the definition of "other health impaired" in the Part B regulations is not exhaustive. The term "other health impaired" includes chronic or acute impairments that result in limited alertness, which adversely affects edu-

---

[2] The Part B regulations define 11 specified disabilities. 34 CFR §300.5(b)(1)–(11). The Education of the Handicapped Act Amendments of 1990 amended the Individuals with Disabilities Education Act (formerly the Education of the Handicapped Act) to specify that autism and traumatic brain injury are separate disability categories. *See* section 602(a)(1) of the Act, to be modified at 20 U.S.C. 1401(a)(1).

cational performance. Thus, children with ADD should be classified as eligible for services under the "other health impaired" category in instances where the ADD is a chronic or acute health problem that results in limited alertness, which adversely affects educational performance. In other words, children with ADD, where the ADD is a chronic or acute health problem resulting in limited alertness, may be considered disabled under Part B solely on the basis of this disorder within the "other health impaired" category in situations where special education and related services are needed because of the ADD.

C. *Eligibility for Part B services under Other Disability Categories*

Children with ADD are also eligible for services under Part B if the children satisfy the criteria applicable to other disability categories. For example, children with ADD are also eligible for services under the "specific learning disability" category of Part B if they meet the criteria stated in §§300.5(b)(9) and 300.541 or under the "seriously emotionally disturbed" category of Part B if they meet the criteria stated in §300.5(b)(8).

III. *Evaluations Under Part B*

A. *Requirements*

SEAs and LEAs have an affirmative obligation to evaluate a child who is suspected of having a disability to determine the child's need for special education and related services. Under Part B, SEAs and LEAs are required to have procedures for locating, identifying and evaluating all children who have a disability or are suspected of having a disability and are in need of special education and related services. 34 CFR §§300.128 and 300.220. This responsibility, known as "child find," is applicable to all children from birth through 21, regardless of the severity of their disability.

Consistent with this responsibility and the obligation to make FAPE available to all eligible children with disabilities, SEAs and LEAs must ensure that evaluations of children who are suspected of needing special education and related services are conducted without undue delay. 20 U.S.C. 1412(2). Because of its responsibility resulting from the FAPE and child find requirements of Part B, an LEA may not refuse to evaluate the possible need for special education and related services of a child with a prior medical diagnosis of ADD solely by reason of that medical diagnosis. However, a medical diagnosis of ADD alone is not sufficient to render a child eligible for services under Part B.

Under Part B, before any action is taken with respect to the initial placement of a child with a disability in a program providing special education and related services, "a full and individual evaluation of the child's educational needs must be conducted in accordance with requirements of §300.532." 34 CFR §300.531. Section 300.532(a) requires that a child's evaluation must be conducted by a multidisciplinary team, including at least one teacher or other specialist with knowledge in the area of suspected disability.

B. *Disagreements Over Evaluations*

Any proposal or refusal of an agency to initiate or change the identification, evaluation, or educational placement of the child, or the provision of FAPE to the child, is subject to the written prior notice requirements of 34 CFR §§300.504–300.505.[3] If a parent disagrees with the LEA's refusal to evaluate a child or the LEA's evaluation and determination that a child does not have a disability for which the child is eligible for services under Part B, the parent may request a due process hearing pursuant to 34 CFR §§300.504–300.513 of the Part B regulations.

IV. *Obligations Under Section 504 of SEAs and LEAs to Children with ADD Found Not To Require Special Education and Related Services under Part B*

Even if a child with ADD is found not to be eligible for services under Part B, the requirements of Section 504 of the Rehabilitation Act of 1973 (Section 504) and its implementing regulation at 34 CFR Part 104 may be

---

[3]Section 300.505 of the Part B regulations sets out the elements that must be contained in the prior written notice to parents:

(1) A full explanation of all of the procedural safeguards available to the parents under Subpart E;

(2) A description of the action proposed or refused by the agency, an explanation of why the agency proposes or refuses to take action and a description of any options the agency considered and the reasons why those options were rejected;

(3) A description of each evaluation procedure, test, record, or report the agency uses as a basis for the proposal or refusal; and

(4) A description of any other factors which are relevant to the agency's proposal or refusal.

34 CFR §300.505(a)(1)–(4).

applicable. Section 504 prohibits discrimination on the basis of handicap by recipients of Federal funds. Since Section 504 is a civil rights law, rather than a funding law, its requirements are framed in different terms than those of Part B. While the Section 504 regulation was written with an eye to consistency with Part B, it is more general, and there are some differences arising from the differing natures of the two laws. For instance, the protections of Section 504 extend to some children who do not fall within the disability categories specified in Part B.

A. *Definition*

Section 504 requires every recipient that operates a public elementary or secondary education program to address the needs of children who are considered "handicapped persons" under Section 504 as adequately as the needs of nonhandicapped persons are met. "Handicapped person" is defined in the Section 504 regulation as any person who has a physical or mental impairment which substantially limits a major life activity (*e.g.*, learning). 34 CFR §104.3(j). Thus, depending on the severity of their condition, children with ADD *may* fit within that definition.

B. *Programs and Services Under Section 504*

Under Section 504, an LEA must provide a free appropriate public education to each qualified handicapped child. A free appropriate public education, under Section 504, consists of regular or special education and related aids and services that are designed to meet the individual student's needs and based on adherence to the regulatory requirements on educational setting, evaluation, placement, and procedural safeguards. 34 CFR §§104.33, 104.34, 104.35, and 104.36. A student may be handicapped within the meaning of Section 504, and therefore entitled to regular or special education and related aids and services under the Section 504 regulation, even though the student may not be eligible for special education and related services under Part B.

Under Section 504, if parents believe that their child is handicapped by ADD, the LEA must evaluate the child to determine whether he or she is handicapped as defined by Section 504. If an LEA determines that a child is not handicapped under Section 504, the parent has the right to contest that determination. If the child is determined to be handicapped under Section 504, the LEA must make an individualized determination of the child's educational needs for regular or special education or related aids and services. 34 CFR §104.35. For children determined to be handicapped under Section 504, implementation of an individualized education program developed in accordance with Part B, although not required, is one means of meeting the free appropriate public education requirements of Section 504.[4] The child's education must be provided in the regular education classroom unless it is demonstrated that education in the regular environment with the use of supplementary aids and services cannot be achieved satisfactorily. 34 CFR §104.34.

Should it be determined that the child with ADD is handicapped for purposes of Section 504 and needs only adjustments in the regular class-room, rather than special education, those adjustments are required by Section 504. A range of strategies is available to meet the educational needs of children with ADD. Regular classroom teachers are important in identifying the appropriate educational adaptions and interventions for many children with ADD.

SEAs and LEAs should take the necessary steps to promote coordination between special and regular education programs. Steps also should be taken to train regular education teachers and other personnel to develop their awareness about ADD and its manifestations and the adaptations that can be implemented in regular education programs to address the instructional needs of these children. Examples of adaptations in regular education programs could include the following:

providing a structured learning environment; repeating and simplifying instructions about in-class and homework assignments; supplementing verbal instructions with visual instructions; using behavioral management techniques; adjusting class schedules; modifying test delivery; using tape recorders, computer-aided instruction, and other audio-visual equipment; selecting modified textbooks or workbooks; and tailoring homework assignments.

Other provisions range from consultation to special resources and may include reducing class size; use of one-on-one tutorials; classroom aides and note takers; involvement of a "services coordinator" to oversee implementation of special programs and services, and possible modification of nonacademic times such as lunchroom, recess, and physical education.

Through the use of appropriate adaptations and interventions in regular

---

[4]Many LEAs use the same process for determining the needs of students under Section 504 that they use for implementing Part B.

classes, many of which may be required by Section 504, the Department believes that LEAs will be able to effectively address the instructional needs of many children with ADD.

C. *Procedural Safeguards Under Section 504*

Procedural safeguards under the Section 504 regulation are stated more generally than in Part B. The Section 504 regulation requires the LEA to make available a system of procedural safeguards that permits parents to challenge actions regarding the identification, evaluation, or educational placement of their handicapped child whom they believe needs special education or related services. 34 CFR §104.36. The Section 504 regulation requires that the system of procedural safeguards include notice, an opportunity for the parents or guardian to examine relevant records, an impartial hearing with opportunity for participation by the parents or guardian and representation by counsel, and a review procedure. Compliance with procedural safeguards of Part B is one means of fulfilling the Section 504 requirement.[5] However, in an impartial due process hearing raising issues under the Section 504 regulation, the impartial hearing officer must make a determination based upon that regulation.

V. *Conclusion*

Congress and the Department have recognized the need to provide information and assistance to teachers, administrators, parents and other interested persons regarding the identification, evaluation, and instructional needs of children with ADD. The Department has formed a work group to explore strategies across principal offices to address this issue. The work group also plans to identify some ways that the Department can work with the education associations to cooperatively consider the programs and services needed by children with ADD across special and regular education.

In fiscal year 1991, the Congress appropriated funds for the Department to synthesize and disseminate current knowledge related to ADD. Four centers will be established in Fall, 1991, to analyze and synthesize the current research literature on ADD relating to identification, assessment, and interventions. Research syntheses will be prepared in formats suitable for educators, parents and researchers. Existing clearinghouses and networks, as well as Federal, State and local organizations will be utilized to disseminate these research syntheses to parents, educators and administrators, and other interested person.

In addition, the Federal Resource Center will work with SEAs and the six regional resource centers authorized under the Individuals with Disabilities Education Act to identify effective identification and assessment procedures, as well as intervention strategies being implemented across the country for children with ADD. A document describing current practice will be developed and disseminated to parents, educators and administrators, and other interested persons through the regional resource centers network, as well as by parent training centers, other parent and consumer organizations, and professional organizations. Also, the Office for Civil Rights' ten regional offices stand ready to provide technical assistance to parents and educators.

It is our hope that the above information will be of assistance to your State as you plan for the needs of children with ADD who require special education and related services under Part B, as well as for the needs of the broader group of children with ADD who do not qualify for special education and related services under Part B, but for whom special education or adaptations in regular education programs are needed.

---

[5]Again, many LEAs and some SEAs are conserving time and resources by using the same due process procedures for resolving disputes under both laws.

Appendix C

Behavior Management Charts

Many variations of behavior management charts exist as do books to explain their use. The following charts are provided as samples. The home management chart depicts the type of chart we used with our son. The daily and weekly school charts have been used successfully by some of the parents I interviewed. For more information about the theory behind behavior management, see Chapters Three and Six.

Chart #1   Home Management Behavior Chart
Chart #2   Daily School Chart
Chart #3   Daily School Record Chart
Chart #4   Weekly School Chart

Sample Home Management Behavior Chart

CHILD'S NAME _____ WEEK OF: _____

	Sun.	Mon.	Tues.	Wed.	Thur.	Fri.	Sat.
NIGHT BEFORE BEDTIME ROUTINE: washes, takes bath, brushes teeth, changes into pajamas, gets into bed, turns lights out on time	3	2	3				
MORNING ROUTINE: gets up, washes, brushes teeth, gets dressed, eats breakfast, is ready on time	2	2	3				
BEDROOM: makes bed, puts books, toys, clothing neatly away by (time)	1	0	3				
HOMEWORK: brings home all necessary materials, completes all assignments by (time) without delays or arguments	3	2	2				
GENERAL COOPERATION AND RESPECT: listens to and follows house rules and directions, cooperates with requests, speaks to and treats other family members nicely	2	2	3				
TOTAL	11*	8*	14**				

RATINGS

Excellent = 3
Good = 2
Needs Improvement = 1
Poor = 0

DAILY TOTALS AND CONSEQUENCES

Excellent Day (12-15 points) Bed 9:30, unrestricted TV/Nintendo time, 50 cents, 2 stars
Good Day (8-11 points) Bed 9:00, 1 hour of TV/Nintendo time, 25 cents, 1 star
Poor Day (0-7 points) Bed 8:30, no TV/Nintendo, no money, no stars

WEEKEND PRIVILEGES = STARS

Excellent week (10-14 stars) = Super Special (e.g. sleep over)
Good week (6-9 stars) = One Special (e.g. rent video tape)
Poor week (0-5 stars) = No Specials

This chart is for an elementary age child whose normal bedtime is 9:00. For younger children—preschool through kindergarten age—it is often best to use a "sticker" or "star" chart. A younger child's chart would have only three behaviors listed. Similarly, rewards would be age-appropriate, e.g., ice cream cone.

Sample Daily School Chart

	DATE:	DAY: MONDAY '89		
SUBJECT	DO YOU HAVE BOOKS/MATERIALS YOU NEED?	HOMEWORK ASSIGNMENTS		
PERIOD 1 READING:	YES/NO HOMEWORK? ☐	ASSIGNMENT: PAGES:		
PERIOD 2 SPELLING:	YES/NO HOMEWORK? ☐	ASSIGNMENT: PAGES:		
PERIOD 3 PENMANSHIP:	YES/NO HOMEWORK? ☐	ASSIGNMENT: PAGES:		
PERIOD 4 MATH:	YES/NO HOMEWORK? ☐	ASSIGNMENT: PAGES:		
PERIOD 5 COMPUTER:	YES/NO HOMEWORK? ☐	ASSIGNMENT: PAGES:		
PERIOD 6 SCIENCE:	YES/NO HOMEWORK? ☐	ASSIGNMENT: PAGES:		
PERIOD 7 SOCIAL STUDIES:	YES/NO HOMEWORK? ☐	ASSIGNMENT: PAGES:		
RESOURCE ROOM:			ARE THERE ANY NOTICES TO GO HOME? YES/NO	
COMMENTS:				
POINTS TODAY:	POINTS TOTAL:	TEACHER(S):	PARENTS:	89P1DEMO

Sample Daily School Record Chart

NAME: _____   DAY/DATE: _____

SUBJECT	WORK COMPLETION				CLASS BEHAVIOR			
Language Arts	3	2	1	0	3	2	1	0
Math	3	2	1	0	3	2	1	0
Science	3	2	1	0	3	2	1	0
Reading	3	2	1	0	3	2	1	0
Social Studies	3	2	1	0	3	2	1	0

RATINGS - Please Circle

Total = _____

3 = Excellent
2 = Satisfactory
1 = Needs Improvement
0 = Poor

Language Assignment:

Teacher initials: _____
Test/Quiz Grades: _____

Math Assignment:

Teacher initials: _____
Test/Quiz Grades: _____

Reading Assignment:

Teacher initials: _____
Test/Quiz Grades: _____

Science Assignment:

Teacher initials: _____
Test/Quiz Grades: _____

Social Studies Assignment:

Teacher initials: _____
Test/Quiz Grades: _____

Richard S. Zakreski, Ph.D.

Previous Assignments overdue:

_____
_____
_____

Sample Weekly School Chart

Name: _____ Date: _____

Ratings
3 = Excellent   2 = Satisfactory   1 = Needs Improvement   0 = Poor

Subject	Work Completion				Class Behavior				Teacher Initials
Language Arts	3	2	1	0	3	2	1	0	
Math	3	2	1	0	3	2	1	0	
Science	3	2	1	0	3	2	1	0	
Reading	3	2	1	0	3	2	1	0	
Social Studies	3	2	1	0	3	2	1	0	
Subtotal	_____				_____				
Total		_____							

Missing Assignments
English/L.A.
Social Studies
Math
Science
Specials

Test/Quiz Grades or Upcoming Tests
English/L.A.
Social Studies
Math
Science
Specials

Index